HUMAN RIGHTS
ODYSSEY

Marion A. Wright

and

Arnold Shankman

MOORE PUBLISHING COMPANY/DURHAM/NORTH CAROLINA 27705

To Alice

ACKNOWLEDGEMENTS

The author acknowledges with deep appreciation the assistance, both temporal and spiritual, of Dr. Leslie M. Dunbar, of the Field Foundation; Harold Fleming, of the Potomac Institute; my brother, Preston L. Wright, of San Francisco; my sister, Mrs. Helen W. Waters, of Hendersonville, N.C.; my wife, Alice, and my secretary, Mrs. Gay W. Franklin, of Ashford, N.C., who typed many of the thousands of words which follow.

Above all am I indebted to Dr. Arnold Shankman, of Winthrop College, of Rock Hill, S.C., for invaluable aid in selection of the material to be used and in preparation of the comprehensive index.

Marion A. Wright

CONTENTS

Human Rights Odyssey

Marion Wright (1895)

M. A. Wright
Winner of State Oratorical Contest, 1913

Marion Wright, 1972, addressing N.C. Coalition, 11th
Congressional District, Asheville, N. C.

Introduction

In recent years scholars have increasingly been turning their attention to Southern history. Tome after tome offers learned discourse on the profitability of slavery, the nature of the black family, the causes and consequences of the Civil War, the reality of the New South, or the history of race relations in Dixie. Of growing interest is the story of the Southern white liberal. Who were the remarkable men and women who braved insults, suffered ostracism, risked losing their jobs and, in some cases, faced mobs to promote equal justice for all? Who sought to foster the climate of tolerance that would hasten the day when Dixie truly rejoined the Union? One such man is Marion Allen Wright, author of the speeches compiled in this book.

In some ways Wright ill fits the stereotyped image of a liberal. Born January 18, 1894, in the tiny hamlet of Johnston, South Carolina, he was the son of Preston Wright, a Confederate veteran who supposedly had received a farewell handshake from General Robert E. Lee at Appomattox, and Octavia Watson Wright, who had attended a women's college in Georgia. Both parents died before Wright's sixth birthday, and the boy, the youngest of ten children, was raised in nearby Trenton by Mabel, one of his older sisters, and her husband, William D. Holland. Holland was a graduate of Furman University. His wife had attended Columbia College in Columbia, South Carolina. Both were gentle, tolerant people, and Wright credits them with instilling in him most of his good impulses. Neither, however, questioned the racial status quo in the Palmetto State. Rather William D. Holland was a well-intentioned paternalist unable to think of the black as a full-grown citizen. This paternalistic spirit is evidenced by his remark in young Wright's presence that Booker T. Washington was "a good darkey."

Living but a few hundred yards from the Hollands was

United States Senator Benjamin Ryan Tillman. Wright and his guardians mistrusted the senator not because of his illiberalism on the race question but rather because he swore and, while governor, had instituted state control over the sale of alcoholic beverages. Despite some misgivings, as a teenager Wright became acquainted with Tillman, and when the senator was in Washington or on a speaking tour, he would stay in the Tillman house to serve as a protector for Mrs. Tillman and her daughters. Whenever the senator returned home from one of his trips he would take Wright into his well-stocked private library and hand him a volume of Plutarch's *Lives* or some other classical work and suggest that he read its contents. Wright later concluded that, deplorable as were Tillman's ideas on race, the man did more good than harm for South Carolina. It was Tillman who brought the state primary system to the Palmetto State and who is credited with having created Winthrop College and Clemson University as state institutions of higher learning to benefit poor white South Carolinians.

At age sixteen Wright went to Columbia to enroll as a freshman at the University of South Carolina. As he left Trenton there was little to indicate a life of dedication to securing justice for blacks, civil rights for all, and religious tolerance for Jews and Catholics. Two incidents in his childhood, however, had a profound effect on him and would later help him to question the racial status quo in South Carolina. The first of these episodes took place around his tenth birthday. The Hollands were building a new house in Trenton and two or three whites had been engaged as carpenters to construct the house. Working with them was a Negro whose job was to push a wheelbarrow and to dig holes at the construction site. One of the whites discovered that a $5 bill was missing from his coat which he had hung to a nail. Without any advance warning he seized the Negro, turned him across a barrel and with a board hit him across his rear. Wright does not recollect that the man, whose guilt was never proven, confessed or that the money was ever recovered. He does remember breaking into tears because, having helped the black load the wheelbarrow with sand and bricks, he had grown fond of the Negro. This was the first time Wright witnessed the strong inflicting brutality on the weak.

The second incident took place when Wright was several years older. At this time he was working for Walter Wise, a local merchant. A well-dressed Afro-American had to change trains in Trenton and while waiting to make his connection he entered Wise's store and deferentially asked if he could wash his hands. Wright, alone in the store at the time, poured water for the man and showed him where soap and towels were kept. Wise suddenly returned and when he saw the black washing his hands he became livid. Shouting that he would have no damn nigger using his wash pan, he snatched a buggy whip from a nearby rack and chased the Negro from his property. Wright was given a lengthy lecture and was warned not to be guilty of such a serious offense in the future. Once again Marion Wright began to wonder what was so different about blacks that they should merit such unfair treatment.

Significant as the two incidents were, it was what he learned at the University of South Carolina that most profoundly influenced his later life. An indifferent student, he irregularly attended his classes, preferring to spend his time at the campus debate and literary societies, in the library, or inside the office of the Columbia *Record*, a local newspaper for which he worked. Though Wright never did receive a bachelor's degree at the university he was most impressed by two dynamic men, President Samuel Chiles Mitchell and Professor Josiah Morse. Contrary to his normal practices, he never missed any of their classes.

In 1909, Mitchell, one of Dixie's ablest educators, was brought to the university to help it regain the prestige it had lost after the Civil War. A liberal, Mitchell, who taught a few classes in political science, encouraged open discussion of such subjects as the need for public schools, public libraries, and public health facilities. Wright does not recall Mitchell speaking publicly about segregation, but "all of the man's words, acts and impulses pointed unerringly to a state's obligation to make no racial or other distinction as between its citizens." Because Mitchell had recommended to a liquidating foundation that its last remaining $400,000 be given to ten needy black colleges, he came into conflict with D.B. Johnson, the president of Winthrop College, who sought the money for his own institution. Johnson visited Governor Cole Blease and protested about what Mitchell was advocating. Winthrop did not get the money.

Blease, as a student at the University of South Carolina, in March, 1888, had been expelled from the Clariosophic Society after conviction of plagiarism in an essay contest. Evidently he harbored a special animosity for the institution. He seized on the foundation grant incident to mount a slashing attack on Dr. Mitchell, who, feeling his usefulness impaired, resigned to accept the presidency of the Medical College of Virginia.

Morse, the other important influence on Wright, taught one of the first courses on race relations in the South. Perhaps because he was Jewish, Morse openly criticized racial discrimination and prejudice. In his classes he used Edgar Gardner Murphy's *The Basis of Ascendancy* as one of his textbooks. This book deeply affected Wright, who later wrote:

> *It was the thesis of the book—a lesson still unlearned in much of the nation—that superiority of one person over another is a matter of individual attainments and excellence with which color has nothing to do. This was revolutionary doctrine at the time. I embraced it without reservation and it has become a permanent part of my personal creed.* .

Morse entertained Wright in his home and the two became good personal friends. The professor invited his student to join a group of University of South Carolina students and black students from Allen and Benedict Colleges in Columbia. This group met informally at the University of South Carolina YMCA and fully and frankly discussed the race issue. Negro suffrage, inferior schools for Afro-Americans, poor medical care for blacks—all were discussed at these meetings.

In Columbia Wright also learned about the menace of religious bigotry. Friendship with Morse and with August Kohn, who provided Wright and his wife Lelia with jobs—her salary having made Wright's legal education possible—made him aware of the evils of anti-Semitism. Through friendship with William Carmack, a Catholic and his boss at the *Record*, Wright became aware of the prejudice faced by members of that Church. During the 1920's, when the Ku Klux Klan espoused anti-Jewish and anti-Catholic sentiments, Wright became a dedicated and able defender of these two faiths.

As noted, Wright did not graduate with his class at the University of South Carolina in 1914. Instead he moved to Winston-Salem, North Carolina, where he taught for a year in the local high school. Two years later, he returned to the university to study law. Reporting was his first love, but being a lawyer was the ambition of most enterprising South Carolinians. Besides, journalists then received notoriously low salaries.

Following his graduation from law school in 1919 Wright decided to move from Columbia to Conway, South Carolina, at that time a bustling town of 1500 near Myrtle Beach. His arrival caused considerable comment.

In 1914, while still a student at the university, he had delivered a noncontroversial but well-received commencement address at the Conway high school. In 1919, because of his previous speech, he was asked to address the Conway seniors. This time he spoke to the commencement audience about civil rights and argued that Afro-Americans should be allowed to vote in the Democratic primary and to serve on juries. This speech met with a rather cool reception. After the twenty-five year old Wright concluded his remarks the chairman attempted to refute all of the speaker's arguments. Wright wisely decided to practice corporate rather than criminal law in Conway. He concluded that his mere presence in a court room as a defense attorney for a black might be enough to persuade the jury to convict the accused. Incidentally, shortly after the commencement exercises the chairman became one of Wright's valued clients.

Unlike most of the rest of South Carolina, Conway had a small black population. Barely fifteen per cent of the town's residents were Negroes, and so there never was any real fear of Afro-Americans threatening "white supremacy." No action was taken to prevent Negroes from voting, but few bothered to register. Despite their ability to vote, Negroes in Conway plainly were second-class citizens. The streets in the black section of town were unpaved, and the sanitary facilities available for Afro-Americans were abominable. Wright was particularly incensed to discover that a Dr. Kelly, the local black physician, was not allowed to treat Negro obstetrical cases in the obstetrical ward of the Conway hospital; rather he had to care for them in the segregated ward reserved for blacks, a ward without obstetrical facilities. Wright's complaints were ignored by the local hospital board of which he was then chairman.

Wright was active in and became president of the South Carolina Interracial Committee, a liberal civil rights organization, and he also organized a group of prominent blacks and whites in Conway. At the meetings of the latter group Wright conducted frank discussions on the race issue much as Dr. Morse had been doing in Columbia.

But Wright was not content to meet privately. A gifted speaker, he often was asked to deliver speeches. Time after time he used his speaking engagements to demand justice for the Negroes, to call for the establishment of more public libraries, and to call attention to the evils of capital punishment. Many of the early speeches were not preserved, but among the earliest addresses that survive is one delivered to the citizens of Marion, South Carolina, on Confederate Memorial Day, May 10, 1927. Going against custom, Wright did not confine his remarks to reciting paeans of praise in honor of the glorious deeds of the Confederate soldiers or to extolling the Confederate women for the many sacrifices they had to endure on the home front. Instead he announced that the time had come "when the political rights of the Negro must have ampler protection and larger exercise." No people, he explained, "can achieve its full stature when deprived by whatever means of any political right." How could anyone, he asked, expect the Negro to observe laws he had had no hand in making? Such was heady stuff for South Carolina in 1927.

The cool reception his speeches sometimes received did not cause Wright to soften his remarks. Like Judge J. Waties Waring, a personal friend of his, Wright did what he felt he had to do. Unlike the judge, however, he was not ostracized and he even served a term as president of the University of South Carolina Alumni Association and later the University Law Alumni Association. Doubtless Wright's wit and charm helped to explain his popularity. Perhaps more important was the fact that he was only able to use the power of personal persuasion to implement racial equality; Judge Waring, on the other hand, carried out his duty to uphold the United States Constitution and this permanently alienated those wishing to deny the Negro his rights.

Many of the Southern liberals who joined the Commission on Interracial Cooperation in the 1920's and 1930's and the Southern Regional Council, its successor, in the 1940's, sincerely believed in segregation. It was their desire to see separate but truly equal schools, hospitals, rest-room and parks for blacks. They disapproved of integration, which they honestly feared was bad for both races. Men like R. Beverly Herbert and Virginius Dabney opposed the Brown *v*. Topeka decision of 1954 with as much vehemence as Richard Russell or Harry Byrd. Wright was different. His mind was blessed with the capacity to grow and to realize that separate could never truly be equal. President of the Southern Regional Council during some of the turbulent years of the 1950's, he often reminded his fellow Southerners that they wasted too much "blood, sweat, tears, and toil. . .to see that a white child and a Negro child do not, side by side, learn their ABC's or the multiplication table." It was Wright's fervent belief that "we must integrate or we shall disintegrate." To well meaning gradualists he questioned the morality of demanding that a citizen "accept future delivery of a present right...a promissory note due at the indefinite date to be fixed at the pleasure of the gradualist."

Perhaps most unconventional of Wright's positions was his welcome of Northerners who called attention to Dixie's shameful treatment of blacks. Outside interference, as such criticism was typically called, did not bother Wright. Fully a dozen years before civil rights workers began to make their treks to Mississippi and Alabama to help blacks gain their civil rights, Wright warned his fellow Southerners:

> *The lament against outside interference, if heeded, would insulate the South against opinion coming from beyond its borders. The Mason and Dixon line would strongly resemble an iron curtain. The South may properly resent any misstatement of the facts regarding its customs, but it should welcome as a sanitative force candid criticism of the true situation from whatever source the criticism may come.*

Prophetically, in 1960, Wright told Northerners that they could not ignore Southern injustice. "The Southern liberal," he observed, "should not be left to fight his battles alone. After all, they are no more his battles than the battles of us all."

During the 1960's and 1970's blacks were registered to vote, were sent to integrated schools, and even were elected to high political offices. This came about, in part, because of outside interference and recognition that Southern liberals needed help.

Writing and speech making were not the only means by which his concern for human rights for all was manifested. For some years he was a member and chairman of the board of Penn Community Services, based at Frogmore on St. Helena Island, South Carolina. That organization's history began during the War Between the States, as Southerners still prefer to call the conflict. Shortly after the start of the war the South Carolina coastal islands fell under federal control. White plantation owners fled inland, leaving behind slaves who were destitute. Quakers, under authority of President Lincoln, began relief work, thought at the time to be temporary. However offering relief assistance led to the establishment of a boarding school for Negro boys and girls which continued to function until the early 1940's.

Supreme Court decisions in the school cases compelled South Carolina to take over education of the black youth of St. Helena Island. During Wright's administration as chairman the name of the institution was changed from Penn Normal, Agricultural and Industrial School to Penn Community Services; a library, day care center and clinic were provided, and, of equal importance, the dormitories, dining and other facilities began to be utilized for completely unsegregated public meetings and seminars, the first such in the state.

Upon the passage of the Civil Rights Act, the Civil Rights Commission was created. That Commission set up advisory committees in each state. Wright was made a member of the first such committee in North Carolina, he having moved to Linville Falls in that state from South Carolina in 1947. Wright became chairman of the sub-committee on employment, and, in that capacity, he prepared reports showing, among other things, that there was not a single Negro in the North Carolina National Guard. Moreover, as for the Tar Heel State's Employment Security Commission, in its Raleigh office there were only ten Negro employees, none above the rank of janitor-messenger. The Commission in the state at large had 945 whites and 51 non-white employees, none of the latter in administrative jobs.

Civil rights for Negroes has been the most important goal for Marion Wright, but it would be a mistake to view him solely as a champion of justice for blacks. His life also has been devoted to encouraging Southerners to establish public libraries, to respect civil liberties of controversial citizens of whatever race, and to abolish the death penalty. Interest in libraries came because Wright realized that "all of us, in this age, must continue to learn while we live." In 1934 he declared that the "only proper conception of the library is that it is an agency for education, that it is an extension of the school system." Libraries opened minds, prepared men and women to be good citizens and responsible voters. A public library was necessary for good government; it was the way to educate the ignorant man whose ballot counted as much as the one cast by the college professor. Ignorance was the enemy, and the library represented one way to educate the masses. Wright, feeling that "a lead pencil in the hand of an uneducated man was as dangerous a weapon as a bomb," insisted that there could be "no embargo on human thought, no quarantine against an idea, and no Chinese Wall isolating culture."

Many who applauded these enlightened views were silent when Wright called for integrated libraries and argued that democracy could not distribute books on a racial basis. Repeatedly during the 1930's and 1940's Wright pointed out the inadequacy of public library facilities for blacks in the Carolinas and argued that a policy of keeping books in libraries exclusively for whites was as damaging spiritually to whites as would be the lack of books. Separate but equal library facilities clearly was not the answer to the problem. Not only was this too costly for the Tarheel and Palmetto States, but it was morally wrong. Doubtless Wright hoped that if libraries could be opened to members of both races, integration of other public facilities soon would follow. But Wright was interested in libraries not only to end segregation; equally important to him was the desire to rid his region of "intellectual and cultural malnutrition."

Not surprisingly civil liberties also greatly interested Wright, who in 1973 served as president of the North Carolina chapter of the American Civil Liberties Union. Decrying censorship and xenophobia, he consistently argued for tolerance and diversity. Coming from a section of the country distrustful of outside influence, he realized that change was not necessarily bad. Variety, to him was not merely the spice of life; it was almost the essence of life. Once he eloquently summed up his thinking on the subject as follows:

*The end result of all that the civil libertarian under-
takes to do is to produce a society in which conformity is not the chief end and aim of man, in which
the goal of the individual is to be not respectable but
worthy; in which a man is free to march to a different
drummer and to follow his own star, wherever it may
lead.*

Sharing Wright's devotion to civil liberties and civil rights was
Mrs. Alice Norwood Spearman, who was a member of the South
Carolina Advisory Committee for the Civil Rights Commission.
She and Wright had served jointly as members of the boards of
the South Carolina Interracial Committee, the Southern Regional
Council and Penn Community Services.

In 1970, Mrs. Spearman, having been a widow for eight years,
and Wright, having been a widower for 13 years, a merger was
arranged and the former Mrs. Spearman is now Mrs. Wright.
Both are recipients of the Frank P. Graham Award given
annually by the North Carolina Civil Liberties Union for
"achievements in defending and advancing civil liberties," the
award to Wright having been made in 1969 and to Mrs. Wright in
1973.

In recent years Wright's concern for promoting civil liberties
has focused increasingly on eradicating the death penalty. For
nearly seventy years, ever since the day he read an essay on the
subject in Benjamin Tillman's library, he has been dedicated to
the abolition of capital punishment. During his student days at
the University of South Carolina, state prison authorities installed
the electric chair to provide a more efficient way to end the
lives of those convicted of capital crimes. In his capacity as a
reporter for the Columbia *Record*, Wright was given the grisly
task of writing news items about the first sixteen electrocutions.
It quickly became apparent to Wright that capital punishment
was reserved for the poor, the friendless, the illiterate, and the
non-white.

Expressing sentiment against the death penalty was

uncommon in the South, but Wright persisted in denouncing what he considered legalized murder in the Carolinas. During the 1960's he assisted in organizing North Carolinians Against the Death Penalty and served as first president of this organization. In 1965, he and Dr. Paul Green, a Pulitzer Prize winning playwright from Chapel Hill, unsuccessfully lobbied for a bill introduced by Representative Ernest Messer to abolish capital punishment in the state.

Interest in the death penalty as a means of punishing capital crime offenders grew in the 1970's. In 1972 the U.S. Supreme Court ruled 5-4 that capital punishment as then imposed by the states was illegal. North and South Carolina hastily made minor modifications in their laws, hoping that their changes might satisfy the high court's objections. On July 3, 1976, the Supreme Court ruled that the new statute devised by North Carolina was unconstitutional; by inference, the South Carolina law, similar to the one in the Tarheel State, was also null and void. Once again there was a rush for new legislation, and Marion Wright was quick to castigate those who "seek to preserve the death penalty as though it were a sacred treasure." Perhaps what most disturbs Wright about the death penalty is its finality. Errors can be corrected in cases of lesser punishment, but after the death penalty has been imposed, no error can be rectified.

On the issue of the death penalty, as on the question of civil rights and civil liberties, Wright is an optimist. He is positive that eventually the forces of reason and religion will ultimately cause men to regard the electric chair and the gas chamber as much relics of barbarity as the thumb screw, the rack, and the stake. In the end, Wright believes, men slowly move upward toward the stars.

Obviously Marion Wright is a most remarkable man. Born when Southern states were disfranchising blacks, he has lived to see Dixie's Afro-Americans reenfranchised and elected to Congress. In fact, one black civil rights leader was named ambassador to the United Nations. Wright has witnessed integration in schools, universities, and libraries. He has seen greater tolerance of civil liberties, increasing condemnation of capital punishment and the election of a Southerner to the presidency of the United States—largely because of black ballots. But as long as he breathes and injustice continues to exist, Marion Wright is not likely to be silent. Rather he will continue to work for his ideal of the millennium. To him "when all victories have been won, government will no longer concern itself with the tastes, the manners, the private morals of men and women, the way they dress, or wear their hair, or criticize their government, or pray publicly or salute the flag."

Arnold Shankman

Winthrop College

The Impact of Alma Mater

Marion Wright enrolled as a freshman at the University of South Carolina in September, 1910, when he was 16 years old, a most impressionable age. He continued as a student for the four year term ending in 1914 without receiving a degree. After teaching in a Winston-Salem, North Carolina high school, he re-entered the university as a law student in September, 1916, and emerged with a law degree in June, 1919. He became president of the Alumni Association and later the Law Alumni Association.

His student days profoundly affected his outlook and motivation. Being an indifferent student, probably his stock of knowledge was not largely increased, but the contacts with fellow students and faculty gave new meaning and purpose to his life.

Among Marion Wright's early surviving speeches was one delivered at the 1925 annual dinner of the ˙Alumni of the University of South Carolina. Wright urged his listeners to develop "a willingness to smash precedent and tradition if they stand in the way of progress" and "a readiness to challenge orthodoxy if orthodoxy be unsound." Wright's well-received oration was not merely a dinner speech; rather it reflected his personal credo. In fact, the title of the speech, "The Pioneer," is an apt description of Wright himself. He has practiced what he preached. For more than half a century after he addressed the U.S.C. alumni his mind and spirit have been devoted to breaking "down every barrier to human advance" and to striking "the shackles from men's minds." Excerpts of the speech appear below.

THE PIONEER

By common consent the most fascinating type in history is the pioneer. Men may remain cold and unmoved by the achievements of generals, statesmen, financiers, inventors and the like; but one must be barren of romance indeed who does not get some kind of thrill out of the exploits of the pioneer. The man who sails an uncharted sea, who blazes a trail thru the Australian bush, who washes his pan of sand in the waters of a California brook, hoping always for the glint of nuggets in the sand, who mushes behind a team of Eskimo huskies along the banks of the Yukon, who sleeps at night in a covered wagon under the stars of a Western sky—the pioneer remains the most picturesque, the most romantic, the most fascinating character in history....

There is little territory left for the activities of the pioneer. But there are vast fields left for his spirit. What is that spirit? It is a divine discontent with the established order, a willingness to smash precedent and tradition if they stand in the way of progress, a readiness to challenge orthodoxy, if orthodoxy be unsound. We South Carolinians have much to be proud of. But is there any section more in need of that spirit than our native State? Do any people excel us in following the beaten trail, in moving in ruts, in thinking in grooves, which is not thinking at all?

This, of course, may sound like treason, but the evangelists tell us that conviction of sin is the first step toward salvation. An admission of our shortcomings is the prelude toward curing those deficiencies. I am emboldened to make some such statements because a South Carolina newspaper, published in what was until recently regarded as the most conservative city in the country, ventured to express the same view in an editorial which won the Pulitzer prize.

We folk in the South have an expression which seems to me to sum up a good deal of our philosophy. That expression is, "If I live and nothing happens," as though the finest fate which could befall us is to go on living without ever having anything to happen....

It is, I hope, no mere setting up of a man of straw to raise the question as to whether or not there is in South Carolina too much moving in ruts and grooves. The great bulk of the population of South Carolina is agricultural. For more than 25 years the boll weevil, sweeping across the Mexican border, leaving desolation in his wake, advanced on South Carolina. His advent was predicted by the experts of Clemson College and the department of agriculture with the accuracy with which eclipses are foretold. Was there any change in farming methods or crops? Not so you could notice it. The old groove was good enough. And after four or five years of the weevil, it is the exceptional farmer in South Carolina who has gotten out of the rut and followed the new methods dictated by the experts. That is true of the great bulk of them. The University may take a high degree of pride in the fact that the one clear voice crying in the wilderness, the pioneer who has blazed the way and spent himself in showing how the pest may be vanquished, is one of her own sons, Mr. David R. Coker of Hartsville.

Isn't the boll weevil merely a symptom? A symptom of the reluctance with which our people abandon ancient habits, of the difficulty with which they make adjustments, of the suspicion with which they regard new ideas?....

Unless intelligent South Carolinians express themselves fearlessly and boldly on public issues whenever proper occasions arise, the legislature may not be expected to be as tolerant as Voltaire, who said, "I detest what you say, but I will die to maintain your right to say it."

It seems to me that it is the peculiar function of college and university graduates to furnish to the states the stimulation of new ideas. As a general rule, the uneducated may be relied upon to furnish the conservative element in abundance. What makes one an educated man is still a moot question, but there would seem to be but little difference of opinion on the point that college training removes part, at least, of the instinctive suspicion of the foreigner, it tends to eradicate the more or less natural hostility of men to new ideas.

Alumni of the colleges and universities of South Carolina should carry into life certain well defined beliefs. I suggest these as fundamental:

That change of customs, habits and institutions is not dangerous

That inability to change is dangerous

That there should be no veneration for ancient institutions merely because they are ancient

That no human institution—even the best of the lot—is perfect

That revolution is a better fate than stagnation

That the scientific spirit should be applied to every institution which surrounds us

The three great movements which have shaken the world have been the democratization of learning, the democratization of government and the democratization of religion. Tremendous battles have been fought at every step of the way. Men died on the gallows to bring learning out of the cloister and bestow it upon all mankind. They died on battle fields and under the guillotine to enfranchise their brothers. They died on the cross and at the stake to make religion the common possession of men. They were bold spirits who dared to challenge the orthodox conception of life. They were pioneers opening up vast unexplored territories for the human spirit.

The process is not complete. It will not be complete this side of the millennium. Government, education, religion, every field of human activity has its frontier. And beyond the frontier still other unknown regions beckon to men. God pity the man who thinks this is a finished universe!....

The real compensations of life are inner and not external. There is a vast compensation in mere self-respect; from being intellectually honest; from leading the strenuous life and fighting the good fight in the cause of truth; from the consciousness that in a small way one is a creator and not merely a creature; from the knowledge that what little force and power one possesses have been spent in making smooth the way of those who come after; a sense of kinship of spirit with the immortals.

Progesss has not come of itself. It has come because men willed it to come. It has come because of a ferment in men's minds, a spirit as deep and restless as the bosom of ocean; a spirit which is destined to break down every barrier to human advance, to strike the shackles from men's minds.

Each man has his part to play in this struggle upward toward the stars.

Tribute to Dr. S. C. Mitchell

On January 23, 1935, at the University of Richmond, Dr. S.C. Mitchell was honored by a testimonial dinner on his 70th birthday. The program featured representatives from all of the institutions which Dr. Mitchell had served as professor or president. Marion Wright, upon whom Dr. Mitchell had had a profound influence, spoke for the University of South Carolina. His address follows.

DOCTOR MITCHELL AT CAROLINA

Beginning about the year 1909 an observer on the campus of the University of South Carolina would have noted the introduction of many new mannerisms into the daily speech and conduct of the undergraduates. Boys who had theretofore been merely "glad" that such and such a thing was true had become "quite happy" at the same state of facts. Those who had been merely "thankful" for some favor received were now "profoundly grateful" for the same favor. One who might have informed another, after some forensic effort that he "had made a good speech," or more likely, that he "had taken the rag off the bush," now extended his congratulations by the statement that the orator "had given us a revelation of power." Freshmen no longer greeted their classmates with an informal "Hey, fellow," but gravely saluted them with "Good morning, young gentlemen." And so on. A somewhat alien note of courtesy, grace and politeness had been introduced into the life of the campus, investing it with peculiar charm.

Those of you who are aware of the fact that Doctor Mitchell had in the year 1909 become president of the University of South Carolina will require no explanation of the epidemic of good manners which had descended upon the student body. There was and is that about him which inspires and lends itself to imitation and the most boorish of freshmen felt somehow impelled to appropriate to his own uses those physical and visible expressions of Doctor Mitchell's inherent polish and grace. Indeed, imitation of him took its place as one of the university's recognized intramural sports, for excellence in which an award of letters, as in football, was seriously considered.

One may initiate mannerisms and afford proof of his success as a mimic. A gesture, a tone, an expression, may be copied and the world called upon to witness the fidelity with which the original has been reproduced. Points of view, social attitudes, deeply held convictions, may be absorbed, may become part and parcel of one's being, the stuff on which he has fed, but demonstrative evidence of this transfusion of ideas is ordinarily difficult to supply. But that this resurgence of manners of which I have spoken was the more efflorescent expression of profounder inner change wrought by Doctor Mitchell upon the of an entire student body within a period of four years I consider susceptible of proof.

New and exotic names began to be bandied about in undergraduate conversation. Cavour and Garabaldi became the daily intimates of the student body, and the unification of Italy was about as well known as the story of the Confederacy. John Huss, who Doctor Mitchell said "was hunted across Europe as we would pursue a mad dog across this campus," Kossuth, Carl Schurz, Savonarola, St. Francis—a whole host of names became clothed with flesh and blood, invested with reality, towering and magnificent figures, who laid grip upon the imagination.

Boys began to dally with bright and shimmering ideas. The great struggles for religious freedom and for freedom of thought and the press became more than musty pages in ancient volumes—they were slow and painful processes not yet complete and in which a man of courage could still enlist. Public roads, public libraries, public schools, public health had strong champions in the student body and were discussed with perhaps more earnestness than eloquence in the literary societies. Discriminations based upon race or color or creed began to be examined objectively to determine upon what, if any, reasonable postulates they could be sustained. In a day when the political powers that be were blowing upon the embers of an ancient prejudice, here and there college men were becoming champions of the Negro's rights. The World Court was as well understood and had as large a percentage of adherents among the student body as among any similar group of men in this country. The first breath of a liberal philosophy—at a time when liberalism was still timid—was in the nostrils of every student.

New heroes were created. South Carolina heroes. James Lide Coker, in industry and philanthropy; his son, David R. Coker, in agriculture; D.A. Thompkins and Lewis W. Parker, in Industry; Charles A. Woods, once an ornament of the circuit court of appeals and a resident of Richmond, in the law; Ambrose E. Gonzales in journalism; Richard I. Manning in government—these men were held up to us as examples far more worthy of our emulation than the cheap and tawdry and spectacular figures who sometimes strutted across the contemporary South Carolina scene.

The boys who lived in and breathed in this spiriting and stimulating atmosphere are now alumni, scattered throughout the country and, in many instances, I regret to report, somewhat bald and portly. I presume that I must also concede that in many instances and to some degree there has been a recession from the lofty idealism of an earlier and a better day. But still they have Doctor Mitchell's stamp upon them. Wherever they are, in the better parts of their natures—in the flaming indignation which they feel in the presence of injustice, in their aspiration for larger and more equal opportunity for the oppressed, in their zeal for a general diffusion of knowledge, in their passion for freedom in the larger sense—they are emanations from, projections of, his electric personality. Such a man lives a thousand lives.

And the alumni wish to acknowledge this debt. They wish to attest to the fact that they live somewhat richer and fuller lives because, for a season and in their formative years, their paths crossed his.

So, Doctor Mitchell, in this volume of letters your old boys speak to you across a score of years. We are not ashamed to wear our hearts upon our sleeves. More, we have tried ineffectually to bind them in a book. May these letters through the years that lie ahead serve often to remind you that from the boundless fount of your own full life, many, many lives have been enriched!

In the fall of 1973 Outlook Publishers issued a Going-to-College Handbook, designed to be helpful to prospective students. The value of a college education was stated in differing terms by authorities ranging from Pope Paul VI to Senator Edward Brooke of Massachusetts. The influence of two University of South Carolina professors—Dr. S.C. Mitchell and Dr. Josiah Morse—on his life was described by Wright under the title "Two Teachers Made a Difference."

TWO TEACHERS MADE A DIFFERENCE

"How did you get that way?"

This is a question often asked of any white Southerner considered "liberal" on the race issue. Happily, the question is asked less frequently as the liberals have become less rare. But in the years before and immediately following Brown *v.* Topeka, those advocating integration of schools and equal rights at the lunch counter were a rare, not to say endangered, species. As a native white Southerner somewhat active in civil rights causes, I have often been queried about the source of my aberration.

I have what is to me at least a partial answer. It is found in the influence of two professors at the University of South Carolina, which I attended from 1910 to 1914 and from 1916 to 1919, when I emerged with a law degree.

Dr. Samuel C. Mitchell came to the university as its president in my freshman year and served during my four-year tour. While I took only one course under him, that in government, it was impossible to be on the campus without feeling the electric energy which flowed from him. He moved always at a half-trot. He spoke rapidly but with inspired diction, never using notes. He established the extension department and placed the university in the forefront of the movement for better schools, roads and public health services.

Looking back on it, I doubt that the issue of segregation was ever put into words by Dr. Mitchell. Indeed, at the time it hardly existed as an issue. But all of the man's words, acts and impulses pointed unerringly to a state's obligation to make no racial distinction between its citizens. He left the state because of his convictions on that issue.

In brief, he recommended to a liquidating foundation that its last remaining $400,000 be granted to ten Southern Negro colleges to establish departments for teacher training. The recommendation was accepted. Winthrop, a white girls' college in South Carolina, had sought the total $400,000. Governor Cole Blease, the then current South Carolina demagogue, seized on the incident to launch an attack on Dr. Mitchell, who, feeling his usefulness impaired, resigned and accepted the task of consolidating three Virginia medical institutions.

When Dr. Mitchell became president of the University of South Carolina, he brought with him as a professor of philosophy, Dr. Josiah Morse. Dr. Morse had been one of Dr. Mitchell's pupils at the University of Richmond. He had absorbed much of his teacher's sympathy and concern for human rights and with the duty of government in protecting those rights. (His first child was named Samuel Chiles Mitchell Morse.)

Whereas Dr. Mitchell had dealt with the problem of the Southern Negro in general terms, Dr. Morse dealt with it in specifics. Indeed, he taught a course on that subject—probably unprecedented in Southern educational annals. Remember, this was in the period of 1910 to 1914.

The textbook used in connection with the course was Dr. Edgar Gardner Murphy's *The Basis of Ascendancy*. Dr. Murphy wrote this book while a professor at the University of Alabama, which is not the least remarkable fact about it.

Dr. Morse was a young, magnetic and an inspiring teacher. Consequently, his classes were always well attended. I took nearly all of his courses. His own influence, plus the thought-provoking quality of *The Basis of Ascendancy*, caused me, for the first time, not merely to question, but to repudiate, the pleasant assumption of my own superiority as a white person over any Negro, however able.

It was the thesis of the book—a lesson still unlearned in much of the nation—that superiority of one person over another is a matter of individual attainments and excellence, with which his color has nothing to do. This was revolutionary doctrine at the time. I embraced it without reservation and it has become a permanent part of my personal creed.

While having the philosopher's detachment, Dr. Morse realized that there is no substitute for experience. Hence, in Columbia, South Carolina, he formed a group of white students from the university and students from Benedict and Allen Colleges, Negro institutions of the city. I was a member of the group which met at more or less frequent intervals at the University YMCA.

These meetings were my first venture into inter-racial activities. They were also my first contact upon terms of equality with black boys of my own age. There were no papers read and no formal agenda. But there was frank and uninhibited discussion of such touchy matters as Negro voting and integration of schools and other facilities.

I think that these contacts at an impressionable age permanently reinforced in my mind the Murphy thesis that the doctrine of white supremacy, on which I had been reared, was a dangerous myth. My contacts with Negroes in all of the succeeding years have been less artificial because of the early association which Dr. Morse brought about.

Marion Wright has always manifested great interest in the youth of America. He recognized that many adults had become too inflexible to change the existing status quo. Moreover, they made a virtue of conforming to whatever was considered proper. This profoundly disturbed Wright who realized that without critical analysis of existing institutions "society will tend to fit itself into a definite mold that will cramp the lives of all its members." It was to the youth that Wright looked for a willingness to consider new ideas and to tolerate dissent. When he went to Rock Hill, South Carolina, on May 27, 1932, to address the graduating class at the local high school, he came, as he noted, "to bury conformity, not to praise it." Excerpts from that speech appear below.

PLEA FOR NON–CONFORMITY

We hear good people deplore the spirit of unrest which is said to be abroad in the land. We hear the fear expressed that those who go out from our schools will not conform to standards of thinking and conduct established by their elders. I come to express no such apprehension. My fear is that they will conform. I come to bury conformity, not to praise it. My plea is for the preservation of the spirit of revolt. The first duty of the educated is the duty of rebellion, rebellion against conditions or institutions which tend in any way to hamper full and free growth and development.

The greatest pressure to which one is subjected on entering into adult life is the pressure which would make him conventional. That pressure is a most elusive thing. You can hardly put your finger on the source of it and you feel baffled in trying to fight back. But it is there, all pervasive, omnipresent. It manifests itself in ridiculous details of conduct. The more trivial and insignificant the detail, the more insistent is the pressure. If you want to learn how strong the pressure is be unconventional in dress. Why, about a year ago the whole Western world was agitated for weeks about whether or not Gandhi would wear trousers or a bath towel when he called on King George. Not what kind of ideas but what kind of wardrobe he would carry to England. More recently the question was whether Andrew Mellon would wear ordinary full length trousers or knee breeches and silk stockings when presented at court. And you may recall that a few years ago there was fierce debate on the question of whether or not a good woman could bob her hair!

Try to be unconventional in your talk. Tremendous events are taking place these days in Russia. Make a speech publicly advocating the Russian theory of government and you will at least be regarded as queer if not deported. If the label of Red or Communist or Socialist or Pacifist may be attached to you, you may be in danger of death or serious bodily harm.

Now the terrible result of universal conventionality is that life becomes dull, boring, flat, inane. It lacks savor and color and charm. Think of being cast ashore on a desert island with a company of people whose one virtue was they did things that were eminently proper and correct and did them in the proper and correct manner. They were all members of the same political party and the same church and the same lodge and the same luncheon club and they had the same views and the same prejudices. Wouldn't it be refreshing after an experience of that sort to sit down for a long talk with some salty, racy and original character who didn't mind stepping on your toes, if the expression of an honest opinion could accomplish that result?

What should give us concern is that one may not have to be cast adrift on a desert island to undergo such a harrowing experience. Some years ago a study was made of what was considered to be a typical American small town. Investigators spent many months studying the life of this community, as Thoreau would have studied the life of an ant hill. The human beings were observed and their characteristics noted with scientific impersonality. The results of the study were published under the title "Middletown." The thing that emerged from the study was the deadly sameness of life in this average American community.

One was a member of a political party because it was the tradition of the family or the group that this was the correct party. One became a Mason or a Rotarian or an Episcopalian because it was customary in one's group to make such affiliation. Schools were chosen for the children on the same basis. A young man's ambition led him toward the ownership of a home in a certain section and membership on boards of directors. A boy developing a talent for music or art was regarded with suspicion. Reading and conversation revolved about safe, sane, and sensible ideas which had been tried and tested throughout the years. The injection of anything original or controversial was taboo. The picture is one of deadly, dull monotony, a living of life according to rule of thumb and fixed routine.

It is a picture of men and women afraid. Afraid of the implications of a new idea. Afraid of any loosening of hold on what is in hand to reach out for the untried. The worst of all possible fears, the fear to think for themselves. Professor Patterson Wardlaw is authority for many well considered statements. He never said anything truer than "When all seem to be thinking alike no one is actually thinking at all." So when we observe entire sections of society motivated by the same impulses, reacting in precisely the same manner to stimuli, apparently agreeing with each other in all fundamental matters, we may conclude that these may all be proper and correct persons but none of them is doing any thinking for himself.

There will hardly be any question of the fact that, certainly in the field of the law, the American who has done the most constructive thinking in the past fifty years has been Justice Oliver Wendell Holmes. He has been a steady and inveterate dissenter, not out of a spirit of pure perversity, but because the operation of an untrammeled mind did not lead him to conclusions held by the majority. With what zest he wrote and with what a zest he lives! And what deep pleasure must have been his as the dissents of his earlier years became the prevailing opinions of the court in his ripened age!

He revealed himself in what he wrote. A Mme. Schwimmer, a Hungarian, applied for citizenship in the United States and was refused because she would not agree to take up arms for the country in time of war. The case went to the United States Supreme Court. Justice Holmes, in one of his militant dissenting opinions, said:

> *If there is any principle of the Constitution that more imperatively calls for attachment than any other, it is the principle of free thought—not free thought for those who agree with us, but freedom for the thought which we hate...I would suggest that the Quakers have done their share to make the country what it is, that many citizens agree with Mme. Schwimmer's beliefs, and that I had not supposed hitherto that we regretted our inability to expel them because they believe more than some of us do in the teachings of the Sermon on the Mount....*

Justice Holmes was unafraid to dissent. Not only have his dissenting opinions enriched the law but his fearless willingness to dissent must have enriched his own life.

So I make the point that the full, the rich, the adventurous life, the colorful, the romantic life is the life lived by those unafraid. Unafraid to dissent. Unafraid to think for themselves. Unafraid to develop hobbies and to preserve unseemly enthusiasms well on into adult life and old age. Not obsessed by what the neighbors will think or say. You recall that Charles Darwin had a neighbor, an estimable old lady, who looked over her back fence and saw Darwin standing for long minutes day after day examining a rose. The old lady became sympathetic and told her friends that she "felt sorry for Mr. Darwin and that she did wish he had something worthwhile to do instead of mooning about his roses." Something worthwhile to do! Fortunately for the world Charles Darwin was not stopped from mooning about his roses by the glances cast at him across his back yard fence.

But it is important not alone for the individual that he should preserve for himself full liberty of thought and action. It is important for the state that such a spirit should be universal. If society is to be other than static, if it is to be adaptable to changing needs, it must have the fertilization of ideas which come from the unafraid. Unless dissents are filed, unless criticism is free and fearless, unless existing institutions are to be subjected to critical analysis, society will tend to fit itself into a definite mold that will cramp the lives of all its members.

During Marion Wright's college days considerable attention was paid to the art of public speaking. There were frequent contests in declamation, debating and oratory. In South Carolina the most important of such competitions was the South Carolina Inter-collegiate Oratorical Contest held annually in Rock Hill at Winthrop College. The University and colleges conducted preliminaries, winners of which met at Winthrop for the finals.

On April 25, 1913, Wright 19 years old and a junior, won first prize with a speech entitled "America and Peace." Woodrow Wilson was then President and such ideas as disarmament and the formation of a body to promote cooperation among nations were uppermost in the public mind. Wright's speech, from which the following excerpts are taken, reflected the rising tide of internationalism.

AMERICA AND PEACE

Progress is the result of concerted action. Leaders of great movements have failed of their endeavors if they have not been able to create a degree, at least, of public opinion in favor of the ends desired. This is true of localities; it is true of nations. An aroused public conscience is necessary and has ever been necessary to compete with social ills. Where this has been had, any enterprise that it has sought to foster has been sure of success. In other words, the crystallization of public opinion about a single ideal is always an epoch-marking event....

Never until recently in the history of the world has there been a blending of international ideals. Each nation has thought in terms of itself, just as a century ago, communities knew nothing and cared nothing about what took place without their borders. But today, with lightning-like means of communication and with an extensive commerce, nations are awaking to the fact that they are a part of the international federation of States and that the principle that "I am my brother's keeper" applies as truly to countries as to individuals.

And with this quickened knowledge of an intimate international relationship, it is not singular that the thought of the whole world should turn itself to the most paramount of all ills. It is not singular that after the spread of Christianity, there should arise a movement in all quarters of the globe, having as its object the promotion of peace among the nations. Public opinion everywhere has crystallized about the high ideal of peace and human society—for the first time in history, internationally federated—is seeking to move forward by lopping of the evil of war....

It has been estimated that the War Between the Sections cost this nation $65,000,000,000, in material wealth. Do you know, that, allowing one dollar for each second that has elapsed since the birth of Christ, the world would stand for five hundred years yet before that vast sum would be exhausted? It has cost this nation $400,000,000 to build the Panama Canal. With the amount wasted in those four years of war, 150 canals, equally as expensive, could have been built, every acre of land within the borders of the country could have been drained and a model school established in every community of 500 population.

Yet this was a comparatively inexpensive war. The campaigns of Napoleon left all of Europe prostrate and bankrupt. The great generals of history have been the central figures of the world's most extravagant enterprise.

Second only in importance to the cost of actual conflict is the expense of preparation for it, the maintenance of a nation's armies and its navies. And again we need not go beyond our own borders to find illustrative facts. Out of every dollar paid into the treasury of the United States seventy cents goes for the payment of debts incurred by past wars and for the maintenance of a fighting force. Think of the enormous drain on a nation's resources, the vast amount of constructive work left untouched by reason of this fact. More than one hundred thousand men are being paid to stand as guards to the national safety and honor.

My friends, I can but believe that the honor of any nation is safest where it resides in the character and in the intelligence of its citizenship. And I believe that that nation is the loser which trades a school or a church for a military outpost.

Another phase of this question. We are building great ships that cost millions of dollars. As has been pointed out, those dollars represent work. Work is stored life. In a memorable battle some years ago, Admiral Togo sank seventeen such vessels of the Russian navy. Think of the thousand upon thousand days of squandered human life that sank with that fleet into the deep!

Of the actual loss of human life on the field of battle, I need hardly speak. Those myriads of men since the world began who have laid down their lives in defense of their flags have become the common heritage of all the earth. However, most of us are hero worshipers and are prone to think rather of the generals who directed the waging of great battles than of the thousands of privates, but for whose loyalty and bravery their causes would have perished.

I saw a picture some time ago that forcibly drives home a great moral. In its forefront there stood the mounted and resplendent figures of Napoleon, Hannibal, Caesar and Alexander, the Great. And stretching far behind on the rocky highway upon which these great generals had ridden to fame, there lay strewn the chilled corpses of millions of victims. And so it has been through all the ages. The steel horse of war has charged steadily forward crushing, in his hurling pace, the good, the brave, the fair, the honored, of every land.

But if wars settled moral issues—if the rule of might acted with wisdom and justice as the arbiter of international affairs—then there might be reason for war. But in ages past avarice and greed have oftener been the cause of war than has a deeply rooted conviction of the justice of it all.

War means a cessation of progress, a stagnation of the current of human achievements. Consider the centuries of war since the world began. They have been barren and gloomy stretches of time wherein tragedy, pathos and famine have been the camp-followers of every army. Art, literature and science have always been shackled during the ages of war. This fact is strikingly illustrated by a comparison of Spartan and Athenian life. The Spartans were strong, vigorous, warlike. Nearly every period of the national existence witnessed a conflict with another nation. On the other hand, in Athens the emphasis was laid on mental and cultural development. Peace was the guiding spirit of the nation. What has the world gotten from Sparta? Nothing but unexampled instances of heroism on the field of battle and perhaps a higher knowledge of military science. But from Athens, the world has gotten all of philosophy, ethics and art. Sparta has given to the world the thrilling and tragic story of Leonidas. Athens has given to the world the teachings of Socrates, Plato and Aristotle, and the literary and artistic work of a hundred others....

Such is the great problem that confronts us. As was said in the beginning, it is the one paramount and universal human ill, and there can be no wonder that sentiment on every hand should be turning against war. The federation of the world has grasped the high ideal of peace. The time will come when it may be said of every land, as it has been said of ours:

No more the thirsty entrance to this soil
Shall daub her lips with her own children's blood.
No more shall trenching war channel her fields
Nor bruise her flowers with the armed hoofs
Of hostile paces.

And with this powerful and concerted movement for peace there comes the great opportunity for this nation to take the lead in declaring for disarmament. Peculiar facts of our history, our isolated geographical position and certain tendencies of our national growth make this nation seem preordained for the great task of leading the peace movement for the world.

The late Associate Justice David J. Brewer, of the United States Supreme Court, said in an address a few months before his death: "It seems to me that there was also a purpose that this republic should lead in the great cause of the peaceful settlement of international disputes. This is a composite nation. It was settled, not by one race alone, but by Englishmen, Germans, Frenchmen and Swedes. And out of these composite races is being formed the nation which, of all on the face of the globe, most fully represents the brotherhood of man. And where there is that brotherhood, there will be no fighting. It seems to me that one of the lessons we may draw from history is that the Almighty has in the councils of eternity the purpose that this republic should stand among the great nations of earth as leader in the cause of universal peace."

The position of Justice Brewer is sustained by Secretary of State, William Jennings Bryan, who said in an address a few weeks ago at Raleigh: "It seems to me that the time is ripe for this republic to take the lead in bringing about peace among the nations, as she has done in advancing democracy everywhere. The most effective step, and the only one about which there can be no question as to its sincerity, is disarmament."

The fact of the isolated geographical position of the United States gives this nation a great advantage in leading the movement for disarmament. Germany, England and France are huddled together and naturally watch with jealous eyes the others' preparations for war. For if one nation is to expand, it means an encroachment on the territory of its neighbor. But America is surrounded by oceans on each side and has near her no potential enemy who would be able to pounce upon her possessions once the peaceful step has been taken....

America has taken the lead in settling a number of international disputes. She is known among the nations as a nation of peace. The United States should show to the world that she deserves the characterization and that this republic will practice in all sincerity the doctrine which it has so proudly upheld.

Such is the great problem that confronts us: Such America's peculiar opportunity. I speak tonight to an audience of Americans and upon each man and woman here there rests the solemn responsibility to lend his influence to so sacred a cause.

You recall how in the days of old, Elisha with his army lay in beleagured Samaria, surrounded by enemies. All escape seemed impossible and the servant of the prophet asked him the question: "Master, how shall we be saved?" And Elisha answered: "Fear not, for they that be with us are greater than the enemy." And the servant beheld the air about him filled with the chariots of an unconquerable host, and on that day the army of the Lord gained a great victory. So, my friends, in this battle for peace, "they that be with us are greater than the enemy," for the cause is of God. And all the world, though it be banded against us, shall not prevail against Him. For it was the mission of the Master to bring "Peace upon the earth, good will to men."

Intimations of Approaching Social Revolution

Until midway of the Twentieth Century the annual observance of Memorial Day was a sacred rite in all states of the South. The event, usually under auspices of the Daughters of the Confederacy, was devoted to keeping alive memories of those who fought under Lee. It was part of the Southern creed that no general in history equalled the skill and genius of Lee and Jackson and no troops equalled in valor and gallantry the troops those generals commanded.

Perhaps much of this praise was not over-blown. General Eisenhower regarded Lee as the greatest American commander and Churchill declared that the struggle of the 1860's was "the last war fought between gentlemen."

On May 10, 1927, Marion Wright was the speaker at Memorial Day exercises in Marion, South Carolina, exercises held in sight of a monument—such as are found in nearly all Southern county seats—a marble shaft topped by the figure of a rifle-bearing Confederate soldier.

Since his father had fought under Lee, Wright was not entirely disingenuous as he extolled the virtues and prowess of the men in gray. He did, however, depart from the script in pointing out the moral obligation resting upon the white South to deal fairly with those whom the war had liberated.

This theme, the moral obligation, as well as the practical benefits flowing to both races from releasing the creative energy of blacks and from their full participation in politics and government, was to be a feature of Wright's speeches for a half century—indeed until a Southern white ex-governor from Georgia was installed in the White House by Negro votes.

In 1927, when the speech was delivered, no South Carolina Negro was permitted to vote in the Democratic primary or to serve on juries. Excerpts from the speech follow.

MARION MEMORIAL DAY ADDRESS

There is no higher test of the culture of a man than his attitude toward those with whom he differs. Especially is that test severe where one is a member of the majority group. Being a member of the majority, a certain majority of numbers, gives one a sense of power, of invulnerability. A consciousness of power tends most naturally to a disregard of the rights and opinions of those less powerful. And so we see our marines in Nicaragua and Haiti.

The white people of the South face and have faced for decades a situation which affords abundant opportunity for the display of the chivalric principle—that principle which recognizes the rights of a weak minority. The close of the Civil War left whites as neighbors of a mass of ignorant black people. A presidential proclamation had stricken the shackles from their feet and the Constitution of the United States had been wisely amended so as to confer on them every privilege of citizenship. And so the two races have remained side by side for six decades.

In that time the Negro has made tremendous progress. His numbers have quadrupled. From empty-handedness he has by the product of his own labors come into the possession of property worth $600,000,000. His schools and colleges have produced graduates in all the professions who are men and women of distinction. In literature, art, music, the drama, his record is one of which the race may feel proud.

Certainly, that material progress would not have been possible without the sympathy and support of white people. Henry W. Grady in his great Boston address laid down the broad principle that toward the Negro the white people of the South stood in the relationship of guardian and ward. Force of circumstances had placed us in such status with the colored man that his progress was largely in white hands. The results sufficiently indicate that there has been a universal consciousness of that truth.

The progress of the Negro has been material, financial, intellectual. I venture now with some trepidation to say that the time has arrived when the political rights of the Negro must have ampler protection and larger exercise. For I do not believe any people can achieve its full stature when deprived by whatever means of any political right.

We want the Negro to become patriotic and law-abiding. Isn't it asking a great deal to expect him to be patriotic while living under a government in the control of which his voice is not heard? Isn't it asking a great deal of him to expect him to observe laws which he has had no hand in making, in interpreting or in enforcing?

Statistics of the last few years show that less and less is the

Negro in the criminal courts. The complexion of jails and chain gangs has radically changed from Negro to white. Isn't the Negro in his increased observance of the law demonstrating capacity to have a hand in determining the kind of law under which he will live?

A citizen must have a stake in his government. No one is going to busy himself about helping in the affairs of a corporation unless he has stock in that corporation. Give a man stock in his government and see how quickly he takes an interest in its internal affairs. The Negro has done more and better than we would have a right to expect. No question has ever been raised as to his loyalty to the government. The race has never produced a traitor. Yet the very government to which he has been loyal has been almost an alien government....

Jolly, chuckling President Taft during his administration went on a 'possum hunt down in Georgia. Several Negroes were members of the party. One said to another:

> "Look, here, who is this fat man we got along tonight?" "Why, man, that President Taft." "What's he president of?" "I don't know, but he's president of something up North."

We sometimes accuse the Negro of being irresponsible. He certainly is not to be blamed for being entirely irresponsible. He couldn't have a very heavy sense of responsibility in regard to his government when he has no voice in determining the kind of government under which he lives, when the government is merely something up North.

The laws of psychology are of universal application. They don't have one application to white men and another to colored men. One way of measuring a good citizen is by his going to the polls, by his serving when called to sit on juries, by his discharge of political duties and responsibilities. Those who seek to prevent the discharge of political duties by Negroes are doing much to make bad citizens out of the members of that race.

But, it may be said, the Negro is making no demand for his political rights. I admit he has shown remarkable patience. All the more reason why the white people should make the first overture. My belief is that when the Negro meets the same educational qualifications as the white man he should have the same privileges. Only superior men are willing to recognize the rights of all others. The kind of superiority worth having is the kind based on moral excellence and on proper respect for the rights of the weak. A really superior person would never feel himself superior or claim that he was.

The fundamental trouble, of course, is to be found in the parallel histories of the two races. Seventy years ago the Negro was a chattel without rights of any kind which a white man was bound to recognize. We have grown up, he with the tradition of slavery and we with the tradition of mastery. In the new adjustment of the races much progesss has been made to the everlasting credit of both. The process of adjustment is not complete. It will not be complete until the white people view with equanimity the exercise of political rights by their weaker brethren.

During campaign years, so-called leaders pander to ancient prejudices. Unscrupulous men dealing with an ignorant electorate blow on the coals of hate. The sons and daughters of Confederate veterans who recognized human rights even when life was at stake ought to rebuke this bankrupt statesmanship. The politician who offers nothing better than groundless hate has no place in this year of grace 1927.

Nor is this sentimental altruism. It is intelligent self interest. One cannot wink at miscarriages of justice in regard to black men without encouraging the disintegration of law which protects the white. One cannot with complacency observe political jugglery to deprive colored men of their votes without being a party to the corruption of institutions which safeguard the liberties of the white. So long as the law of compensation and retribution is operative we dare not fail to help the Negro. We can only hold him down by holding ourselves down to the same plane.

Not only do we in the South undergo a racial test of our chivalry, our sense of fairness. We also undergo a religious test. The population of the South is preponderantly Protestant. I have not seen the statistics but I imagine that not more than five per cent of the people of the Southern States are Catholics. Here again is the sense of power, which power imposes a test of a crucial sort on those who wield it.

I feel free to speak with frankness for the reason that, so far as I know, all the members of my family and my forebears for generations have been Protestant. So I am not concerned especially with the rights of Catholics, but I am concerned with the rights of human beings everywhere to worship God according to the dictates of their own consciences, or not to worship at all.

That right, of course, is guaranteed to us by the Constitution of our nation and by the Constitutions of all American States. But some of those who are loudest in their protestations of Americanism appear to forget this fundamental principle of the American creed. While shouting for us to uphold the flag they tear to tatters the principles which the flag represents.

It is not enough that a thing is guaranteed by law. That guarantee must be backed up by public sentiment if it is not to be meaningless. The public by a cynical attitude toward those whose religious beliefs may not jibe with those of the majority may nullify the Constitution as effectively as it could be done by amendment or court interpretation.

Is it setting up a mere man of straw to inquire if there is not abroad in the land a spirit which would curtail the religious freedom guaranteed by the Constitution? The Constitution affirms that no man shall be disbarred from holding public office on account of religious belief. Yet in the year 1927 we have seen the charge circulated publicly as well as privately and insiduously that a governor of a great State was disqualified for the presidency because he happened to worship in his own way. Shades of Thomas Jefferson. Men have bled and died to guarantee him that right, a right which a temporary and powerful majority now seeks to abrogate overnight.

Who is the real enemy of his country? Is it the soldier who in fair and open combat makes war against its flag? He, of course, is an enemy. But the archenemy of the nation is that man, living under the protection of its institutions, enjoying the freedom, dearly bought, which it confers, yet who turns his back on the principles which have made it great.

The history and tradition of the nation are insulted by every effort to curtail religious freedom and by every effort to proscribe those whose form of worship is somewhat different. The first settlers who touched its shores were impelled to cross the seas by the thought that in the wilderness which lay beyond the Atlantic a religious haven from persecution might be found. The colonies, one by one as forms of government developed, wrote this jealously guarded principle into their fundamental law. The Declaration of Independence, while a political document, breathes this universal craving of the newborn nation. The Statute of Religious Liberty, framed by Thomas Jefferson for Virginia, was adopted in essence by every state. And when the Articles of Confederation had given way to a more permanent Union, that great principle was firmly imbedded in its texture. On such meat have we fed. Of such beliefs have we imbibed from our national youth to this day. Any man who turns his back now on that principle for political or other reason befouls the very nest in which he is reared. Wherever this monster of religious intolerance rears its head let us strike it down.

I have spoken of racial and religious matters merely as illustrating the entire problem. That problem is to apply to controversy in whatever field the principle which recognizes human worth and dignity on whichever side of the question it may be found.

To belittle and disparage one's opponent one must be an incurable egotist. One must be positively convinced of his own infallibility in order to say that one who differs with him is a knave or a fool. The Romans with a broad wave of the hand referred to all those who lived beyond the limits of the Eternal City as barbarians. And we to this day in a slightly more modest fashion express the same belief. We say that Mr. So-and-So is a pretty good fellow to be a Yankee, the inference being that, of course, not having been born in the South, he couldn't be quite as good a fellow as I am. We say that Mr. Borah is an able man to be a Republican, the implication being that, not being a Democrat, you wouldn't expect very much of him anyhow. And so on.

Why, our conceit, as some one has pointed out, has actually influenced our attitude toward colors. We say that a thing is as black as sin. We say that a coward has a yellow streak. The Bolshevists are Reds. A bad taste is a dark brown taste. But when someone has been unusually nice to us, he has treated us white. Our color, white, so a synonym for all that is good and fine.

The inevitable effort of large majorities is to make the minority conform to its own views; to reduce mankind to types and fit men into common molds. All too often is the effort made to stifle thought and speech when thought and speech run counter to popular belief. By such a course is life robbed of much of its color and charm and variety. The atmosphere in which genuises are bred is the atmosphere in which no shackles are placed on the human mind.

As Montesquieu long ago pointed out, the danger about a democracy is that the rights of minorities may be disrespected. It is true that the majority rules. But a majority demonstrates its capacity for ruling by refraining from tyranny. The real test of capacity for government is to be found in the respect which is shown to the rights of minorities. It was said long ago that "The strong shall bear the infirmities of the weak." By the same token the strong must respect the rights of the weak.

The strong become stronger by such a course. They grow in that department of life where growth is worth-while. With the generous attitude toward the weak there comes an accession of moral power. There is vast compensation in mere self-respect, in the consciousness that power has been put to sacred uses, that we have been large enough to live side by side with the weak without trampling them under foot or flaunting their convictions.

When the Conferderate War came on, it was opposed by certain able South Carolinians. Among them was James Pettigru of Charleston. Throughout the War he maintained an attitude of passive opposition. The fact that he stood practically alone did not alter his course. In other societies he might well have been branded traitor and shot at sunrise. But not in Charleston, South Carolina. He lived out his allotted span with the admiration and respect of his associates. And admiring fellow citizens have marked his last resting place with a bronze tablet to perpetuate his memory. The State University named its law school in his honor.

That incident is typical of the spirit of the South in the Sixties. The Confederate soldier, even under stress of war, preserved the amenities of conflict, respected the dignity and worth of his opponents. Surely, those of us who inherit the land which he honored, can give no higher evidence of our admiration for him than by applying the principle of chivalry to present day human relations.

". . .The time has now arrived when the way should be prepared for the exercise by the intelligent members of the colored race of the right of suffrage guaranteed by the Constitution."

Thus Wright told a meeting of the Parent-Teacher Association in Columbia, South Carolina, on May 3, 1928. The time was significant because many Democratic politicians in the South were raising the hallowed cry of "white supremacy" to keep the rank-and-file members within the "White Man's Party." And because of the anti-Catholic campaign already being waged against Al Smith, Wright injected a reminder of the Jeffersonian, and American, principle of religious liberty. Excerpts follow.

CHALLENGE TO WHITE SUPREMACY AND RELIGIOUS BIGOTRY

This is not the time for generalities. This is not the day when one should hesitate to speak his real convictions because those convictions may happen to clash with the convictions of those who hear him.

With that preface, let us consider one of the chief tools in the hands of South Carolina politicians. Every campaign year men go about our State blowing on ancient coals of hate. The battle cry is directed against the Negro. We are told that he must be kept away from the polls. The same men who speak with great eloquence in favor of the Eighteenth Amendment* to the Constitution propose a course directly in conflict with the Fourteenth and Fifteenth Amendments, which provide that no one shall be deprived of his right to vote on account of his race, color or previous condition of servitude....

Negro progress would not have been possible without the sympathetic understanding and assistance of white people. I believe that the time has now arrived when the way should be prepared for the exercise by intelligent members of the colored

*The Prohibition Amendment.

race of the right of suffrage guaranteed by the Constitution. Such right cannot be longer withheld except by a process of deception and fraud more stupefying intellectually and more stultifying morally to the white race than to the colored.

Every white citizen whose opinion is worthy of consideration wants members of the colored race to develop to the limit of their capacity. Certainly, the people who send missionaries to Africa for the development of the natives there and to China and to India for the development of the natives in those countries, is committed in his own heart to the doctrine that every individual should follow the universal law of growth to the utmost.

But can any people attain full growth and rise to full stature when deprived by whatever means of the right to participate in the government under which they live. Descendants of those men who fought from the swamps of the Pee Dee to Yorktown and Valley Forge to establish the principle that taxation without representation is unjust, and that the humblest of men has a right to a voice in determining the kind of government under which he lives will not at this late day change front on that principle when its application would benefit the members of another race....

Yet, this year and for long years to come, we will hear strident voices raised in protest of any program which looks toward conferring any political rights upon members of the colored race. The point that I am making is that those voices are addressed to prejudiced hearers; that prejudiced hearers are ignorant hearers; that with the removal of ignorance, prejudice will largely disappear and the advocates of depriving men of rights guaranteed to them by the Fourteenth and Fifteenth Amendments of the Constitution will find themselves without an audience.

So, the spread of education and the betterment of the type of education afforded, which are primary concerns of this organization, will result inevitably in a tendency toward the purification of politics.

I have referred to the Negro because he represents the deepest rooted and most elemental of all our prejudices. There are numbers of others—religious prejudice, class prejudice, and social prejudice resting on no logical basis or foundation.

STATUTE OF RELIGIOUS LIBERTY

We say that we are Democrats—Jeffersonian Democrats. Yet, how many of us subscribe in practice and in thought to the majestic Statute of Religious Liberty which 150 years ago Jefferson had adopted by the legislature of the State of Virginia:

Well aware that the opinions and beliefs of men depend not on their own will, but follow involuntarily the evidence proposed to their minds; that Almighty God hath created the mind free, and manifested his will that free it shall remain by making it altogether insusceptible of restraint;...

—that our civil rights have no dependence on our religious opinions any more than on our opinions in physics or geometry; that therefore the proscribing any citizen as unworthy the public confidence by laying upon him an incapacity of being called to offices of trust and emolument unless he profess or renounce, this or that religious opinion is depriving him injuriously of those privileges and advantages to which, in common with his fellow-citizens, he has a natural right;...

—that the opinions of men are not the subject of civil government nor under its jurisdiction;...

—and finally that truth is great and will prevail if she

is left to herself; that she is the proper and sufficient antagonist to error, and has nothing to fear from the conflict unless by human interposition disarmed of her natural weapons, free argument and debate; errors ceasing to be dangerous when it is permitted freely to contradict them.

We, the General Assembly do enact, That no man shall be compelled to frequent or support any religious worship, place or ministry whatsoever, nor shall be enforced, restrained, molested or burdened in his body or goods, nor shall otherwise suffer, on account of his religious opinions or beliefs; but that all men shall be free to profess and by argument to maintain their opinions in matters of religion, and that the same shall in no wise diminish, enlarge or affect their civil capacities...

The logic and reasoning behind this statute makes its appeal and brings conviction to every thoughtful mind. Yet, would it not be far from the truth to say that 150 years after its adoption absolute liberty of thought in matters of religion has been secured for this country? Is it not obvious to anyone who reads the newspapers that religious prejudice is as active and vitriolic in form and tone today as it was in the days of the sage of Monticello?

So long as unreasoning prejudices exist, there is tinder for the spark of the politician; and, by the same token, there is work for those sincerely interested in their government.

Forecast of Future (1933)

Areas of interest with which he would be absorbed for the rest of his life were revealed on November 17, 1933, in a speech Wright made at Columbia, South Carolina, before the American Association of University Women.

Treatment of the criminal; lynching, at that time of fairly frequent occurrence in South Carolina and employed exclusively against blacks; removal of a professor for teaching the theory of evolution; the role of women in public affairs, and the function of education in a democracy—his comments on such themes reveal the bent of his mind.

Excerpts from the speech follow.

TREATMENT OF THE CRIMINAL

When Richard I. Manning became Governor, he brought to that office a passion for the humanities. From a long familiarity with conditions in South Carolina he knew that the penal institutions of the state were, in many instances, harshly administered; that jails were vermin infested and unsanitary; that the fee system of feeding prisoners had naturally led to the dishing up to them the cheapest kind of slop that would support life; that men shivered throughout winter nights under insufficient covering and that in chain gang camps all too often the lash drew blood from bared backs.

Governor Manning set up a board of disinterested and patriotic men and women, having something of the scientific approach to crime and punishment. One of its chief functions was the supervision of the state's penal institutions. One of the bright pages of the state's history was written by that board. It ameliorated the rigors of punishment. It banished the lash. It brought cheer and hope to men in prison camps.

But a few years ago by a stroke of the pen the State Board of Charities and Corrections to all intents and purposes passed out of existence. The state took a step backward toward savagery. One of the ironies of the situation was that the pious and well-meaning chief executive responsible for this step* issued a stern order that there must be a weekly prayer service at the reformatory for Negro boys. Their bedding might be vermin infested, their food unfit for human consumption, and a leather strap occasionally used, but, by the Everlasting, those boys were going to be prayed for!

How history does repeat itself! You recall what Macaulay said about Charles I:

> The advocates of Charles, like the advocates of other malefactors against whom overwhelming evidence is produced, generally decline all controversy about facts, and content themselves with calling testimony to character.

> We charge him with having broken his coronation oath; and we are told that he kept his marriage vow! We accuse him of having given up his people to the merciless inflictions of the most hot-headed and hard-hearted of prelates; and the defense is, that he took his little son on his knees and kissed him! We censure him for having violated the articles of the Petition of Rights, after having, for good and valuable consideration, promised to obey them; and we are informed that he was accustomed to hear prayers at six o'clock in the morning!

And so the boys at the reformatory were going to be prayed for.

In 1918, the State established a reformatory for girls. Its creation marked a great forward step in the penal policy of the state. It was projected on curative and corrective lines and substituted training under relatively normal conditions for confinement in jails and penitentiary. Some years ago one

*John G. Richards.

governor found that the matron in charge was from Massachusetts, I believe, or, at any rate, was not a native South Carolinian. You remember the horror aroused by the discovery. An edict removed the contaminating influence. The doctrine that, regardless of merit, salaries must be paid to home folk, was enunciated. And the Acts of 1933 contain a notation that the section making appropriation for the girls' reformatory was vetoed by the governor and the veto sustained by the House. And so another experiment in the humanities came to an inglorious end. Were the educated women of the state sufficiently vocal?

LYNCHING

In one field, an age-long battle still continues. And I am happy to say that there are developments to encourage every intelligent and patriotic citizen. I refer to the struggle to eradicate lynching. One examines the statistics with pride that their number should have been so greatly reduced and with shame that lynching should to any extent still persist. So long as there is in any year a single victim of mob violence we cannot rest. Those outbursts of savagery which occurred at Walhalla, Union, Aiken, Clinton and Ninety-six, and which might have occurred anywhere in the State, are too fresh in our memories to permit any feeling of immunity.

And while I am on the subject let me say that I, for one, am not concerned with the nice discussions sometimes carried on in the press as to how many constitute a mob and whether or not, when one is taken from a jail by four men or a half-dozen and strung to a convenient limb, he has been actually lynched. The victim is not concerned, nor are the members of his family. Some persons apparently take the view that the honor of the state is less involved if only three or four men are required to overpower a sheriff and take a prisoner from the jail than if two or three hundred were engaged in that activity. I do not believe the honor of the state is affected in proportion to the number required to do the job.

Because of the pretext on which lynching survives women may be of greater value, perhaps, than men in stamping it out. As important as resolutions may be, lynching will not be ended by resolutions. It should be discussed by women in their clubs. They may induce their pastors to preach about it. They may write to their local newspapers about it. And, if a threat should appear, they may by 'phone or telegraph harry the public authorities into providing police protection. And if still it occurs they may contribute toward the employment of detectives to fix the guilt. If members of the mob should become known, the women may show their scorn and contempt for such members. And they may assist in forever driving from public life any condoner of or apologist for lynching, anyone who utters or endorses the sentiment "To hell with the Constitution."* The educated women of the state should adopt the life-long motto of Voltaire—"Crush this infamy."

ACADEMIC FREEDOM

At another State institution a few years ago an able professor who taught biology as he knew the subject and in the light of modern science was removed from his post. The policy of the State was declared to be that freedom to teach must be qualified to conform to the public mores—that the teacher must forego his traditional function of stirring the intellect and leading it into new and strange worlds....

If teachers may be ordered to desist from teaching the truth of biology, why may they not be ordered to desist from teaching the truth of astronomy or of philosophy or any truth whatever?

*Governor Cole L. Blease.

ROLE OF WOMEN

In an ideal state of society one pictures women as being primarily interested in art, literature, the drama, and as investing life with charm and color and grace. These clubs that study Chaucer and Shakespeare and architecture and landscape gardening and interior decorating—they reflect the great quality of cultured womanhood which has its expression in the realm of the beautiful and the inspirational. And thereby they temper the harshness of existence. No one would seek to modify or to limit such activities.

But new occasions demand new moods. The times now do not call for virtues exclusively of that sort. Politeness and restraint may be overdone. There can be no academic detachment from lynching—a black body with a broken neck is laid on your door-step, and what are you going to do about it? A young girl is thrown into a cell with habitual offenders—can there be any serene contemplation of that? Men are brutally beaten by guards in chain gang camps—can there be any drawing away of the skirt from that? There can be no peace for a sensitive soul when injustice or brutality is anywhere to be found. An Amazonian ferocity may have its place, even in the heart of the cultured.

Tolstoi tells of a Russian noble lady who attended the theatre and wept bitterly at the drama there enacted but who was unmoved upon emerging to find that her coachman had frozen to death in her absence. Those tragedies of the novel, the stage and the film which move us so profoundly have their counterpart every day in the South Carolina scene. The real test of the depth of our emotion is how we react, not to fiction, but to life.

Long devoted to the cause of public libraries, Wright addressed the South Carolina Citizens' Library Association at Clemson College in January, 1934. He closed his remarks with these prophetic words:

PLEA FOR PUBLIC LIBRARIES FOR NEGROES (1934)*

...The trend of judicial decisions of the United States Supreme Court makes it apparent that Negroes will be sitting on juries in South Carolina and voting, in Democratic primaries if they want to. Like it or not, it is around the corner. With 750,000 Negro population in South Carolina that part of our population has been debarred from many of its rightful privileges, and it is a part that is going to come into its own. If you are going to extend suffrage to 750,000 citizens only slightly removed from illiteracy, the state for self-preservation must bring to these citizens a higher degree of interest and information than they have heretofore had. If this meeting considered only the extension of culture for white people it would be very regrettable. But these facts also appeal for libraries for Negroes far more strongly than ever before.

*This speech is printed in *The Library Journal* (1934), pp. 558-59.

Wright returned even more forcibly on February 11, 1939 to this theme before the same group in a meeting at Columbia, South Carolina.

PLEA FOR PUBLIC LIBRARIES FOR NEGROES (1939)

The object of local libraries, I think we may agree, is to elevate the cultural standards of the community.

Now, there was perhaps a time when the standards of one community might have been maintained without reference to the standards of every other community. Those days have gone forever. These are the days of good roads, the automobile, trade, commerce, newspapers, magazines, the radio. The standards of one community are sensibly or insensibly affected by the standards of every other.

There can be no Chinese wall about culture.

There can be no quarantine against an idea.

There can be no embargo on human thought.

Justice Cardozo* coined a fine phrase and a true one when he said that every community is affected by the "push and pressure of the Cosmos."

I don't know how you feel about it but I am glad that there are men in control of the national administration who realize that this elusive thing called culture transcends state lines. It is an article of interstate commerce. And hence the administration—certainly with my complete approval—proposes a policy of national aid to education, including national aid to libraries.

It is opposed on the ground of state rights. I question the right of any state to remain illiterate—to impose a social and economic drag upon every other State.

If we may indulge in prophecy, I believe that some of us here will live to see the creation of an international commission on

*Benjamin N. Cardozo, Associate Justice of the United States Supreme Court.

libraries. Because there is not even national immunity to an idea. Ideas infect us all. The ideas which prevail in Italy or Germany, for example, may have profound repercussions across the Atlantic.

But that is another story. It merely accentuates the view that we are taking a short first forward step when we come to think of the state as the proper unit of library service.

Let me say this, too, because I think it is germane and I think it should be said: There is no such thing as white culture and black culture. If a state cannot live half slave and half free, culture cannot exist where a population is half literate and half illiterate. We don't want to make the mistake of thinking of libraries as existing only for one race.

The Citizens Library Association was created to express and to foster the view that libraries are matters of statewide rather than local concern. With that purpose it is entitled to the enthusiastic backing of every librarian. Enlightened self-interest should prompt us to give it full support.

It is true that the local library is our particular section of the trench which we must hold at all hazards. But we may win the local engagement and lose the general battle because other sectors have not been held.

The shoe maker should stick to his last. But he will be a better shoe maker if he considers the shoe in relation to the foot, the foot in relation to the body and the body as a fraction of human society.

So the local library is but a unit in a statewide effort to make all South Carolinians thoroughly literate.

If any one date could be given to mark the beginning of the New Reconstruction it would be 1941. Relations between the United States and Japan were growing more strained in the Pacific; Hitler's forces held most of Europe and reached deep into Russia. The United States, not yet in the war, readied its armaments and extended all-out aid to those nations which resisted the aggressors. On June 25 of that year President Franklin D. Roosevelt, yielding to pressure from Negro leaders and the exigencies of the defense program, issued Executive Order 8802, establishing the Committee on Fair Employment Practices. No quick miracles in racial justice were worked, but thus began a small stream that gradually became a torrent of social change. A few weeks before the President's move, on April 29, 1941, Wright spoke about civil rights to workers in adult education from the Southeastern States who were then meeting in Knoxville, Tennessee.

ADULT EDUCATION'S TASK IN DEVELOPING CIVIL RIGHTS

I suppose, if one wanted to be argumentative about it, he could successfully maintain that civil rights have always existed; that men have always had the "unalienable rights" so eloquently expressed in the Declaration of Independence. Neither that document nor any other document *created* those rights. There has been a long and honored succession of documents—Magna Carta, Constitutions, Statutes, court decisions—which *gave expression* to such rights, but did not call them into being; they existed long before hieroglyphics were employed, long before Gutenberg.

The lawyers, with their professional passion for exactitude, make a neat distinction. For centuries they have used a phrase, "To have and to enjoy," which aptly suggests the idea that it may be one thing to have property or a right but something else again to enjoy that property or right. A right is of only academic value if one is not permitted to enjoy it, to exercise it, to assert it upon appropriate occasions. For example, every defendant has the right to be heard by counsel. That fact would be small consolation to one forced to go to trial without a lawyer. He would hardly be sufficiently philosophic to grasp the point that his right still existed in all of its pristine strength and beauty and that all that had happened to him had been that he had not been permitted to assert that right.

Viewed in that light, civil rights are not developing. They have always been. What is developing is an awareness of these rights, a determination to assert them and an impatience with a society which, by direct action or by evasion or subterfuge, thwarts one in his aspiration fully to exercise and to enjoy all of his civil rights.

This impatience, I must state at once, happily for us in the South, is not limited to one race. As deeply as a great many of our Negro citizens must feel upon the subject, they may be assured that their white neighbors in growing numbers share their resentment. I speak from the record. I get the bright side of the picture before you first. North Carolina since 1936 has each year spent more for Negro education than it spent for both races in 1900. In the Southeast, from no public schools at the end of the Confederate War, advance has been made to where there are more than 2,000,000 Negro pupils, taught by 40,000 Negro teachers, in school. In the same area there are 80 Negro colleges with an enrollment of 12,000 students. The value of school grounds and buildings has increased from $8,000,000 in 1915 to $50,000,000 in 1940. Of largest significance for this group is the fact that in the Southeast illiteracy has dropped from four-fifths to less than one-fifth of the Negro population. Surely, this is a record in which all of us may take pride. It is a record made by editors, leaders, publicists, of both races. And it should not be forgotten that in the making of that record the rank and file of both races have borne the load.

But having said so much, one would be far less than candid if he did not go further and say that there is a decidedly unpleasant side of this same picture. I shall not buttress the argument with figures but shall merely point out—what is within the knowledge of all of us—that in the South a distinct line of cleavage runs between the two great racial groups. The civil rights of those on one side of that line are reasonably secure; the civil rights of those on the other side are frequently, if not systematically, violated.

They are violated in spite of many solemn pronouncements and protestations. They are violated at great cost to our consistency and to all principles of logic.

Each campaign year a great deal is said and written to the effect that every citizen should vote. But a great deal of ingenuity has been spent in devising means of keeping Negroes away from the polls.

Citizens are urged to serve upon juries when they are summoned. But due precautions are taken to see that few, if any, Negroes ever have the opportunity to serve.

We are constantly preaching that every boy and girl must be educated. But we spend three or four times as much to educate the white girl or boy as we do to educate the Negro boy or girl.

We become apoplectic at Hitler's re-establishment of the Ghetto. But we tolerate as a matter of course zoning ordinances and Jim Crow laws which accomplish the same result.

And so on through the whole shameful category of discrimination.

Let me say this to the credit of our courts, State and Federal. They are striking down these barriers to the natural aspirations of a race as rapidly as they are presented for judicial review. The unfortunate thing is that lesser mortals so conduct themselves that the issues arise. Only the major discriminations ever attain to the dignity of an issue for judicial determination. It is the large field of the trivial, and, hence, the unlitigated—a field which has its own overtones of drama and pathos and tragedy—that mere private citizens such as you and I may give expression to whatever nobility of purpose we may possess.

Adult education's task in developing civil rights is, primarily, to prepare large numbers of people properly to exercise those rights when the opportunity arises. We must move at once—we are already too late—to give to thousands of men and women some kind of preparation for performing the fundamental duties of citizens. Discrimination has been a tragedy. It would be almost an equal tragedy if, with the barriers of discrimination removed, one should not be qualified properly to exercise the rights he has so long sought. The courts with monotonous regularity are exploding one by one the little legal fictions which petty minds have labored to develop. The most important job now confronting us in the South is to see that those upon whom the boon of full citizenship is conferred are qualified for its enjoyment.

A lead pencil in the hands of an illiterate man in a voting booth may be to the state as dangerous a weapon as a bomb. The vote of the illiterate or semi-literate is fully as potent mathematically as the vote of the most learned and upright. The illiterate man is usually the prejudiced man. Upon prejudices do demagogues grow and thrive. One might say that illiteracy is the fertile breeding ground for demagoguery.

One who has read widely and deeply is not apt to be swept off his feet by appeals to his deeper prejudices and emotions. When candidates blow upon the embers of ancient hatred and antagonisms, the well-read man does not toss his hat into the air. He smiles contemptuously and remarks to himself that the device of the candidate is shabby and threadbare with age. One who is familiar by reading with the demagogues of ancient Greece and Rome will not be bowled over by the relatively inartistic performances of our local talent.

Nowhere is illiteracy capable of accomplishing more tragic results than when it is enthroned in a jury box. The ordinary trial is a highly emotional proceeding. One whose prejudices lie close to the surface will find it difficult to arrive at a verdict which reflects the application of cold reason to the facts of the case. You may as well expect to gather figs from thistles as to expect to gather rational and intelligent opinions from minds which have been deprived of such nourishment as books afford.

The mythical man in the street is fully aware of that difficulty. He has a phrase which aptly expresses it—"a good jury lawyer." What is connoted by the phrase is that one need not be particularly versed in the law so long as he knows human nature, so long as he is adroit and skilled in making subtle appeals to the prejudices of those who sit upon the jury. By such antics a well educated and well-informed man is left relatively cold and unmoved.

But not *entirely* cold and unmoved. One of the greatest of our jurists, Justice Benjamin N. Cardozo, has pointed out that even the judges are not utterly unaffected by the great tides and currents which engulf the rest of men. "I have found," he writes, "no trace, not even the faintest, of the power of favor or prejudice in any sordid or vulgar or evil sense, among the judges whom I have known. But every day there is borne in on me a new conviction of the inescapable relation between the truth without us and the truth within. The spirit of the age, as it is revealed to each of us, is too often only the spirit of the group in which the accidents of birth or education or occupation or fellowship have given us a place. No effort or revolution of the mind will overthrow utterly and at all times the empire of these subconscious loyalties."

Surely, we ask too much of the semi-literate voter or juror when we demand that, in the clamor of appeals to his emotions, he shall give ear only to the still, small voice of reason.

What is the implication of all this to those of us in the Southeast who are workers in the field of adult education? One answer fairly proclaims itself. Books, books, books for all our people. Is it not more or less idle, with events moving as rapidly as they are about us, to content ourselves with teaching men and women how to read while giving them little or nothing to read, with creating a hunger for reading but doing little or nothing to satisfy that hunger?

In his monumental work, *Southern Regions*, Dr. Howard W. Odum says that in 1930 in the Southeast there were more than 600 counties without library service as compared with only 46 counties in the Northeast and only 19 in the far West. The circulation of books in the Southeast is about one-sixth of the national average. And we spend for libraries about one-sixth of the amount spent by the average American State. As pitifully inadequate as are library facilities for white people, they are practically non-existent for the Negro population.

Now, making all due allowance for the innate excellence of our people—about which we hear every campaign year—and facing the facts squarely in the face, is it reasonable to expect that in the Southeast there will be found as much exchange of ideas, as well formed or expressed opinions, as highly developed critical faculties, as are discoverable in those sections where books are available to all the people?

Fortunately, there are signs of quickening life in the library movement in the Southeast. More and more are library trucks found out in the cross roads and backwoods. And though our section may boast of many spectacles of natural beauty, there is none that exceeds in significance or importance these bearers of the materials of learning to those who hunger for them.

These trucks, when viewed in their proper light, are instruments of adult education. For the effort to make books available to every citizen is of the essence of educational endeavor. It is impossible to conceive of a worker in the field of adult education being uninterested in the library movement. As well conceive of a doctor who is uninterested in the fight on tuberculosis. Teachers in adult schools are interested in libraries not as something collateral to education or as merely germane to it, but as something that lies at the very core of education.

What may workers in the field of adult education do in developing civil rights? Let's turn the question around and ask: What may we do in developing civil rights in the field of adult education?

I would answer, in part: Be bold. For when one is bold enough he is honest in his dealing with facts, because he has no fear of the consequences of disclosure of the truth.

If we were bold enough we would proclaim that:

Illiteracy is much more general among Negroes than among whites.

The need for schools and teachers is much more acute.

But we are spending vastly more, per capita, on education of whites than on education of Negroes.

That is not just.

A state which pursues an unjust policy has within it the seeds of critical weakness.

I should like to see constant war made on the idea sometimes expressed that Negroes receive in their schools benefits in proportion of the taxes they pay.

In the first place, that is pure assumption which may or may not be supported by the facts.

In the second place, we do not follow that policy to its logical conclusion and discriminate between white children upon the same basis. By such a policy a great many white children would receive no education because their parents pay no taxes. All pretense of a *public* system would be abandoned by such a procedure.

In the third place, isn't the proper conception of money that it represents work and the Negro sharecropper or mill hand may have contributed his full share to the tax dollar which a landlord or company treasurer pushed across the collector's window?

If we were bold enough we should drive out of any man's vocabulary such expressions as "white supremacy" or "superior race." I don't know that you are familiar with those expressions in Tennessee. I hope not. Of course, we never hear them in South Carolina. But I read the papers occasionally and every now and then run across those phrases in remote states. They should be driven back into the woodwork or into the slime of the pit from which they sometime emerge.

Woodrow Wilson said many years ago "I care not how wise and good a master may be, I will not have a master." And President Roosevelt said a few nights ago "There has never been, there will never be, a race capable of ruling another."

Those who bandy about such phrases as "white supremacy" are curiously unaware that they parrot sentiments which come to us over the radio in foreign tongues and in strident accents from lands across the sea. They are sentiments which should never find lodgment upon American soil.

It is possible that too much emphasis may be placed upon civil rights and not enough upon civil duties. In all that we think or say upon the subject the relationship between the two should be kept in mind. The press should be free but its very freedom should impose voluntary restraints of decency and honesty on all that is published. We insist upon freedom of speech but a wise freedom of speech recognizes that other men have ears that ought not to be unduly offended or shocked. Where government does not exercise legal authority in such matters the individual must recognize the authority of reason. The whole system will crash if he does not.

The ship of state must answer to the rudder of reason or it will answer to the rock of disaster.

So the extension of civil rights should be greeted both gladly and solemnly. Gladly, because the individual has greater liberty for the development of his powers. Solemnly, because the use of power calls for wisdom and restraint.

Race relations in the wartime United States grew strained as the Negro minority and its leaders chafed under ancient injustices. Negroes became more vocal and demanded and received greater political attention after 1941. Wright, in a move calculated to rally enlightened South Carolinians and to inform the nation, wrote the following piece for public release. Nineteen other prominent South Carolinians signed with Wright and the essential moderation, even conservatism, of the declaration, especially toward the end, is noteworthy.

The moderate tone was no doubt due to the fact that the statement was a consensus. The paper was circulated by mail and many of those who received it did a bit of editing before signing. The result was that its original boldness was somewhat tempered. The statement did, however, serve notice that there were white South Carolinians of some influence who were challenging the established racial patterns.

A STATEMENT ON THE RACE PROBLEMS
IN SOUTH CAROLINA

The presence of two races in South Carolina means that this state has had, and has, a race problem. It will continue to have such a problem for as long as the two races live side by side. It is a problem of the adjustment of the two races to each other. Prior to the adoption of the XIV and XV Amendments to the Federal Constitution, this problem existed only in its social and economic aspects. Since the adoption of these, it has a political aspect as well.

The problem has always been nationwide. In the days of slavery the people of one section of our country transported and sold the slaves while those of another section bought them. The evils of the system were shared by the North and by the South. From the earliest days the Negro was set apart from the whites in his economic and social status in all parts of America. As time has passed, wherever the Negro has congregated in significant numbers, barriers of one kind and another have been erected to maintain a virtual separation of the two races.

By-products of this policy of separation of the races and segregation of the Negro have been:

1. The Negro has been denied equal opportunity with the whites.

2. His economic advancement has been retarded.

3. His social status as a servant and a menial has remained relatively fixed.

4. He has been discriminated against in provision for public education.

5. He has not always been accorded unbiased treatment in the Courts in spite of the efforts of many of our Judges.

6. He has not received his share of civic improvements, including playgrounds and general recreation facilities.

7. In the Southern States he has been denied any official part in the government under which he lives.

Some of this discrimination has been more or less inevitable, and is not as blameworthy as it sounds. Unless much of it is changed, it will be blameworthy enough.

In spite of these restrictions and handicaps, the Negroes of America, three generations removed from slavery, have made phenomenal progress which is a source of pride to them and should be a source of gratification to the whites. In the main the Negroes have been orderly and law-abiding. Annual reports of law enforcement agencies show that the percentage of arrests and convictions of Negroes during the past twenty years has decreased sharply as compared with those of whites. When occasion has offered, they have been patriotic. They have developed in the field of business, they have shown solid accomplishments in the arts and sciences, they are actively engaged in the major professions, and they are successfully carrying on educational endeavors. The pride that they feel in these attainments necessarily makes them restive under the restraints that are imposed upon them. It is our hope that the gratification which the whites should feel in this progress of the blacks will lead to a modification of these restraints as a means of advancing the interests of both races and of promoting a better feeling between the two races.

Social equality is not a part of the Negro problem in South Carolina. The Negroes disclaim any interest in it. And it must be obvious to anyone who gives unprejudiced thought to the subject that social life is of individual making and is not to be determined by groups or races. Whatever advancement the Negro may make in an economic way, however far he may go in his intellectual accomplishments, and however much he may finally mingle with the whites in public, it is inconceivable that he could have any social relations with whites that were not acceptable to both parties. The emphasis that is placed on this subject is an unworthy one, an unreasoning appeal to fear and prejudice and is calculated to prevent a fair and just consideration of our race problem in its fundamental aspects. The use that has been made of it by candidates for public office has had unfortunate effects on our political standards, is based on error and misconception, and, if allowed to go unchallenged from this time forward, is certain to retard the necessary racial adjustments.

We ask the citizens of South Carolina to give thought to the following suggestions:

1. White people of this State should take a serious interest in the race problem. If groups could be organized in different parts of the State to study and discuss the question, much good might result.

2. Provision should be made for Negroes to serve on juries. Negroes should be allowed representation on boards which have to do with administering affairs that involve Negro citizens and their property; Negro policemen should be provided in Negro residential districts; and public conveyances and facilities provided under our State segregation laws should be as safe, as hygienic, and as comfortable for one race as the other.

3. We should enlarge our educational efforts for the Negro. He should have better schools, better teachers, more adequate transportation, and provisions for education at college levels, including graduate instruction.

4. The question of the Negroes' position in industry is more of a private than a public matter. His admission to membership in labor unions and his employment in association with white workers are matters that must be worked out on the basis of an employer-employee relationship. Such inhibitions as now exist for the Negro in this regard can be lifted only by time and, only then, by the white and Negro worker developing a mutual respect and understanding for each other.

5. Negroes employed in domestic service should receive wages commensurate with their training, experience and capacity to serve; their hours of

employment should be agreed upon and adhered to; they should be provided with clothing suitable to their employment; and they should be encouraged to look upon their work with dignity.

6. The problem of Negro suffrage in South Carolina has no immediate solution. Many Negroes in South Carolina are qualified by every standard to vote and to hold office. But the great masses of them have not advanced to the point where the white people are willing that they should play a dominant part in politics. We have ordered our political affairs so that we put no qualifications on white suffrage, so we can make no qualifications as to the Negroes. It is all or nothing. The Negroes have been patient as to this, but some of them are impatient. We see no early solution. We do not believe that disenfranchisement of all Negroes in South Carolina can endure indefinitely, and we hope that a careful study of this problem may, in the end, result in a plan of suffrage for the state that will be to the better interests of both races.

Finally, we want to make it clear that we are prompted in this statement by our affection for and interest in our state. Our primary interest is in the white people. Their predominant position in this state imposes upon them the responsibility that they shall deal fairly, justly and even generously with the Negro citizens. The only white supremacy which is worthy of the name is that which exists because of virtue, not power. Good morals, to say nothing of religion or democracy, require that there shall be drastic revision in our attitude toward our colored citizens. Such revision will require the best thought and finest intentions. It is to these that we appeal.

The discrepancy between Southern pretensions and the realities in areas of government and religion was exposed in a speech made by Wright nine years before the decision in the school desegregation cases. The speech was made on March 15, 1945, at Spartanburg, South Carolina, before the Spartanburg War Education Center. It was printed and distributed throughout the state by the South Carolina Division of the Southern Regional Council.

The anomaly of the white church's professed devotion to the brotherhood of man while turning Negroes away from the altar and of governmental professed devotion to pure democracy while turning Negroes away from the polls and jury panels was laid on the consciences of white hearers with rare candor in a bastion of segregation.

The speech was, in part, an appeal to the sense of fair play which is in the Anglo-Saxon tradition. It also made the point that a wide gap between practice and pretension is, in the individual, damaging to personality, a kind of moral schizophrenia. That kind of double life was, at the time of the speech, a common phenomenon. Excerpts follow.

FACING FACTS IN SOUTH CAROLINA

Should we not face the fact that there is a wide discrepancy between our pretentions and our practices? Let me illustrate what I have in mind.

One of the things of which the state may be proud is its relatively large church membership. In that field and in the contributions which we make to the churches as compared with our incomes, we are considerably above the national average. This is naturally a cause for satisfaction and pride.

Now, if religion teaches anything, it teaches the brotherhood of man—a brotherhood which is not limited or circumscribed by considerations of differences in race and color. Yet the same people who, with so much sacrifice, support their churches, tolerate mouthings of politicians and editorials in some quarters—happily greatly reduced in number—about "white supremacy." We seem strangely unaware that when we talk or write or think about the superiority of one race over another, we are echoing sentiments that lie at the heart of Nazi philosophy.

There are no people more outspoken in their professed attachment to the principles of democracy than are the people of South Carolina. Now, if democracy means anything, it means equality before the law and equality of opportunity to make a living.

Yet, are we not reasonably complacent in the face of a system designed to exclude Negroes from the polls, from jury service, from holding public office or, indeed, from receiving the same pay as a white man for service rendered?

We live under a Constitution framed by white men and interpreted by Courts composed of white men. These Courts have said that the Constitution means that there shall be no exclusion from a political primary or from jury service because of color. *Our* Constitution and *our* courts.

Yet we have seen two or three successive Legislatures using all of their cunning to escape the consequences of a judicial decision.

Even now there is pending in the Legislature a bill designed to spend almost eight million dollars upon the white colleges of South Carolina and only two hundred and fifty thousand dollars on the lone state Negro college.

We profess a devout attachment to Anglo-Saxon principles of fair play. Yet we see public funds distributed between the races for parks, playgrounds, hospitals and the like on a basis which cannot remotely be called fair....

So there exists this wide discrepancy between our pretentions and our practices. There will, of course, always be a gap between the ideal and the actual. Even in the exact science of mechanics a tolerance of one-thousandth of an inch is permitted in airplane motors—a negligible failure to attain perfection. But as this margin of error increases the machine becomes inefficient and finally it destroys itself. The spiritual entity is subject to the same law.

We cannot go on being split personalities. We do damage to our own natures by pretending one thing and practicing another. The subjective effects upon us of a policy of subterfuge and evasion may be more damaging to us than would be even the lack of schools. There is a question of morals involved and we can't run away from a moral issue.

Facts are stubborn and disagreeable things. They lose none of their disagreeable character by being ignored. Those who ignore them do themselves lose character.

A meeting such as this and similar meetings which are being held here and there throughout the State give cause for hope that men and women in private life and with no axe to grind, are moving more rapidly and courageously than are their so-called leaders. But the leaders will always respond to public pressure.

The first duty of a citizen of this state is, therefore, to create here the spirit and atmosphere which will permit anyone to discuss facts, however disagreeable, and to advocate a course of action which may break with tradition but which will square with what is honorable and right.

74

With all the furor about busing which now rages in some white quarters, it is interesting to note that in 1945 no Negroes rode on school buses in South Carolina. White children, of course, did. Few white voices protested this inequity, as they did not protest exclusion of blacks from the polls.

In an address at Marion, South Carolina, on December 4, 1945, before the alumnae of Winthrop College, then the state college for women, Wright made a frontal attack on the state's official policy toward its black citizens.

In South Carolina, as in many Southern states, lynching of blacks by white mobs during Wright's youth was of frequent occurrence and was rarely, if ever, punished by the courts or rebuked by public officials. By 1945 the shameful practice had virtually ended.

A leader in the crusade to stamp out lynching was a Southern white woman, Mrs. Jessie Daniel Ames. Mrs. Ames, a dynamic individual possessed of unusual ability as a speaker, addressed groups of women all over the South. She read at every meeting a petition to the sheriff of the county that he use all force necessary to protect prisoners in his custody and informing him that he would be held accountable for failure to do so. Inspired by the Ames oratory, women in droves signed the petition, which was personally delivered to the sheriff by a committee of women. Almost immediately lynching came to its end.

Excerpts from Wright's speech follow.

NEW DEFINITION OF LYNCHING

In my boyhood every few weeks I was accustomed to read grisly accounts of some lynching that had occurred somewhere in South Carolina. When have you read such a story? In the 35 years from 1882 to 1917, there were 163 lynchings in South Carolina, an average of slightly more than four a year. For the ten years from 1917 to 1927 there were only 14, or 1.4 a year. I regret I do not have later figures but we know that lynching has been practically stamped out in South Carolina.

Many causes produced this happy result, not the least of which must have been the instinctive recoil of intelligent women from such manifestations of barbarity....

Lynching is merely the ugliest and most debasing expression of racial prejudice. Its result is to deprive a person of life without process of law. There is a narrow margin of difference between life and liberty. A good many millions of men have been willing to exchange one for the other. To deprive a citizen of liberty without due process of law is but one degree removed from so depriving him of life.

A substantial part of liberty in a democracy is the exercise of the right to vote. (Women who fought so long and so gallantly for the ballot know this better than I.) Our Constitutions, written by white men, and our courts, filled by white men, have said that no one shall be deprived of his right to vote in a general election or in a primary because of his color. Yet I have a letter from an intelligent, educated Negro man who says that in one South Carolina county 162 qualified Negroes have presented themselves to register and been denied solely because they were Negroes. That was Marion County.

Men may be lynched without being strung up on telegraph poles.

Let us take pride in our educational progress. But let us realize that it has its ugly features. No buses haul Negro children to school. There are disparities in the amount spent per capita for the education of the white and the Negro child that outrage our sense of what is fair and right.

Thirty-one years ago one of the ablest and most inspiring educators* that the State had within its borders urged a policy of creation of a school of education at the State Negro College at Orangeburg. He was driven from the State by a politician

*Dr. S.C. Mitchell.

then at the helm*—certainly, not the least price we have had to pay for placing demagogues in high office. And in 1945 a bill was introduced to spend almost $8,000,000 on the white colleges and only $250,000 on the lone State Negro College.

I am an alumnus of the University of South Carolina. You are alumnae of Winthrop College. Surely neither school would have done much for us if it had not taught us to think first of the State and next of our alma maters.

And civilization will have done but little for us if it has not taught us to think first of humanity and then of race....

PLEA FOR ACTIVISM

What may the individual do? I have no right to advise further than is implied from the fact that you invite me here and that you hear me tolerantly.

First—all of us, men and women alike, must take an active interest in public affairs. It is no longer sufficient that one shall pay his debts, be law-abiding and respectable. That course, however commendable, does not keep the infecting and corroding fingers of demagogues from throttling the State.

Second—we should have the utmost sympathy with those who seek to discharge the first duty of the citizen, viz. to vote. But sympathy is not enough. We may inform our boards of registration that we do not approve of evasion and subterfuge and violation of law done in our names. We may go with qualified Negroes to places of registration amd observe for ourselves the treatment they receive. We may be prepared to testify, if necessary, as to any discrimination observed. If we are honest in our profession that democracy is the right kind of government for Americans, we will not fail to give these little proofs of our devotion to principle.

*Governor Cole L. Blease.

Third—We may let our school boards know that we approve of fairness in division of school funds and facilities. We doubt that it is fair that all white children shall ride, and all colored children shall walk, to school. And is the time not at hand when we should make the store houses of knowledge represented by our libraries available to all men and women of every race?

Fourth—we may urge our legislators to divorce the reform schools from penal management and make them really reformatories. And we may work for the establishment of a reform school for Negro girls.

I think that somewhere in the Bible there is something about a people whose women "shall be as a cornerstone polished in the similitude of a pearl." That is a very choice metaphor. Grace and strength. The aesthetic and the practical. Culture and power. They should be inseparable.

By 1949 the pace of the New Reconstruction had markedly quickened. President Harry S. Truman won his 1948 victory, despite a Dixiecrat bolt from the Democratic party, and demanded Federal action in the civil rights area, including a permanent Fair Employment Practices Commission. Integration in all of the nation's armed forces began after Truman's executive order of 1948. In Wright's own state, Judge J. Waties Waring of the United States District Court enraged many white Southerners by his decisions, especially those which made it possible for Negroes to vote in Democratic primary elections. As white standpatters raised the ancient cry about "outside interference," Wright, now an active leader in the work of the Southern Regional Council and other such organizations, eloquently defended the "sanitative force" of honest, frank criticism regardless of its source.

"OUTSIDE INTERFERENCE" IN CIVIL RIGHTS*

A lament frequently heard in the South is that far more rapid progress would be made in solving its difficult racial problem if it were not for what is termed outside interference. Those who use the phrase do not seem accurately to have defined it. But, having recourse to Webster, we find that "interference" is inter-meddling, a clashing or collision. "Outside" presumably relates to that portion of the United States lying north of the Mason and Dixon line. So the phrase seems to brand as a meddler any person living beyond the territorial limits of the South who seeks to change Southern policy or attitude, whose efforts or activities come into collision, or clash, with the local folk-ways.

Nowhere in the country is there thought of using physical

*Printed in *New South* (March, 1949), pp.6-8.

force in changing Southern custom. The interference which draws Southern fire lies in the field of expression of opinion of the one hand, or congressional action on the other. The Southern protest, therefore, seems to demand that adverse opinion shall be muffled and orderly legislative processes be suspended insofar as either affects Southern racial relations. Since the opinion which is most potent, which hurts, is usually editorial opinion, the demand is that non-Southern editors shall forego their usual right of criticism. Presumably the Southern editor is not to be similarly ham-strung.

This Southern resentment—which is, of course, white resentment and is not felt by all whites—seems to take no account of the dual nature of American citizenship. One may be a citizen of South Carolina or Mississippi but he is also a citizen of the United States. It is by virtue of American, rather that state, citizenship that a citizen pays federal income and other taxes, has his conduct supervised or controlled in many fields, and is drafted into military service. Citizens of South Carolina and Wisconsin, in the national sense, are fellow citizens. Each has a legitimate interest in the welfare of the other, an interest evidenced on its lowest level by the fact that federal taxes taken from one are spent in part in the State of the other.

NATIONAL PROBLEMS

President Roosevelt was entirely accurate in describing the South, not as an economic problem or a local economic problem, but as the *nation's* economic problem No. 1, a phrase which rasped on Southern ears. It is the problem of the man from Wisconsin or California or New York, as well as the man from South Carolina or Mississippi or Georgia. The theory which generally prevails in federal government policy and is subscribed to by intelligent men everywhere is that the resources of the nation must be used to eliminate weak spots in the nation's economy. In its simplest terms, this means spending in South Carolina money raised by taxes in Wisconsin. Federal aid to education, libraries, roads, health, will naturally be more generous in poorer than in wealthier states. The poorer are the Southern States. Hence, the citizen living north of the Mason and Dixon line is going to have a progressively larger dollar-and-cents stake in his neighbor to the South. Whatever contributes to Southern poverty touches the pocket nerve of the man from Wisconsin.

If the Southern Negro, because he is a Negro, is kept out of employment for which he is qualified, or is paid less than the white for similar services, or if he is required to pay higher rent for inferior housing, or if his credit terms are unnecessarily harsh, or if he doesn't get his proper share of health or educational facilities, and if these conditions tend to keep the South economically backward, then they are properly subject to interest, comment, and action by outsiders. It is not necessary here to determine that such conditions do exist. But inquiry into the possibility of their existence and editorial comment based upon bona fide belief that they do exist would seem to be entirely authorized.

STAKE IN SOUTHERN VOTERS

But the outsider's stake in the South is much more than economic. It is also political and governmental. Laws governing the Wisconsin citizen have been made in part by Cole Blease and Ed Smith and Huey Long and Tom Heflin. South Carolina voters sent two, Louisiana one, and Alabama one, of those worthies, to the United States Senate. Their choices presumably reflected the best judgment of voters of those states as to the qualifications of a United States Senator. The qualifications of a senator or congressman depend upon the qualifications of the voters by whom he is elected. The qualifications of Southern voters, therefore, are a matter of genuine concern to the citizen of Wisconsin or Minnesota or Pennsylvania—and, of course, vice versa.

No formula for producing the perfect voter has been devised. But adequate free public libraries and an efficient public school system do not seem to hurt. If Negroes in the South are excluded from "public" libraries and if their schools are relatively inefficient, such exclusion and inefficiency are of acute interest to all Americans, North as well as South. Judge Waring's* courageous decisions mean that the Negro is going to vote, is voting. How shall he vote? With what judgment? His schools and libraries, built in the future partially by federal funds, will help to provide the answer. Whoever shall contribute by his taxes to those funds is entitled to express himself on how they shall be spent. That would not seem to be inter-meddling. Incidentally, the rest of the country may be expected to show some reluctance in spending tax money to help provide the Southern States with the luxury of separate and duplicating school and library systems for the two races.

Not only is the Negro voting; he is serving on Southern juries, thanks again to judicial decisions. The kind of juror he will make will be influenced by the same factors which shape him as a voter. The Oregon apple grower who must sue on an account in a Georgia court, the Grand Rapids furniture manufacturer whose case is brought in Alabama, the motorist from New Jersey who accidentally runs down a Louisiana pedestrian—all are interested in the calibre of twelve men in a jury box, in what lies within their skulls. As communication and commerce

*J. Waties Waring of Charleston, S.C.

among the States are accelerated, this interest will become more general and intensified.

END OF ISOLATION

It may be said with assurance that all factors operating throughout the country are hastening the end of Southern isolation. More and more the South has impact on the rest of the States and they have impact on the South. Leaving out of account a sense of public morals and humanitarian impulses, which lie at the base of much criticism of Southern discriminatory practices, economic and political considerations are sufficient to bring criticism into being and to keep it alive and vigorous.

Factors in the international scene operate with power equal to that of those closer home. As a nation we are engaged in a great effort to impress borderline or doubtful nations with democracy's superiority to communism. The freedom of the American citizen, his right to determine by his vote the character of his government and its official personnel, his complete equality of opportunity with every other citizen—these are large guns in our arsenal. But in part they are spiked or their aim deflected by every incident which seems to belie these noble pretensions.

The exceedingly rare lynching of a Negro, the long and arduous struggle which he has had to secure the ballot, the inferior position assigned him in housing and employment, his segregation in schools—all of those compose our Achilles' heel in the propaganda war. The issue of that struggle is of such profound and crucial importance to mankind that one who criticizes the official Southern attitude may hardly be deemed guilty of inter-meddling in a purely local affair.

NOT ABOVE CRITICISM

The protest against outside interference pre-supposes either that Southern policy is above criticism or that there exist within the South critics sufficient in number, skill, and courage to subject the customs and institutions of the region to objective analysis. The view that policy is above criticism will hardly be asserted outside of Klan circles. The courts with almost monotonous regularity are declaring that much of the policy is indefensible in law, to say nothing of morals.

The per capita circulation of local newspapers in the South is the lowest in the nation. Southern magazines of opinion are so few in number and so limited in circulation that they may be left out of consideration. It is no exaggeration to say that the average Southerner is subjected to less locally originated editorial opinion than is the average citizen of any other section of the country.

Local newspapers, with exceptions so small as to be negligible, are owned, published, and edited by Southern whites. Their subscribers are white; their advertisers are white. Is it not going a little far to expect complete objectivity and candor of a white Southern editor in discussing the duty of his subscribers and advertisers to members of a race which brings him no bread and butter? The politicians are probably no more practical fellows than the editors and they are hardly examples of courageous leadership in this ticklish field. Ellis Arnall ventured to run a little ahead of the pack in Georgia and Herman Talmadge took over.

The Northern editor is not subject to reprisal. He may not have been born and reared with the race problem, which fact may deprive him of first-hand knowledge. At the same time he may have the objectivity and lack of prejudice which go with physical detachment. The liberal white Southerner should, and no doubt does, regard the Northern press as an ally in the constant struggle which he carries on.

The lament against outside interference, if heeded, would insulate the South against opinion coming from beyond its borders. The Mason and Dixon line would strongly resemble an iron curtain. The South may properly resent any misstatement of the facts regarding its customs, but it should welcome as a sanitative force candid criticism of the true situation from whatever source the criticism may come.

Such, at least, is the view of the writer, a life-long Southerner.

Probably no Southerner was more vilified because of his liberal racial stand than was J. Waties Waring of Charleston, South Carolina, Federal judge for the Eastern District of South Carolina. It fell to Judge Waring's lot to write decisions equalizing teachers' salaries; requiring South Carolina to admit Negro students to the University of South Carolina law school unless a separate but completely equal law school was established; opening the Democratic primary to Negro voters, and, in dissent, striking down segregation in the public schools.

Waring's decisions aroused hostility among a great majority of white South Carolinians, whose reaction was vocal, bitter and, in many instances, obscene. Unruly mobs vandalized their house and verbally abused the judge and his wife. Congressman L. Mendel Rivers of Charleston obliquely defended such acts, prompting Wright to write him on November 16, 1950. In his letter Wright sharply castigated the Congressman for his activities:

> *Since your thoroughly childish utterances about this shameful incident have probably brought you praise from the illiterate and the depraved, I think it may be well for you to know that among your constituents who do not sign with a cross mark and who can count without using their fingers and toes, you have been remarkably successful in inducing acute nausea.*

An unpenitent Rivers responded that he considered Wright's letter "insolent."

Sadly, Wright was one of very few South Carolinians to speak out in behalf of the Warings. Charleston society ostracized the couple. Evidently the so-called better elements of the city could not forgive the apostasy of a native Charlestonian of distinguished ancestry. Waring, however, would not modify his views. He once explained to a reporter that "by being a judge I have gradually acquired a passion for justice."

While the school desegregation case was pending before the United States Supreme Court Marion Wright visited the Waring home and wrote this impressionistic report of J. Waties Waring, man and judge. One year later, on November 6, 1954, Wright was the principal speaker at a testimonial dinner given by the state NAACP for the then expatriated Judge and his wife.

SOUTH CAROLINA VENDETTA

The retirement on February 15 of United States District Judge J. Waties Waring of Charleston, South Carolina, probably marks the end of a campaign of abuse and persecution of a judicial officer having few, if any parallels in the history of this country. Since July 12, 1947, he has been the object of almost daily attacks by South Carolina officialdom, a section of the press of that state, the Ku Klux Klan and a host of anonymous bigots making use of the mails and telephone to get to him their scurrilous and obscene messages. Mrs. Waring, no less than the judge, has been brought under this sniping fire. Charleston, which indulges the quaint fiction that it is aristocratic—whatever that may mean—carries on an elaborate social boycott of the Warings. It is hardly surprising that, upon his retirement, they are moving away from the judge's native city. They will make their home in New York.

"It is time for South Carolina to rejoin the Union."

So wrote the judge in an opinion filed July 12, 1947. These words, directed at one phase of South Carolina's segregation policy, touched the State upon an exposed nerve. The decision struck down the system the State had set up to deprive its Negro citizens of any effective participation in politics, and, hence, in government, a system devised by "the best legal brains in the State." The judicial condemnation of the morals behind this effort was apparently not so much resented as was the reflection upon the lack of shrewdness of its authors.

Some years ago Governor Olin D. Johnston, now Senator, purpled upon reading a decision of the United States Supreme Court in a case from Texas. That decision held that the plaintiff, a Negro, was entitled to vote in a Democratic primary even though forbidden by the party rules. Negroes were so forbidden by party rules in South Carolina. In Texas there were statutes regulating conduct of primaries. There were such statutes in South Carolina. There was language in the decision which aroused belief in Governor Johnston that a different result might have been achieved in Texas if the State had had no such statutes but had left political parties entirely free to make their own rules. That seemed the way out for South Carolina. Certainly, if the situation in South Carolina could not be distinguished from the situation in Texas, Negroes of the Palmetto State would, upon a proper case, be granted the right of participation in primaries. In that state, of course, this means the Democratic primary.

Governor Johnston thereupon convened an extraordinary session of the legislature. There was nothing Oriental or disingenuous about the call for the session. "It now becomes absolutely necessary that we repeal all laws pertaining to primaries in order to maintain white supremacy...White supremacy will be maintained in our primaries. Let the chips fall where they may."

So the legislature ripped approximately 150 statutes out of the books. The state convention of the party eliminated from its rules all references to statutes. When George Elmore, Negro, stood before Judge Waring, asking that he be permitted to enroll in the Democratic party and to vote despite its rules against Negro participation, the party was able to say with engaging innocence that its status was exactly the same as a private social club.

Judge Waring was unimpressed. "Racial distinctions," he wrote, "cannot exist in the machinery that selects the officers and lawmakers of the United States; and all citizens of this state and country are entitled to cast a free and untrammeled ballot in our elections. If the only material and realistic elections are clothed with the name 'primary,' they are equally entitled to vote there...The primary held by it (the Democratic party) is the only practical place where one can express a choice in selecting federal and other officials."

And so, the Negroes voted in South Carolina.

What manner of man is J. Waties Waring?

Physically there is nothing ascetic about him. In his seventy-second year he is erect, vigorous, apparently athletic, although he engages in no sport and takes very limited exercise. There is no equatorial bulge fore or aft. His greying and stiffish hair, standing up from the scalp, conveys the militance suggested by Justice Holmes' cavalryman's mustache. His rather full and broad mouth lies between an ample chin and an overhanging beak of a nose and is set in pothooks. The whole effect is one of firmness. Here is not a man to be pushed around.

I saw him first at his desk in the post office building which also houses the federal court for South Carolina's Eastern district. It may be that immersion in such austere and formal surroundings, in which as federal judge he wields great power, has a subjective effect upon him, causing him to appear somewhat cold and brittle, detached and distant. But some hours later in his Meeting Street home with Mrs. Waring and his married daughter and son-in-law, who had come down from New York, he was transformed, a warm and pleasant, if not a gay and witty, companion.

One of his favorite entertainment tricks is an authentic imitation of the bantam rooster swagger and coconut grater voice of an editor who daily attacks him. Each morning at breakfast the Warings read the editorials. "We find him enjoyable when taken right between coffee and orange juice," remarked the judge. These quaint editorials are clipped and preserved for the amusement of out-of-state guests. "It shows them the operation of the pre-Confederate mind."

Out-of-state guests, you will observe. It is almost mathematically accurate to say that no white South Carolinian ever visits the Warings, though formerly both Judge and Mrs. Waring had a large number of white friends and entertained extensively. That was in the days before the case of Elmore *v*. Rice and its companion case of Brown *v*. Baskin, of which more will be later said. It was also, some Charlestonians will tell you, before the divorce of Judge and the first Mrs. Waring, which was obtained by her in 1945.

Insofar as impartial opinion may be gotten in Charleston, it supports the statement of Judge and Mrs. Waring that, while there was some defection of Charleston associates on account of the divorce, this was limited to the elderly and primly correct social circle living "below Broad Street," a thoroughfare roughly dividing the echelons of Charleston society. The mass desertion of the Warings came after and as a result of the primary case decisions, and, more particularly, after the decision in Brown *v*. Baskin.

It might have been naively assumed by those who did not know the masters of the Democratic party in South Carolina that the decision in the Elmore *v*. Rice case, unanimously affirmed by the Circuit Court of Appeals (composed, by the way, of three white Southern judges) and the Supreme Court of the United States, would have put an end to efforts to exclude the Negro from the Democratic primary. Not so. Like John Paul Jones in a worthier cause, the party had just begun to fight. The Democratic convention on May 19, 1948, almost a year after Judge Waring's decision in the Elmore case, adopted new rules. These limited membership in the Democratic clubs to white persons and required of all those seeking to vote in the primary an oath which provided, among other things, that the prospective voter believes in and will support the "social, religious and educational separation of races," in "the principle of States Rights" and "is opposed to proposed federal so-called F.E.P.C. law." A rather neat little device for rendering completely nugatory the former decision of Judge Waring.

David Brown, a Negro from Beaufort, brought suit against

officials of the party, seeking an order granting him membership in one of the Democratic clubs and enjoining the requirement of the oath as a prerequisite to voting in the primary. In addition to the permanent injunction, a temporary injunction was sought relating to the then imminent primary.

Judge Waring, native born and lifelong resident of Charleston, with eight generations of Southern ancestry behind him, with Confederate and slave owning antecedents, always a Democrat, heard the motion for the temporary injunction.

"It is important," his order read, "that once and for all the members of this party be made to understand—and that is the purpose of this opinion—that they will be required to obey and carry out the orders of this court, not only in the technical respects but in the true spirit and meaning of the same...It is time that either the present officials of the party, or such as may be in the future chosen, realize that the people of the United States expect them to follow the American way of elections...It becomes the duty of this court to say to the party officials that they will have to obey the true intent of the law...and that no excuse or evasion in the future will be tolerated...Any violation of the terms of the order, or of the law as set forth in this opinion...will be considered a contempt and will be proceeded against and punished." From the bench he announced that punishment would not be a mere fine but would be imprisonment.

Under the aegis of this order 35,000 South Carolina Negroes voted in the Democratic primary of 1948 without disorder or incident.

Later, on November 26, 1948, the injunction was made permanent. The Circuit Court of Appeals again unanimously sustained the action of the lower court. The appellate court was asked to hold that Judge Waring should have disqualified himself because of "personal bias" against the defendants. This contention was overruled with the observation "A judge cannot be disqualified merely because he believes in upholding the law, even though he says so with vehemence."

While Judge Waring had one of the election cases under consideration, a defender of public morals dropped a suggestion into the mails:

"You must realize the fearful racial hatred that will follow any adverse decision that you may render in the present case under your consideration against the white people of your own state.

"We again trust that we will have your co-operation in a favorable decision for the white people which will in the end do more justice to the Negroes themselves than the past decisions that you have been making."

The signature—Knights of the Ku Klux Klan—was in red ink.

There have been other communications bearing the Klan's signature. The campaign of abuse by anonymous telephone calls, round the clock obscenities shouted indiscriminately at the Judge or Mrs. Waring, seems to show central organization and direction. On March 12, 1951, at midnight, while the Warings were in New York where he was holding a term of court, shadows from a burning cross danced over the grey wall of the handsome Meeting Street home. On another occasion a rock was hurled at night through their living room window. An anonymous pointed reminder came to Mrs. Waring:

"Every time you open that sloppy mouth of yours you make it worse for you and a disgrace to your race. Write another speech and look for K.K.K. They may visit you today."

Mrs. Waring, 55, strikingly handsome and vivacious, silvery haired, mother of a son killed in the Pacific and two other children who live in the North, is neck deep in the fight. In a Thanksgiving Day program last year in a Charleston Negro church, she placed herself unequivocally on the side of the Negro in his struggle for legal rights. That gave some foretaste and caused some mutterings. But in January of this year before the Negro Y.W.C.A. all of her batteries were unlimbered;

"You Negro people have already picked up the torch of culture and achievement from the whites down here. They are sick, confused and decadent people."

"You know," Mrs. Waring observed, "South Carolina officials proceeded to prove my point." She might have been thinking of:

Governor Thurmond—"Coming from another section of our country, she does not understand or appreciate our problems. But it is quite apparent that she is following the Truman line and speaks for the Trumanites in South Carolina."

State Senator Edward Cantwell—"I hold him (Judge Waring) in contempt. I hate him and detest him, and I wish they would run him out of the state."

Representative John D. Long who introduced a bill appropriating $10,000 to finance impeachment proceedings, which bill has this revealing preamble: "Whereas, a resolution to impeach Federal District Judge J. Waties Waring, of Charleston, South Carolina, on the grounds that he and his northern-born wife have advocated a Negro revolution against white supremacy has been drawn up and will be presented in Congress."

The joint resolution by Representative Garrett "to appropriate necessary funds to purchase two one-way tickets for Federal Judge J. Waties Waring and his socialite wife to any point of their choice provided they never return to the state of South Carolina; and further to deduct from the $800,000 allocation for an animal science building at Clemson College the necessary funds to erect a suitable plaque to Federal Judge and Mrs. Waring in the mule barn at said college."

The resolution to investigate the Florida divorce secured by the first Mrs. Waring.

The resolution adopted by the South Carolina Sheriffs Association condemning Judge and Mrs. Waring for uttering "statements that seem coldly calculated to wreak vengeance upon a people who, in his mind, have been convicted of decadence...These utterances, if followed to a logical conclusion, could but lead to a mongrelization."

The vaporings of certain South Carolina congressmen, and the outpourings of certain South Carolina newspapers.

Those are examples taken from the higher levels of criticism. The Get Waring Movement, you may be sure, had its grass roots. Witness the following printable excerpts from anonymous letters addressed to one or both of the Warings:

"Can you blame some people for asking each other if you have Negro blood in you?...If you continue your practice of breaking up homes, and getting divorces, it would surprise no one if your next husband would be a Negro."

"What is any lower than the nigger-loving whites? The nigger is all right in his place and that is right where we are going to keep them."

"If you love the Negro so much you can live with them. Your daughter can mary and raze a family in some states. There is to much pride about any refine people mixing with negers."

"Dear nigger lover: How much are nigger outfits paying you? Why don't you have yourself examined by a doctor. It must be something wrong with the pair of you....It is a shame somebody did not drop a bomb over you last night...The country in time will get rid of crooks like you and the Truman bunch."

"We do not agree with what you say about our southern states. You know what this means when you get to Charleston."

"Haven't you any more sense than to try to force them (Negroes) on all good honest democratic American people just for your own selfish pride. They are much happier as they are and the white people are also...You better be putting your efforts towards Christianity that is good for you and an award far greater for you and everyone awaits us who know Him."

The deeply pious tone of the last quoted letter crops out occasionally in the correspondence. But the overwhelming majority of these hundreds of anonymous missives reek of the livery stable. Yankee. Divorce. Nigger loving. These are the central ideas. But sex and the bodily functions are the vehicles for developing these themes—words usually reserved for the backyard fences and public toilets. The scrap books and drawer full of these untold obscenities would provide a field day for a first-rate Freudian.

"But this one," said Judge Waring with a smile, passing over a post card from Spartanburg, South Carolina, "is the one I like best. It is clean and a masterpiece of condensation." There were printed letters an inch high—DROP DEAD!!

"A confused and decadent people?" Well, for what they are worth, there are the exhibits from Governor Thurmond on down.

Judge Waring talked earnestly of these letters. "They are tragic in a way. The language of newspaper critics, while bitter, is always parliamentary. The papers constitute the arsenal of ideas for the campaign against me. The ideas which the papers chastely express lend themselves to expression in vulgar and obscene terms by those who can't write correctly. Those who write these letters do the best they can with the material the papers furnish. The writers have been stimulated to attempt a task beyond their powers."

"The papers would be quick to condemn the letters. They are quick to condemn the Klan. They eschew the term 'white supremacy.' But they daily give aid and comfort to the Klan and the white supremacy crowd because they express the sentiments of those groups. They run the interference while the the other boys carry the ball. They peddle the same wares sold under the white supremacy label."

The Judge was speaking from the book, as is the habit of judges.

The Charleston *News and Courier* on August 26, 1937, carried the following editorial:

"Again let it be said and clearly understood that were the *News and Courier* a democratic newspaper, if it believed in democracy as President Roosevelt believes in it, as he described it in his North Carolina speech last week, it would demand that every white man and woman and every black man and woman in the South be protected in the right to vote. It would demand the abolition of all "Jim Crow" cars, of all drawing of the color line by law. That is democracy. But the *News and Courier* is not a democrat. It fears and hates democratic government. The *News and Courier* believes in Democratic government—Democratic with a big 'D' and that is another word for a measure of aristocratic government that ought to be more aristocratic than it is."

And on July 20, 1938, the following appeared:

"In South Carolina, the Democratic Party, has been, so far as the Negro vote is concerned, a Fascist party, and that is why the *News and Courier* 'cooperates' with it. In the North the Democratic party has become so democratic that it turns Southern stomachs."

So the opposition in the Get Waring Movement—South Carolina officialdom, a section of the State's press, the Klan and the horde of ignorant and vicious whites who feel that their world will topple about them when the Negro becomes a full citizen. Judge Waring has had a major role in the emergence of the Negro; in addition to primary decisions, his order in one case brought about equal salaries for Negro teachers and in another gave South Carolina the hard alternatives of (1) ceasing to maintain a law school for whites, (2) maintaining a similar school for Negroes or (3) admitting Negroes into the law school of the State University. The separate school was established.

In a case from Clarendon County, South Carolina, the Judge on June 21, 1951 wrote a dissenting opinion repudiating the doctrine that a state acts within the 14th Amendment to the Constitution of the United States when it provides separate but equal school facilities for Negro and white pupils. The case is the first to attack segregation *per se* on the elementary school level. After reviewing the testimony of certain witnesses for plaintiffs, Judge Waring wrote:

"From their testimony it was clearly apparent, as it should be to any thoughtful person, irrespective of having such expert testimony, that segregation in education can never produce equality and that it is an evil that must be eradicated...I am of the opinion that all of the legal guideposts, expert testimony, common sense and reason point unerringly to the conclusion that the system of segregation in education adopted and practiced in the State of South Carolina must go and must go now.

"Segregation is per se inequality."

The other two judges of the three judge court, John J. Parker and George Bell Timmerman, upheld the separate but equal doctrine. An appeal from their decision is now before the Supreme Court.

But this would be a badly distorted picture if the impression should be created that hatred of Judge Waring approaches being unanimous in South Carolina. Far from it. The press of the state generally has not taken up the hue and cry, regarding his decisions as being inevitable and correct statements of the law. Outside of ancient Charleston and environs, if one may judge from the letters and telegrams (these not wearing the mask of anonymity) there is a substantial body of white opinion which applauds the judge's course. From outside the state there have come literally thousands of commendatory messages.

The Negro people, of course, both at home and abroad, have elevated him to sainthood, a role for which he is ill-adapted and which gives him acute discomfort.

"After all, I have done nothing except perform very plain duties. For merely doing his duty a man is not entitled to anything approaching adulation."

But wherever he goes throughout the country Negro men and women—bell hops, red caps, college students, teachers—come forward to press his hand and voice the gratitude of their race.

"Of course," the judge admitted, "it does appeal to the ego which I guess we all have. And a few words like their's make up for a lot of those anonymous letters," pointing to the drawer which contains that literary collection.

Sitting and talking with the Warings in their gracious and well-appointed home, it is hard to realize that the letters exist, that they are there in a drawer—within arm's reach—or even that people exist who could laboriously spell out such fetid exhalations and entrust them to the mails. They are so in contrast with the evidences of urbane and civilized living with which the place abounds. To be sure, there is nothing showy or ostentatious or suggesting luxury. But there are superior paintings and etchings—sedge-bordered lagoons; old, old gateways yielding glimpses of formal inner courts; balconies of lacey wrought iron suspended from Corinthian columns; sleek yachts stooping before the wind; live oaks, massive, gnarled, bent with years and shrouded with venerable moss; ebony street vendors with head-borne baskets of flowers or vegetables—scenes hauntingly familiar to anyone who knows his Charleston and Carolina low country. Whoever lives here, one would be sure, must have a deep attachment for the peninsula lying between the Ashley and the Cooper; he has brought so much of it within doors.

But inevitably the eye comes to rest upon one of the smallest objects in the airy high-ceilinged living room. It is a bronze head of a small Negro boy, delicate, appealing, sensitive, filled with indescribable pathos. It is by Barthé, the Louisiana Negro sculptor. It was impulsively presented to Mrs. Waring by Mrs. Robert Lehmann of New York, grand-daughter of William Jennings Bryan, at one of the innumerable parties and receptions—all out of the state, of course—at which the Warings have been guests.

For the Warings are in, but not of, Charleston. They are light years removed from the habits of thought, the social attitudes and the scale of moral values which prevail in this most ante-bellum American city. The Warings will be dust and another generation of Charlestonians will occupy the peninsula before the Warings are forgiven for performing a simple act, an act scripturally symbolic of the brotherhood so universally professed—breaking bread with Negroes.

I asked Judge Waring if any white Charlestonian had publicly given him support.

"Not a one."

"What about the Churches?"

"You know," he replied with evident feeling, "that has been

the most disappointing feature of the whole matter. I am unable to understand how ministers who Sunday after Sunday utter the ancient cliches about brotherhood never translate them into action, apply them to specific local situations. Untouchability in India and the Ghetto in Germany draw fire but segregation here at home does not.

"It probably is all a matter of courage. One preacher did come to see me and expressed complete agreement with all I had done. "Why don't you tell your congregation that?" I asked. For reply he drew his finger across his throat, indicating that, if he did so, he would lose his ecclesiastical head. I guess it's just a matter of not having enough courage."

Probably that, but possibly also not having read so widely of the literature on this country's race problems. In the Waring's living room there is a collection of books on a circular table within easy reach of the judge's favorite chair. Some of the titles may be significant: Tannenbaum's *Slave and Citizen*, Asch's *Mary*, Davis and Gardner's *Deep South*, Myrdal's *An American Dilemma*, various volumes by Jefferson, Lillian Smith's *Killers of the Dream*, Cash's *The Mind of the South*, Lumpkin's *The Making of A Southerner*, Walter White's *A Man Called White* and Henry Lee Moon's *The Balance of Power*.

If the mind of a man is not wholly impervious to new ideas, if it is in any degree plastic or malleable, if it grows by what it feeds on, if it is not insulated against the impact of another's thinking—well, those books must have done something to Judge Waring. They and a bronze head from its perch upon the mantel. Something did—and the cord which bound him intellectually and socially to Mother Charleston was snapped.

That the predilections, personal beliefs and bent of mind of judges enter into the formulation of judicial decisions has long been recognized. Theodore Roosevelt in 1908 wrote in a message to Congress:

"The decisions of the courts on economic and social questions depend upon their economic and social philosophy;

and for the peaceful progress of our people during the twentieth century we shall owe most to those judges who hold to a twentieth century economic and social philosophy and not to a long outgrown philosophy, which was itself the product of primitive economic conditions." Sounds a little like another Roosevelt.

Justice Cardozo in *Nature of Judicial Process* advanced the same thought. "My duty as judge," he wrote, "may be to objectify in law, not my own aspirations and convictions and philosophies, but the aspirations and convictions and philosophies of the men and women of my time. Hardly shall I do this well if my own sympathies and beliefs and passionate devotions are with a time that is past."

Whatever entered into the mind of J. Waties Waring, the individual—such as books on his round table—flowed from the pen of J. Waties Waring, the Judge.

He feels that the apparent unwillingness of South Carolina to respect the Negro's constitutional rights is of a piece with prevailing attitudes toward lawlessness generally.

"With us," he said, "unfortunate crimes of violence are frequent, and the public is not greatly concerned about them. For instance, it has never occasioned any great surprise or ill feelings that Governor Thurmond's father killed a man and was tried for murder, or that the former Chief Justice, Eugene Blease, was tried for murder.

"The nullification and secession movements grew out of the sentiment that we would not observe laws we didn't like. The Dixiecrat movement in 1948 was just another evidence of the secession spirit."

For bucking this tide of local sentiment Judge Waring has paid substantial penalties. He has learned the truth of what Mr. Mencken wrote thirty or more years ago in his corrosive *The Sahara of Bozart*:

"Entering upon such themes (the cultural equality of the Negro) one must resign one's self to a vast misunderstanding and abuse. The South has not only lost its old capacity for producing ideas, it has also taken on the worst intolerance of ignorance and stupidity...All who dissent from its orthodox doctrines are scoundrels. All who presume to discuss its ways realistically are damned. I have had, in my day, several experiences in point. Once, after I had published an article on some phase of the eternal race question, a leading southern newspaper replied by printing a column of denunciation of my father, then dead nearly twenty years—a philippic placarding him as an ignorant foreigner of dubious origin, inhabiting 'the Baltimore ghetto' and speaking a dialect recalling that of Weber and Fields—two thousand words of incandescent nonsense, utterly false and beside the point, but exactly meeting the latter-day southern notion of effective controversy."

To the positions taken by Judge Waring in his decisions or addresses there has been no sane or reasoned reply. This has been true as to Mrs. Waring's blunt remarks. There has been a counter-attack on purely personal grounds—"incandescent nonsense utterly beside the point"—involving endless use of the terms "socialite," "Yankee," "divorcee." To such a state are upholders of white supremacy reduced.

I asked the judge about the penalties he had endured. He replied:

"For merely thinking and talking differently from your fellows, you are marked as being queer and unfriendly. For putting those thoughts into action, as I have tried to do, you are put down as a traitor to your class and state.

"As a result I have been completely abandoned by many friends and acquaintances. Probably the most serious phase of this abandonment is loss of contact with lawyers. They physically evade me and dodge around corners in order to avoid the business, political or other consequences if the impression should be created that they were friendly to me.

"I knew some pleasant and amusing people whose very frivolity was attractive. They left me.

"Then there is the discomfort of living in atmosphere of tenseness and ill will. There is a feeling of being on guard. I do not mean physically, though threats of violence are not uncommon, but, rather, of watching every word and act to be sure that they are not subject to misconstruction.

"All of those things, of course, detract from normal and happy living."

What was the other side of the ledger, what compensations to off-set these penalties?

"There have been plenty of compensations," he began. "They more than off-set the penalties.

"Of course the first great gain is the complete knowledge that one's actions have been right, not only right because, in the matter of court decisions, there have affirmances and complete approval nationally, but right because the conscience of the world approves of these actions, and right because one's own conscience says so, and that is the greatest gain there is.

"The absence of social contacts has necessarily caused my wife and myself to be thrown more closely together and to be in constant communication and dependent upon each other's society, and that has been an enormous boon. It happens that we have a great many interests in common on practically every line of thought and endeavor. And it has given us the opportunity to fully develop and appreciate the intellectual and emotional contacts and connections. It has developed our love and our friendship and has given us the opportunity to read and study subjects in which we are both interested and in which we wish to make further inquiry and gain knowledge.

"Another gain has been the outside contacts. We both have a considerable correspondence with people all around the country and even some outside, and when we go away, we now have the opportunity of meeting people throughout this country who are worthwhile, not because of achievements of prominence, but because they have inquiring minds. We have met literally hundreds of people with whom we would have never had any contact and whom we never would have met and many we never would have heard of but for the fact that South Carolina has chosen to advertise us as Americans and humanitarians and opposed to oppression. Too, it came as a great surprise to find out how many individual thinkers there were who wanted to know more about these things.

"I feel that this ostracism here has allowed me to take part in what might be termed a true crusading movement in which many hundreds and thousands of good people in this country are enlisted and performing various parts. But for this alignment, I would never have had such an opportunity.

"Some day the civil rights battle will be won. I hope I may be pardoned a sense of pride in the thought that I shall have had some small part in the victory."

(He might have added that from all sections of the country—except the South—he had received honors, distinctions, awards such as have come to few American judges.)

Since the Judge was in this self-revealing mood and there was still a quarter-hour before dinner, I asked if he felt that Charleston would ever soften its attitude toward him, come to think a little more kindly of the work he had done. There was a long pause. Finally:

"In my lifetime, no."

A native South Carolinian, my mind turned to the career of James Louis Pettigru, brilliant and courageous lawyer of Charleston, who opposed nullification and secession when those fevers ran high. As a result he was Charleston's loneliest man in the decades before Fort Sumter was shelled and during the war which that shelling announced until his death in 1863. He lies buried in St. Michael's churchyard in Charleston. As a boy Waties Waring absorbed the epitaph, from which the following extract may be pertinent:

"In the great Civil War he withstood his People for his Country but his People did homage to the Man who held his conscience higher than their praise and his Country heaped her honors on the grave of the Patriot, to whom living his own righteous self-respect sufficed alike for Motive and Reward."

Charleston may do it again.

Aftermath of the Decision

No one development more signified and quickened the pace of the New Reconstruction than did the Supreme Court's unanimous decision of May 17, 1954, against segregation in the public schools. The separate-but-equal doctrine, which dated from the decision in 1896 in Plessy *v.* Ferguson, had been under steady attack for two decades before 1954; a number of the Supreme Court's decisions from 1938 on, largely in the realm of state-supported higher education, had sharply limited and nibbled away at the Plessy formula. But the Court in 1954 met the issue head-on and, speaking with an impressive unanimity and moral authority, buried the legal fiction of separate-but-equal once and for all.

Marion Wright had correctly anticipated this momentous development. Yet, as he admitted in later years, he and many other liberal observers underestimated the depth and amount of Southern opposition to desegregation. This aspect of the New Reconstruction became manifest only gradually and after white extremist groups and politicians had moved into action.

The Supreme Court's decision in 1954, and its decree a year later implementing the decision, forced Southern whites to decide: would they actively assist, passively accept, or bitterly oppose the greatest tide of racial change since the years immediately after the Civil War? The gradualists, Southerners who looked to changes at some far-off, unspecified date, were especially confronted with the dilemma of deciding. In his speeches and written essays, Wright often dealt with the fallacies of gradualism and the obligations of the Southerner.

It was Wright's goal to transform Southern society into one that did not dwarf its men but rather encouraged their growth into giants. The ability to grow, he realized, could come only with a truly new South, one that came to grips with the Confederacy realistically, recognizing that the Civil War in the South had been waged to defend an ignoble institution. Dixie had fought gallantly for a cause that should have been lost, and now one hundred years later it was time to turn away from the past and to educate the young, black and white, to treat one another as brothers and sisters.

Wright was aware that the process of integrating the schools would be hard for both races and would reveal hidden antagonisms. When addressing Southerners sometimes Wright told of an elderly Negro woman in New Orleans, her hands bleached from the washtub. Shortly after school riots in that city she sadly confided, "I washed for those people for thirty years and I wouldn't have believed if I hadn't seen it that they would run in the house and pull down the shades while that crowd threw rocks at my grandchild."

It was precisely because such incidents did occur, Wright argued, that integration of schools was necessary, for this would foster democracy and would prove more beneficial to whites than to blacks. In February 1971, he noted:

> *It is as damaging to the personality to be shut in as to be shut out. Whites create ghettos for themselves. It is more important that the White Southerner know the black than that he know the European. Whites and blacks here are neighbors and neighbors must know each other if they are to get along and build a better society. Such knowledge begins in the schools.*

Delay, gradualism would not work, for all the world, even the peoples of Latin America, Africa and Asia, were "aware of the shabby and fraudulent tricks used to deny rights to people of color in the South, aware of burnings, boycotts, and bombings."

> *You know a man can secure a reputation for wisdom merely by saying, "Let's not move too rapidly." He can secure a reputation for goodness merely be saying "This thing is wrong and some day we must get rid of it." Such men are the meanly wise, the feebly good. Bigotry takes many forms. In none is it more detestable than in the assertion that mere procrastination will accomplish the results which all good men seek.*

These words, spoken by Wright before the Men's Club of Trinity Episcopal Church in Buffalo, New York, on May 6, 1952, set forth a theme to which he often recurred. That theme was in response to the plea for gradualism in re-adjusting Southern race relations. Gradualism was another term for non-action.

The attack on gradualism was more fully developed in the following essay.

SEGREGATION AND GRADUALISM

One who grew up within ear drum burst of the sulphurous oratory of Cole Blease and Cotton Ed Smith and who read almost daily the vaporings of Bilbo, Heflin and Gene Talmadge finds it hard to believe he still lives in the same region. The old fire and brimstone are gone from Dixie. Southern politicians, where not actually converted to the spirit of a new day, are at least tamed by the votes and purchasing power of the South's Negro citizens. Seldom nowadays does one hear of white supremacy; yet *Dixie Demagogues*, published in 1939,* records that the phrase was the blockbuster in the arsenal of spokesmen for the South in that fairly recent day.

With few exceptions, every responsible public official and

*Allan A. Michil and Frank Rhylick; Vanguard Press.

newspaper in the South concedes that segregation will not forever—or even much longer—be a part of the Southern pattern. There is general admission that it cannot be reconciled with democratic concepts of government or with the tenets of Christianity or Judaism. The tide of public opinion in this country and abroad, which runs so strongly against the practice, has not been deflected at the Mason and Dixon line. Segregation, it is now clearly seen, multiplies many Southern problems by two and imposes an unnecessary financial burden on those least able to bear it.

So the avowed white supremacist is now almost non-existent. Where found, he is a shabby and discredited figure, speaking no opinion but his own and having no following except among the illiterate and unwashed.

But, by a sort of political transmigration, the white supremacists of a decade or so ago have become the gradualists of today. They concede, at least privately, that segregation will go but they contend that the process is being artificially speeded to the hurt of both races. They are apparently a quite sincere group. They speak of evolutionary changes. They take the geologist's view of the operation of social forces. These forces, it would seem, exist independently of human effort and move of their own volition. To attempt to expedite them verges upon tampering with Divine Law.

The gradualists are most elusive and difficult to combat. They agree with all the arguments against segregation; they disagree only as to timing. Ultimately, yes, they say, but not now.

For some time I have been corresponding with one of the ablest representatives of the gradualist school, a South Carolina lawyer of distinction and integrity, who is light years removed from the Cole Blease[1] and Ed Smith[2] philosophy. He was, indeed, active in the inter-racial field until the irrepressible

[1]Gov. Cole L. Blease.
[2]U. S. Senator Ed Smith.

segregation issue presented him with hard alternatives. What he writes may be accepted as the best expression of the gradualist attitude. It should be carefully examined since, wherever the opposition to integration exists, it wears the gradualist label.

My friend writes: "I think it will do infinite harm to go too fast"; "We are making great progress now—why run any risk?"; "The Negro might have been better off if he had gotten the same things by white action ten years later."

Nowhere in the letter is there suggestion of another step forward which may be taken *at this time*. In a long and wide acquaintance with gradualists I never knew one with a time table, one who proposed that we integrate in this field now, in another in two years, in another five, and so on. He never tells you how fast he wants to go, merely that you are going too fast.

Several years ago I spoke before the South Carolina Library Association and the South Carolina Historical Society. In both talks I urged the view that South Carolina could not afford two public library systems, one for whites and one for Negroes, and that the public library offered the logical starting point for integration. The suggestion, of course, was not adopted, though I believe every person present would have described himself as a gradualist.

Incidentally, as late as 1941 only four Southern public libraries, two in Kentucky and two in Texas, offered library service to Negroes upon the same terms as to whites. According to *New South*, $20,000,000 would have to be spent in the South on Negro libraries to meet standards of equality.

Being upon terms of some intimacy with the then president of a State University Alumni Association, some years ago—before the rash of law suits—I wrote him suggesting that he appoint a committee to study the question of admitting some Negro students to the graduate school. That suggestion went unheeded, though I am quite sure the president considered himself a gradualist.

Of course, the Negro has made great progress in the last twenty-five years, credit for which the gradualist seems often to claim. But the cold, hard fact is that Congress, the Roosevelt and Truman administrations and the courts brought about most of that progress. The Eisenhower administration in the field of civil rights moves in the same great tradition. In addition, there has been the industrial migration to the South. Men from New England who operate the modern machines of 1954 are not too much impressed. by a feudal social and economic system. They have their impact—a grim jest at the expense of certain Southern governors who importuned them to move South.

The gradualist concedes that segregation is an evil thing which ultimately must go, but only by degrees. Tuberculosis is an evil thing, too. But no one proposes that we give it up gradually, reducing the number of deaths a few thousand a year, so that the people may become accustomed to getting along without it. The human race has had tuberculosis a long time; it would be shocking to get rid of it all at once—such would be the consistent parallel argument. Segregation has probably brought as much anguish to mankind as tuberculosis ever did, but the plea of the gradualist is that we get rid of it a little at a time, weaning the people off from an indulgence to which they are sentimentally attached. It would never do, they say, to act firmly and promptly.

Yet within the same month, the Catholics and Quakers in North Carolina abolished segregation in their churches and Sunday schools—at one swoop. Theaters and restaurants in Washington did the same as to their services. Thirty thousand Negroes voted in the South Carolina Democratic primary the first year they were admitted. And so on. Sudden, sharp, dramatic change—and no riot or bloodshed. Conversion for men or states involves no gradual break with a past one sincerely wishes to renounce.

But despite the fact that these changes and many others equally significant have occurred in the sight and hearing of all Southerners—have occurred peaceably and produced a sense of relief that the nonsense and hypocrisy of segregation were finally ended—my South Carolina correspondent and the entire gradualist school continue to predict serious disorder upon the integration of the two public school systems. Of course, it must be conceded that the making of such predictions by prominently placed white citizens tends to foster such disorder. The predictions create in the minds of men of both races the belief that riots are expected, natural, inevitable. The League of Nations was done to death and the United Nations may be by men who kept repeating "It won't work."

What the gradualist is really saying is that it will be natural and inevitable for whites to flout the law of the land as declared by their courts, to resurrect on the individual level the doctrine of nullification, and to go flatly contrary to everything they have been taught in church and Sunday School. If that premise should correctly depict the mentality and character of the Southern white, how bogus would have been his claim to being superior and how insecure his right to be called civilized! But the falsity of the premise is demonstrated by the peaceful transition everywhere evident.

What of these changes would the gradualist like to see undone? Negroes on juries? At the polls? Members of police departments? Drawing equal pay with white teachers? Enjoying the same transportation facilities in interstate commerce? Absorption into white military, naval and air force units; Admission into white graduate schools and seminaries? Every one of these steps was opposed upon the going-too-fast ground. Every future step, I am afraid, will be so opposed by the gradualist.

One of the comforting reflections of the gradualist is that the Negro has done well here under slavery and segregation. As my South Carolina correspondent strikingly puts it: "If I has been a black and could have I would have run into the net of the first Yankee slaver I could find."

Either my friend or Patrick Henry is merely rhetorical. Henry, I believe, preferred death to slavery. Generations of Americans have been taught that his choice was the proper one for a man to make—the same choice which the Israelites made when they fled the palaces of the Pharoahs. There is an unexpressed premise underlying the argument; that is, that the full belly is the greatest good. It is at the poles from Woodrow Wilson's "I care not how wise and good a master may be; I will not have a master"....

What would be thought of, of course, would be a condition of enforced servitude—a master and servant relationship of the antebellum kind. That slavery has no champions, no defenders. But in a practical and broader sense, slavery is a lack of privilege to do what free men do. There was the slavery of chains which merely restrained and limited locomotion. There may be the slavery of law and custom which commands; Use the rear seats. Don't sit in that grandstand. Don't go in that waiting room. Don't eat in that restaurant. Don't use that library. Don't attend that church. Don't go to that school.

Why? Because you are Negro. That slavery is subtle. The chains don't show.

But law and custom may be hard masters. Wounds to the spirit may be deeper than mere leg sores produced by shackles.

Slavery is but half abolished, emancipation but half completed, while millions of Americans are denied the right to use all of the institutions, instrumentalities and facilities of government upon precisely the same terms as every other citizen. When the Negro fights segregation, he is fighting a sinister and pervasive form of slavery.

Certainly, the Negro has done well here. But it seems to be specious reasoning to conclude that, since he has done so well with so many doors shut in his face, he would have done worse if all doors had been open.

When the Negro fights segregation, it is because he realizes that he *must* fight; that freedom is won, not conferred or handed down as a gift from above. When he demands an end to segregation *now*, he acts in the tradition of the Barons at Runnymede, who did not demand the vote this year, jury trial ten years from now, freedom from imprisonment for debt still later. Their demands were a package deal, with no taint of gradualism about it.

My South Carolina correspondent departs somewhat from the gradualist line to express fear of what would happen to white prisoners in the hands of a Negro sheriff. It is a fear which no doubt exists in the minds of many white Southerners but is seldom put into words. One would be more impressed with this alarm if those who give it utterance had shown equal concern about treatment of Negroes by white police officers. Police brutality—white police, that is—toward Negro prisoners has been fairly common and well authenticated in the South. It has been widely tolerated. So the fear is apparently not of brutality *per se* but of brutality inflicted upon whites.

Probably a great many white Southerners would show up rather poorly on the couch of a good psychoanalyst. They suffer from a sense of guilt. They do not fear original or unprovoked brutality on the part of a Negro sheriff so much as they fear reprisal.

Obviously, my friend would not contend that the white sheriff was brutal because white. His brutality is a purely personal quality. Similarly, the Negro sheriff, if brutal, will be so not because he is Negro but because of purely personal qualities. Brutality, as any other characteristic, is dissociated from color.

But the question about brutality is somewhat revealing. It implies, of course, a conviction, not frankly avowed, that white men are less brutal than Negro men, or that, merely because they are white, they are better qualified to govern. If one really believes that, is he not, without wearing the label, a white supremacist? And how far is a believer in white supremacy removed from being at heart a good Klansman?

It is precisely such considerations as these which make one accept with great reserve the strictures of certain Southern governors on the Klan. They dealt gingerly, if not respectfully, with the Klan in the days of its real power—in the McAdoo and Al Smith days. They kicked the Klan only when kicking was safe, if not actually fashionable. Nor did they lift a finger for equal Negro education until a prospective court decision sent chills down their spines.

In two instances Southern governors reveal their inner convictions, give us glimpses into the devious operations of their minds. The governors of Georgia and South Carolina* threaten to close the public schools rather than give up segregation. (Happily, they seem to stand alone among Southern governors in their shameful proposals.) When they announce that course they act pursuant to a certain belief. That belief is that it is somehow degrading to whites to be associated with Negroes in a classroom—despite the fact that three-fourths of the country's children are so associated. Such association leads to intermarriage and the corruption of racial purity. The blood of whites would be debased by such mingling. So runs the argument of these spokesmen of the polyglot race in this melting-pot land. Of course, it is not phrased that bluntly but it is the unexpressed major premise of their contention.

The whole structure of segregation rests upon this conviction of the superiority of whites over Negroes. Ed Smith, Bilbo and Cole Blease shouted it aloud—white supremacy. It has become a little unfashionable nowadays to be so forthright. So the phrase is shunned but the philosophy embraced, though by fewer men every passing day. When the philosophy is embraced, there is aid and comfort for every wearer of a mask and burner of a cross. Granted the premise of superiority, there follow in remorseless sequence arrogance, intimidation, brutality, even in extremes, extermination. Witness the Aryans of Adolf Hitler.

My correspondent may be said to be representative of a great deal of Southern opinion when he expresses resentment that "idealists in *other sections*" engage in some criticism of the official Southern attitude on school segregation. Those who advocate segregation—and their numbers rapidly dwindle—suffer from sensitiveness. A striking feature of that sensitiveness is that

*Herman Talmadge and James F. Byrnes.

it is felt that criticism loses its value if it travels any considerable distance. Criticism is seldom met head-on, on its merits. What right do you have? Who are you to tell us? When all other arguments fail the *argumentum ad hominem* is trotted out.

The country as a whole does not share this provincialism. It is generally agreed that Lord Bryce, Montesquieu and De Tocqueville are among the best critics of our government. The best study of the race problem in the United States was made by Gunnar Myrdal, a Swede. These foreigners were the best critics, not in spite of their detachment, but because of it. The detached and unembroiled critic has a vantage point not granted to those closely involved. For that reason we insist that our judges and jurors have no interest in the controversy before them.

But, of course, "outsiders" have the right to speak their minds. Only in the most limited and primitive sense are they outsiders. There is involved a moral issue which is not merely regional in scope. The impact of Southern practices is felt throughout the world. A New Englander or Westerner keeps silent at his peril. The bell tolls for him, too.

Those Southerners who want a fair analysis of the segregation issue—their numbers daily increase—welcome expressions from "idealists in other sections." For local critics labor under a great handicap. They live under the tyranny of time and place. There is massive group pressure upon them. There is the feeling that they are disloyal—to their state, to the white race, to "our way of life"—if they happen to think and speak as civilized men everywhere else think and speak. In such an atmosphere it is difficult to express a larger loyalty—to the human race, to abstract principle, to honor itself. In spite of all that, above the clamor and din of mean and strident voices, more and more often in the South are heard the calm and compelling tones of reason and conscience.

My South Carolina correspondent praises a certain Southern

governor* for not endorsing integration "which no one espoused thirty years ago."

This seems to make a virtue out of resistance to change. That in spite of the fact that the world has been worked over thoroughly in the last decades. If the mind of a Southern governor is unchanged, that fact merely means that he has an unusual capacity to remain impervious, a well developed allergy to new ideas, a marked ability to repel the impact of events. He has insulated himself against other men's thoughts, imposed a one-man embargo upon interchange of opinion.

The conclusions of thirty years ago were merely the points at which the men of that day became tired of thinking. That any idea was not then entertained affords no reason for rejecting it now. Its merits must be tested by conditions now prevailing. Such conditions, including the ever enlarging world importance of the customs of any one region, dictate an immediate end to segregation.

*James F. Byrnes.

In August, 1955, Emmet Till, a black youth from Detroit, visiting in Mississippi, was killed by three white men who dumped his body into a sluggish river bearing the Indian name Tallahatchie. The slayers were never brought to trial. The murder was one of a long series of dastardly felonies against blacks and their white sympathizers which made the name of Mississippi a synonym for unpunished racial crimes.

At the time Senator James Eastland of that state, Mississippi's governor and the governors of South Carolina, Georgia, Louisiana and North Carolina were issuing inflammatory statements urging resistance to the Supreme Court's desegregation decisions and plotting legislative maneuvers to circumvent such decisions.

Wright saw a cause and effect relationship between such utterances and parliamentary procedures and racially motivated brutalities. He wrote the following expression of his sense of outrage and submitted it to various Southern newspapers. None accepted it for publication.

MURDER ON THE TALLAHATCHIE

They fished the body of the little Negro boy out of the Tallahatchie River.

He had, it is said (by whom, no one knows), made "ugly remarks" to a white woman. And so, without warrant, arrest, trial, jury, conviction or legal sentence, he is kidnapped and slain and his body dumped into the river. It is doubtful that he had committed any crime. If any, the punishment could not have exceeded thirty days. But they fished his body out of the Tallahatchie.

How many thousands of white men have made "ugly remarks" to Negro women—and still breathe the free air and walk upon the green grass under the blue sky?

The lips upon which turtles have gnawed speak to the capitals at Jackson, Columbia, Atlanta, Baton Rouge and Raleigh.

Hear me, you Governors.

I was your fellow citizen. I lived with you under the same flag and constitution. I had, in theory and on paper, all the rights you enjoy. But I didn't have them in practice and in fact. I am dead and you are alive.

I charge you, you Governors, with a part of the guilt for my death. Oh, no, you didn't lay hands upon me or pull a trigger. You were in your comfortable offices or homes or elsewhere, when my skull was shattered and the red stream mixed with gray spurted from the wound.

But you have planted and nurtured an idea, a belief. Beliefs are the things which cause men to act. Beliefs of illiterate and brutal men may move them to murder. Sow an evil belief deeply enough and widely enough and the harvest of foul deeds is assured. You gave the prestige and benediction of your office to an idea—an idea which came to fruition along the mud flats of the Tallahatchie.

What is that idea?

It has two prongs. One is that men of one race are somehow superior to men of another race. A German named Adolf Hitler was possessed by that idea. Thousands of men of my race and yours gave their lives to destroy that idea—they came to their deaths on honorable battlefields, not in river slime.

The other prong is that it may be respectable and right to evade the law. Since May 17, 1954, you or your predecessors have preached that doctrine to your people. On that day a court of white men, interpreting a constitution written by white men, declared that you and I have equal rights. But you have spat upon my rights.

You have devoted all of your cunning and guile to thwarting the law. You have taught your people that they may select the laws by which they will abide and flout those they do not select. This law you chose to flout had to do with school attendance. The law two Mississippians chose to flout had to do with trial by jury and punishment for crime. Surely their right of selection is as good as yours.

The same constitution guaranteed the right of attendance upon a school of my choice. Can you complain if you choose to deny the one and some of your constituents choose to deny the other?

Some of you rail against the Ku Klux Klan. The Klan doesn't take you seriously. You are its best allies. Because, in essence, you and the Klan preach the same doctrine.

If you will look closely, you Governors, you will see more than a thread of connection between what you say and what two Mississippians did.

Beliefs may be the prelude to murder. Think upon that, my Governors, before you next use air waves or printer's ink to spread your poison.

By the time Wright made this talk to the Fellowship of the Concerned on March 6, 1956 in Columbia, Southern opposition to desegregation had erupted into ugly violence. The admission of Miss Autherine Lucy to the University of Alabama brought riots in February, 1956. Southern legislatures were busy passing scores of new laws designed to thwart integration and to harass those who advocated it. The fact that a presidential election loomed ahead added special political tensions to a racial situation in the South which seemed to be deteriorating rapidly.

"Cunning men with perverted minds seek to fasten an immoral regime upon us," Wright declared. "Shall Christianity stand idly by, dumb, mute, while this infamy is being perpetrated?"

The Fellowship of the Concerned was an organization composed largely of Southern church women. The moving spirit was Mrs. Dorothy Tilly, long active in Methodist church affairs. She was a staff member of the Southern Regional Council and, in organizing and supervising Fellowship activities, acted under the Council's sponsorship. The relative ease with which desegregation was accomplished in the South is due in large part to the fact that in many Southern communities women, organized under the Fellowship's banner, secured acceptance of the new order.

THE MORAL ISSUE

Who among us ten years ago would have believed that in South Carolina in the years 1955 and 1956—

A professor of education at the University of South Carolina* would have been fired because he made a temperate criticism of a governor's speech and publicly expressed an honest opinion on educational policy?

A teacher at Mullins would have been fired because he asked

*Prof. Chester Travelstead.

a Sunday School class if they felt that throwing eggs at a Negro girl was Christian conduct?

A Baptist minister at Batesburg would have been fired because he voted his conscientious beliefs on a matter of church policy?

Hundreds of Negroes would have been thrown out of work, had their credit cut off and become displaced persons, threatened and put in mortal terror, because they exercised the American right of petition?

Would you have believed it? Would anyone living under the American flag have believed it?

Yet those things happened, happened before my eyes and yours, happened before the shocked and unbelieving eyes of the nation and all mankind. They happened in a state that calls itself—proudly—democratic and Christian.

As appalling as are the events themselves, they are mere symptoms of a disease which afflicts us, a distemper that devours.

The disease is intolerance. I do not at the moment refer to intolerance of people. I mean something far worse—intolerance of ideas, of opinion. I say it is far worse because ideas and opinions are more important than the individuals who entertain them. The individual perishes but ideas are the life blood of society, the thing which gives society vitality and causes it to evolve imperceptibly but surely into adaptations better suited to human needs. In that sense ideas are immortal.

How did we get this way?

I am not historian enough or philosopher enough to give any authoritative answer to that question. I suspect that, if we sought original cause, we would be back in the 16th and 17th centuries (if no farther) and at the side of men with ropes who ranged Africa in search of human prey, in the steaming holds of vessels which brought captives to the young nation, and on thousands of tidewater plantations where the beautiful and the base in our society had their common roots in the soil of slavery. The problem of how the races shall get along with each other was not of Negro creation.

If you ask the question "How did we get this way, how did we get to the point that terror is being used to prevent men from expressing their honest beliefs?"—if you ask it, you will be told by many in high places that it is because of something that occurred on May 17, 1954—that one decision by one court brought us to this pass. It is a very slick and glib answer and suits the purposes of those who give it. But it is far, far from the truth.

We will be told that because a scapegoat is a psychological necessity for those having guilty consciences. It is very convenient having nine men sitting there in Washington to whom we may point and say, "These are the villains. But for them all would be quiet below the Potomac." You see, if we say that often enough and loudly enough we accomplish certain pleasant results.

First of all, we will convince *ourselves* that *we* had nothing to do with creating the illegal, immoral and unconstitutional conditions the court had to correct.

We may hope to divert the attention of others away from ourselves, the really guilty, and to the men who have exposed our guilt. No one hollers "Stop, thief!" more loudly than the fleeing pickpocket.

And we may conceal our mental bankruptcy in dealing with integration after the decision by continuing to whine that the decision was wrong. The poorest player usually is the one who most often cusses the umpire.

Those who now assail the decision of May 17, 1954, claim to have been shocked and amazed by the court's action, as though there had been nothing in judicial history to forecast the result. If their surprise is genuine, they had been blind to the signs and trends of the times. For to all reasonable men, lawyers and laymen alike, the handwriting had long been on the wall. Their blindness was the blindness of those who *will* not see.

Take the case of Plessy *v.* Ferguson, on which they rely and of which we hear so much. That case was decided in 1896. It was not remotely concerned with schools; it was concerned with transportation by train. What it held—all that it held—was that a passenger on an interstate train could not complain of separate accommodations so long as the accommodations were equal. There was a moving dissenting opinion by Justice Harlan in which he strongly contended that separateness because of race was, in itself, a badge of inequality, a needless humiliation of a passenger, and in violation of the constitutional prohibition against state action discriminating against a citizen because of his race. There was the warning finger, lifted in 1896.

The dissent was significant, not merely because it spoke for enlightened public opinion throughout the country, but because able dissents have a way of becoming ultimately the views of later courts. If I had the time, I think I might cite a hundred cases from the Supreme Court records in which the minority view has later become the majority view. In at least a dozen cases the great dissenter, Justice Holmes, had the deep satisfaction of seeing his conclusions in dissent later be adopted by his brethren. Truth has a way of triumphing—ultimately—over error.

So, the warning finger. In 1896, mind you.

Now, for the handwriting on the wall.

The State of Missouri sought to discharge its duty to Negro graduate students by setting up scholarship funds under which such students might be educated in other states. A Negro student sought admission to the State University. He was refused upon the ground that education fully comparable was provided by scholarships to institutions located elsewhere. The court struck down the contention, holding that the state could not thus discriminate between white and Negro students. The spokesman for the court was that conspicuous New Deal subversive, Charles Evans Hughes. The word *"Mene"* appears on the wall. Earl Warren was an inconspicuous citizen at the time.

In an Oklahoma case, a Negro student named McLaurin had legally won admission to the University, but had to use separate classroom, library and cafeteria accommodations. He again went into court to have these restrictions removed. In ordering them removed the court said:

"These restrictions were obviously imposed in order to comply, as nearly as could be, with the statutory requirements of Oklahoma. But they signify that the State, in administering the facilities it affords for professional and graduate study, sets McLaurin apart from the other students. The result is that Appellant is handicapped in his pursuit of effective graduate instruction. Such restrictions impair and inhibit his ability to study, to engage in discussions and exchange views with other students and, in general, to learn his profession.

"Our society grows increasingly complex, and our need for trained leaders increases correspondingly. Appellant's case represents, perhaps, the epitome of that need, for he is attempting to obtain an advanced degree in education, to become, by definition, a leader and trainer of others. Those who will come under his guidance and influence must be directly affected by the education he receives. Their own education and development will necessarily suffer to the extent that his training is unequal to that of his classmates. State-imposed restrictions which produce such inequalities cannot be sustained."

Mene, Mene appears on the wall.

In the Sweatt case from Texas, it was clearly recognized that a law school for Negro students had been established and that the Texas Courts had found that the privileges, advantages and opportunities offered were substantially equivalent to those offered to white students at the University of Texas. Apparently, the Negro school was adequately housed, staffed and offered full and complete legal education, but the Supreme Court clearly recognized that education does not alone consist of fine buildings, classroom furniture and appliances but that included in education must be all the intangibles that come into play in preparing one for meeting life. As was so well said by the Court:

"....Few students and no one who has practiced law would

choose to study in an academic vacuum, removed from the interplay of ideas and the exchange of view with which the law is concerned."

That decision was the final *Tekal, Upharsin*. And who do you think wrote it? That Yankee outsider meddling in our affairs, Justice Fred Vinson, from Kentucky. Where was Earl Warren at the time? Why, he was the efficient Republican Governor of California.

So, what happened on May 17, 1954, was not a bolt out of the blue. Already segregation had been outlawed in graduate schools, colleges and universities, in inter state travel, in housing in real estate covenants, in labor employment and in other fields. The decisions had been written by judges of all shades of political belief. The one thing that they had in common was a conviction that no man should be forced to endure legally inflicted penalties because of the color of his skin....

Boycott, intimidation, repression—those are not the end of the trail. They are sign posts on the path to brutal violence and murder. A governor who advocates "interposition" is also, by that act, an advocate of cross-burning, egg-throwing bombing—though he may lack the intelligence to perceive it. The "respectable" Citizens Council, in advocating economic boycott of Negroes, is blood brother to the Klan. Emmett Till was done to death in Mississippi by men who took their cue from governors and senators.

Let us keep certain points clearly in mind....

Depriving a color minority of its rights under law will be the first step toward depriving other minorities of their rights under law, such as Catholics, Jews, labor unions and any other group which does not have its hands on the power of government.

If public officials today may wink at a denial of my rights tomorrow they may wink at a denial of yours. Winking may become a habit, you know.

The rights and liberties of *none* of us are safe under government which deprives any of us of *his* rights and liberties The bell tolls for us, too.

Let me lay a question upon our consciences. I should like to see it lie there and writhe and burn and gnaw until an answer is forthcoming. What is the duty of a Christian church or a Christian association in these times?

If there is anything of reality in what I have said, we in South Carolina live in a time of moral crisis. Cunning men with perverted minds seek to fasten an immoral regime upon us. They presume to act as our spokesman, our agents. Shall Christianity stand idly by, dumb, mute, while this infamy is being perpetrated?

The glorious chapters in the church's history were not those in which it remained quiescent in the presence of vice, perhaps even carried the torch for libertine monarchs, gave ecclesiastical backing to corrupt governments.

Not again in our generation will Christians have so rich and rare an opportunity to exert whatever moral authority and power they possess. Crises winnow wheat and chaff. If the churches and associations such as this now act—exhibit in their own membership the actual brotherhood of *all* mankind, assume the leadership of all forces of enlightenment, move to the attack upon the powers which seek to throttle our spiritual growth—they will perform in the noble tradition of the faith and prove their right to wear the name of Christian.

In the 1950's men began orbitting the earth. There was talk of "putting a man on the moon." Mars and other planets no longer seemed to lie beyond human reach.

At the same time in the Southern United States massive efforts were under way to prevent black and white children from attending the same school. The incongruity of this cosmic view of human aspiration and the narrow, constrictive view of human relations engaged Wright's attention. The phenomenon was discussed on April 9, 1958, in an address before the Greater Atlanta Council on Human Relations.

SEGREGATION *V*. THE SPACE AGE

This is a day in which our imaginations soar with our satellites. None of us is so dull-witted that he does not visualize as happening within his life time, or certainly within the life time of his children, easy and safe flights to the moon and slightly more arduous journeys to Mars and other planets. All eyes are toward the future and toward the skies. Men look up and ahead. At no time in all the tortured history of mankind has the next decade seemed so alluring and beckoning.

The prospect is so rosy and enticing that it is almost inconsiderate to direct our attention elsewhere; almost a brutal intrusion to turn our thoughts from the bright future to the dark past. I don't want you to think for a moment that I am insensitive to the romance of the times. My own space helmet hangs conveniently in a closet. But, of course, there is always connection between past and future. If we seem to stray from contemplation of tomorrow's fair vision, we shall, I hope, a little later return to that congenial occupation.

So—to the past. And when I say past, I *mean* past. Pre-historic past. In that day the most conspicuous feature of tribal life was the tabu. Every tribe had them, as every primitive tribe has them today. Men may not eat the heart of a deer; to do so would make them timid, whereas they gain courage from eating the heart of a lion. If one should touch the foot of a chief he would die of scrofula, later known as the "King's disease." There were elaborate rules men must observe to keep from offending the gods. Incantations must be spoken at birth. Marriage, war, death—every human custom or occupation-was hedged about with tabus. A great part of the time, attention and energy of the tribe was devoted to preserving these tabus in pristine vigor. They were a way of life, and, as such, sacred to primitive minds.

Every tribe had as part of its social system special rules regarding aliens or foreigners. It was generally permissible to steal from them though not from members of the tribe. Kipling wrote of "lesser breeds without the law." An alien was strange, unknown, and therefore, dangerous. In *The Golden Bough*, Sir James Frazier writes: "Of all sources of danger none are more dreaded by the savage than magic and witchcraft, and he suspects all strangers of practicing these black arts. To guard against the baneful influence exerted voluntarily or involuntarily by strangers is, therefore, an elementary dictate of savage prudence."

PRIMITIVE SUSPICION

This primitive suspicion of the foreigner carried over to later generations of men otherwise civilized and cultured. Dr. Frank Graham has collected many instances. To the Greeks, he points out, the world was made up of Greeks and barbarians; to the Israelites; of Jews and Gentiles. Aristotle, the Greek, rated low the intelligence of the people to the north of Greece. Cicero, the Roman, later considered the Greeks to be given to much talk and more ineptness, held that Syrians were fit only to be slaves, that Britons were "incapable of learning, too stupid to be slaves and unfit to be a part of the household of Athens," and called the inhabitants of the Iberian peninsula wild and barbaric people. A thousand years later a resident of the Iberian peninsula, Said, an Islamic scholar of Toledo University, said that the races north of the Pyrenees were "of cold temperament, never reached maturity, were tall and of a white color, but lacked keeness of intellect." In the late eighteenth century the Emperor of China scorned receiving an ambassador from the British King and made it clear that such a presumptuous suggestion came from "outside barbarians," who had nothing to contribute to the superior Chinese civilization, and could not be considered by the Emperor of the favored people of the "Celestial Kingdom." In this country the white man used "redskin" as a term of contempt, and the Indian so used "paleface." None here has forgotten that Hitler's Germany regarded as inferior everyone who was not of pure Aryan blood.

Of course, from the vantage of 1958, we may smile indulgently at the primitive tabus and those later assumptions of racial or national superiority. But it is hardly fitting or becoming to smile when we reflect upon the woe and misery which men have endured because of their belief in such nonsense. Such beliefs have through the centuries produced not merely the short, sharp agony of war but the prolonged and subtle and refined torment of spirit which follows discrimination.

Nor are we justified in using the past tense as to such beliefs. In certain of our state capitals—not all—are men highly placed—irresponsible men in responsible positions—who apparently cling to such dangerous and repudiated concepts. Some of these men are coarse and they use harsh language. Others, suave and oily, use polished speech. But their basic ideas are the same. They are the ideas of the tribal chief of 5,000 years ago.

IRONIC

If I may illustrate: The Governor of North Carolina, my state, uses good grammar. He never champions "white supremacy" in so many words; he employs euphemisms that are supposed to be becoming to moderates, though the euphemisms mean white supremacy and nothing else. Recently, he was interviewed in company with a Michigan congressman, who remarked that many Southern Negroes were moving to Michigan. "Yes," Governor Hodges replied, "we are sending them up to you as fast as we can." How ironic that a governor of *all* the people considers 35 per cent of his constituents as undesirable citizens! No doubt when Adolf Hitler drove a certain Jew into exile he chortled that it was good riddance to bad rubbish, though the rubbish turned out to be Albert Einstein.

The principal concern of the tribal chieftain, as I have said, was to preserve the tabus which constituted what they no doubt called their "way of life." A large part of tribal time, attention and energy went into strengthening the tabus, adding to their rigidity and meting out punishment of their infraction. To the chief and, it must be admitted, to a majority of the tribe, these tabus were not, as we now know, completely meaningless; they were felt to be moral principles of the highest order, reflecting the strength and virtue of the tribe.

I hope that what I have said thus far may have suggested to you the point which I should now like to drive home. That point is that every one of our customs which flow from segregation is nothing more nor less than a primitive tabu and that those who strive to maintain them have merely failed to distinguish between a tabu and and a moral principle. All of the turmoil and social upheaval and personal tragedies we now endure flow from the dominance of the aboriginal over the cultivated intellect.

Let us examine some of the tenets of the creed of the segregationist, keeping a sharp watch for any suggestion of a moral principle which may lurk in any of them.

Basically and generally, they seek to regulate association of human beings with each other. Whites must sit in the front and Negroes in the rear of buses. In theaters whites must occupy the lower floor and Negroes the balcony. Members of the two races may not play on the same golf course, use the same swimming pool or even ocean. They may not read together in the same library or eat together in the same restaurant. They must occupy separate waiting rooms at railroad or bus stations or airports. The men who fought together in Germany or Korea must be members of separate American Legion posts when they have returned home from enduring common dangers. They must not risk incurring the wrath of God by worshipping Him jointly. Nor must they damage young minds by having them trained in the same schools.

CODE OF CONDUCT

Underlying all of this elaborate code of conduct is the basic premise that somehow members of the white race would undergo some debasement or contamination if exposed to members of the Negro race under the condemned circumstances. But not under *all* circumstances. There is one important exception. That is, the master and servant relationship. It is quite all right for whites to have Negro cooks, maids, wash women, gardeners and chauffeurs where the relationship is far more personal and intimate that under the proscribed conditions.

Why the difference? There is but one answer: The master and servant relationship is consistent with the idea of superiority of the whites; the other relationships are consistent with the idea of equality of members of the two races. Up with that, as Mr. Churchill would not say, your segregationist will not put.

SPIRITUAL HEIRS

The point is important because it lets the air out of the principal contention of the modern segregationist. The old fashioned segregationist was a hardy and forthright individual. Your "Cotton Ed" Smiths and Cole Bleases and Vardamans openly and unequivocally championed white supremacy. They didn't flinch from use of the phrase. The modern boys have become soft and effete. They no longer use the term and, in fact, disclaim the entire idea. They are, for the record, of the separate but equal school, bearing down on the word equal. But when they fully uphold the master and servant relationship, with all the personal and intimate contact associated with it, and condemn the purely formal and conventional and incidental contacts detailed in the segregation code, it becomes evident that equal status is the last thing they will concede. The present day breed of segregationist politician is spiritual heir of the cruder demagogue of an earlier and a more forthright day.

Reverting to the segregation code, it is evident from our brief resume of its essential features that what and all that it does is to impose limitations upon the right of association. It outlaws normal contact between individuals of different color. It does so for the sole reason of the supposed detriment suffered by the white person from such association.

Now, habitual and constant conformity to a moral principle, theoretically at least, makes one, if not wiser, certainly better. Do you see in any of this baffling code the slightest suggestion of a moral principle? Would the scrupulous observance of every one of its provisions for an entire lifetime make one wiser or better? Rather, would it not, by the contraction of his sympathies, by the narrowing of the circle of his associates by the exclusion from his full friendship of an entire segment of human beings, however worthy, by the hostility and arrogance which flow from an assumed superiority—would not the faithful observance of all the rules make one smaller, meaner, something more of the brute and less of the divine?

Religion and philosophy are concerned with the principles by which men should live. Can the segregationist refer us to any system of religion or philosophy, holding the allegiance of civilized men, which conjures a white man to ride in the front end of a bus, or to leave a restaurant if a Negro should enter, or not to share with him a book in a public library, or to withdraw his child from school if a colored child should also there seek light and truth, or to have his name stricken from the rolls of his church if a person of another color there sought the solace of religion?

So the segregation code seems to have little in common with any moral principles of which we are aware. On the contrary, it is a system of tabus, of things men are forbidden to do, which would fit perfectly into the primitive tribal life of 5,000 years ago. The motivations of tribal tabus are suspicion of those of another tribe or color, belief in the superior excellence of the tribe of which one is a member, and fear of contamination from association. In India today, despite the devoted labors of Gandhi and Nehru, there are millions of outcasts whose very shadow is believed to contaminate those Brahmins upon whom it falls. Such are also the motivations of the segregation code.

TRIBAL TABUS

The role of the tribal chief deserves somewhat fuller attention than we have given it. Murdock writes in *Our Primitive Contemporaries*, "The chiefs are the custodians of tradition, the censors of etiquette, the masters of ceremonies." Upon their shoulders rests primarily the burden of seeing that the entire congeries of tribal tabus is preserved—that, for example, no soldier shall eat the knee of an ox, lest, like the ox, he should become weak in the knees, and unable to march; that no male animal shall be killed at the home while a soldier is away at war; that no person who has helped bear a corpse to the grave may enter a house until he has undergone a ritual of purification; that shorn hair and clipped fingernails must be a carefully buried, and so on. All of these tabus constitute the tribal "way of life" which the chief feels he must defend.

It is a matter of historical record that the office of chief evolved into the office of governor. I think it is equally a matter of proof that the primitive tabus evolved into the segregation code of the Southern states. The defense of that code by certain of those governors is a classic example of atavism. They are in 1958 playing the role of a Timbuctoo chief of 2,000 years ago.

SIGNIFICANT KINSHIP

There is a species of kinship of vastly larger significance than relationship by blood. In this country, at least, by refusing to establish royalty as an incident of the newly created union of states, by abolishing the right of primogeniture and by decreeing that the father's misdeeds should impair no rights of the son, we relegated blood relationship to the realm of the governmentally and officially unimportant.

The kinship which *is* important is the kinship of spirit. Not what corpuscles run through our veins but what ideas run through our brains—there's the rub. Between certain Southern governors and certain African chiefs there is a kinship more momentous and more ominous than any mere blood relationship. In the insistence by chief and by governor that no hand shall be laid upon irrational custom there is a kinship of spirit which transcends the affinity of blood.

I return now to the point which I tried to make a moment

ago. That is, that those who strive to maintain segregation fail to distinguish between moral principles and a mere system of tabus. How much of this failure is due to perversity and how much to pure ignorance I do not know. If the former, there can be no palliation; if the latter, there is still no excuse for, in this age, ignorance is not compulsory. In John Erskine's phrase, there exists a "moral obligation to be intelligent." All of the facilities for enlightenment are available if they were only used. None is so blind as he who will not see.

May I press the analogy to the tribal mentality a little further. As I said somewhat earlier, much of the time, energy and attention of the chief went into preserving and strengthening the tabus. Naturally, agriculture, industry, education, the arts, suffered from this concentration of thought and effort upon non-essentials, upon maintenance of "a way of life." In the competition between tribes, that one forged ahead which first diverted tribal energy away from pre-occupation with its caste system and applied it to more seemly pursuits.

What have we been witnessing in the South, particularly since May 17, 1954, the date of the first segregation decision? With notable exceptions which history will honor but which we do not have time here to discuss, what has been the absorbing engrossment of our political leaders? Any headline reader, any school child, can give the answer. It has been the devising of ways and means to preserve the region's caste system. I have no way of proving it, but I think you will agree that far more than half of the time, thought, effort and energy of our governors, legislators and public officials generally has been devoted to shoring up the shaky edifice of segregation. That item has been No. 1 on any political or legislative agenda. Education, science, the arts, the humanities—all of those functions of government which tend to improve the lot of the citizen—have been relegated to secondary position. What matters it that a man is poorly fed, or clothed, or housed, or unemployed, or his children poorly educated, or justice poorly administered, in face of the dire threat that young people of both races shall together learn that two times two equals four?

ENORMOUS EXPENDITURE

All of this blood, sweat, tears and toil have been spent, essentially, to see that a white child and a Negro child do not, side by side, learn their ABC's or the multiplication table.

On some of the French battlefields a plowman occasionally turns up a stone battle axe or an arrow lying alongside a rusted 75 millimeter gun or the remains of an exploded tank. Five thousand years intervene. The tools have changed—but men?

If one could believe in re-incarnation, in whose person would we now look for the shade of the tribal chief who, in History's dewy morn, impaled upon a spear that fellow creature who violated the caste system of the group? Well, it wouldn't be among this company or in the person of anyone who has a sincere attachment of the Bill of Rights or who is genuinely devoted to democratic principles.

Can there be any doubt that the Southern states have suffered from this enormous expenditure of official energy upon the task of maintaining our caste system?

GREATER LOSSES

It might be possible to ascertain the dollars actually poured down this rat hole, though I am not sure how it would be done. But the greater losses are indirect, and not measurable in dollars. The other American states move forward on many fronts while we mark time. They strengthen their school systems to meet the demands of this age. They build up their public libraries. They enlarge their parks. They strengthen their public health services. They do all of this while we debate—debate who shall go to school with whom; how to keep certain people out of our libraries and out of our parks. When it comes to public health, one of our states took time out to fire a white doctor for eating with a Negro nurse. Another has under consideration a requirement that donations to the blood bank shall be accompanied by certification of the color of the donor.

Let us disregard the facts that, by such antics, we make ourselves a national laughing stock and that, by the turmoil and uncertainty we have created, we discourage Northern investment here. The important fact remains that wise government requires the closest attention of the best minds. Far from giving it such attention, we are frittering away our energies grappling with a mock issue. The same energy applied to compliance with law would long since have devised a plan of integration satisfactory to the courts, and we could have kept step with the other American states in their advance toward proper goals of government. As it is, while we stop to bolster our caste system, the procession of progressive states leaves us in the lurch.

I think I may perhaps demonstrate how we lag because of our concern with caste. Just a very few years ago in the national government the witch hunt was on in full cry. Senator McCarthy, notably, and other lesser inquisitors, blasted reputations ruthlessly in the effort to find Communist influence in government. It took some years for sanity to be restored and for the senate and the country to call a halt on such inquisitions. Even now the army, the State department and all other branches of government are quietly, almost furtively, re-employing the discharged, purging records, issuing passports long withheld, making formal apologies, and, generally, seeking to atone for the reckless disregard of constitutional rights and human sensibilities manifested by Senator McCarthy and the senate and house committees on un-American activities. The whole country has breathed a sigh of relief that this orgy of brutality is ended.

STATE COMMITTEES

But, mark you, it is merely beginning on the state level in the South. In South Carolina, Florida, Georgia and Louisiana—no doubt there are other states—they have created, or plan to create, their own *state* committees on subversive activities. This means that, despite the existence of the F.B.I., especially charged with the duty of detecting subversion and especially equipped for that purpose, and despite the existence of congressional committees having duties in that field, these states now will devote time, attention, energy to catching Reds. And, of course, in the view of these committees any person or organization that believes in upholding the Supreme Court decisions in the segregation cases is a Red.

My point is that, in their zeal to maintain the caste system, these states will now, on the state level go through the orgy of investigation and persecution which the nation as a whole has repudiated. The energy of the states will be dissipated on a futile enterprise when it should be applied to solution of the legitimate concerns of government. No wonder we lag behind the procession.

INVESTIGATIONS

There is, of course, an ironic touch to these investigations. They ostensibly seek subversives. A subversive, by definition, is one who seeks to undermine the foundation of his government. The foundation of our government is the Constitution. Hence, one would suppose, the committees would attempt to ferret out those who act contrary to constitutional provisions, who deny rights guaranteed by the constitution, or who use unconstitutional means to attain their ends.

But those who sponsor the legislation creating the committees and who will conduct the investigations are members or supporters of the notorious White Citizens Councils, organized, financed and maintained for the sole purpose of denying to millions of people their constitutional rights. The country has recently been treated to the spectacle of Senator Eastland, proceeding directly from addressing these Councils all over the South, spewing his particular type of venom, to conduct investigations of honorable men and women and honorable organizations who are suspect only of favoring due observance of law. If he wanted to look subversives in the face he should have cast his eyes around him at his council meetings. By the way, I wonder if the man has a good mirror.

Of course, Senator Eastland has no connections with Moscow. Of course, he mortally hates Communism. But he is apparently unaware that not all subversion is manufactured in Moscow. There is an equally detestable American brand....

....[Our] trait of equating the evil with the foreign affects our use of color in description. A bad taste is dark brown taste. A coward has a yellow streak. Prose that is too rich or frothy is purple. A guilty man is caught red-handed. A thing is black as sin. But when we have received unusually kind and considerate attention, we have been treated white. Our color, white; hence a synonym for the good, the pure, the beautiful.

You see, we make our own vocabulary, coin our own terms. You recall Aesop's fable of the man and the lion who were looking at a statue of a man standing with his foot on the neck of a prostrate lion. The man remarked that the statue correctly showed the relationship of the parties. Replied the lion "If a lion had been the sculptor, the lion would have his foot on the neck of the man."

EXCEPTIONS

But, to return to matters governmental—
Such, then, are the pre-occupations of certain of our statesmen—not all, thank God. For the exceptions, for those who have resisted the mass pressures of the times, special niches will be reserved in History's hall of fame. But such are the pre-occupations of the majority at the dawn of the satellite age.

One is reminded of what Robert Louis Stevenson wrote of the French poet Francois Villon:

> *The world to which he introduces us is blackguardly and bleak. Paris swarms before us, full of famine, shame and death; monks and servants of great lords hold high wassail upon cakes and pastry; the poor man licks his lips before the baker's window; people with patched eyes sprawl all night under the stalls;...the drunkard goes stumbling homeward; the graveyard is full of bones...*
>
> *In our mixed world, full of green fields and happy lovers, where, not long before, Joan of Arc had led one of the highest and noblest lives in the whole story of mankind, this was all worth chronicling that our poet could perceive. His eyes were indeed sealed with his own filth. He dwelt all his life in a pit more noisome than the dungeon at Meun. In the moral world, also, there are large phenomena not cognizable out of holes and corners. Loud winds blow, speeding home deep-laden ships and sweeping rubbish from the earth; the lightning leaps and cleans the face of heaven; high purposes and brave passions shake the sublimate men's spirits; and, meanwhile in the narrow dungeon of his soul, Villon is mumbling crusts and picking vermin."*

How modern is every word of this. In this day how much intellectual rubbish is being swept from the earth, including man's most dangerous myth—the inviolability of caste. What high purposes and brave passions *now* shake and sublimate men's spirits—including the passion for equal and exact justice and opportunity for every man and woman, every school child. And, with such a back-drop of stirring and whirling events, how dwarfed and shrunken appear those who seek to interpose their puny wills and desires against history's onward surge.

SCALES MUST FALL

Surely, scales must fall from eyes. Surely, none is so deaf that he cannot hear the message of the satellites. The beeps which come to us from chill and distant space tell us of temperature, radiation, all the secrets of the ionosphere, but they tell us something vastly more important.

They tell us that the globe which we all inherit is now so diminished and shrivelled that every man is our next door neighbor. In this enforced intimacy friendship with all men is our most priceless possession. We must make friends and be friends with all mankind.

And so we move into the age of space. What mental equipment shall we carry with us on this leap into the unknown? What shall be our credentials as citizens of the brave, new world? Shall we go as Neanderthal men, weighted down with the suspicions, fears and hatreds of our Adamic ancestors? Or shall we go as men and women, erect and unafraid, recognizing every other man and woman on this now tiny orb as full and equal partner in the most fundamental and enduring of all enterprises? That enterprise is to develop human capacities for good to the ultimate limit of their potential.

If we shall enter the new age in that spirt and with that high resolve, we shall slough off some traces of the gross and the brutish; prove that we are indeed made a little lower than the angels.

The May 17, 1954, decision of the Supreme Court and subsequent decisions relating to desegregation of public schools were followed in practically all states of the Confederacy by parliamentary efforts to evade the law. Governors, legislators and, in many instances, boards of school trustees, connived to preserve segregation. Their legalistic efforts were followed by violence perpetrated by whites upon blacks and their white· sympathizers.

In an address before the Community Relations Conference at Nashville, Tennessee, Wright pointed out the causal relation between such legal maneuvering and the foul and brutal deeds of unsophisticated advocates of apartheid.

ANATOMY OF THE RESISTANCE

I appreciate the opportunity you have given me to come to Nashville and Tennessee. Of course I have been here before—as who hasn't? The architectural beauty of the Hermitage and the natural awe-inducing grandeur of the Smokies assure you of a perpetual flow of reverent visitors. For many decades now, because of those—and many other—points of compelling interest, the eyes and thoughts of the nation have turned to Tennessee.

And, though I venture timidly into the delicate area of politics, and do so for a limited purpose only, I feel compelled to say that your two able United States Senators have within recent years brought you added fame. Their refusal to sign the notorious Senate Manifesto and their uniformly correct position on civil rights have been enlightened and courageous actions. Senators help to create images of their states. The image of Tennessee has received new luster from the high and noble stand of Senators Kefauver and Gore. As the television commercials have it, no other Southern state can make that claim!

It is nothing but fair that I thus express our appreciation.

There have been many occasions in other areas of the South when I have expressed chagrin and disappointment. No one wants to become known as a public scold, fit for the ducking stool. So he must seize upon such rare opportunities as come his way to utter praise where it is deserved.

Lest I imperil anyone's tax-exempt status, let me hasten to say that no member of this organization or of the Southern Regional Council has conspired or confederated with me in the preparation of these remarks—"an ill-favored thing, Sir, but mine own"....

It is quite natural that Tennessee, through its senators, other public officials and state policy, should cling more tightly to pure democracy than do some other states. Geographically it is not Deep South. It had no extensive acquaintance with slavery. It enjoys neighborly contact with border states. Industry came early to your great valley. Those factors have given it national, rather than regional, consciousness and identity. The tides of enlightened world opinion do not break here upon a stern and rock-bound shore.

But more important than all of these is the brooding presence of Andrew Jackson, one of the early and great champions of the common, the small and the weak individual. He left his stamp upon the entire nation, but surely that stamp is nowhere more deeply implanted than here where he lived and wrought and died.

He faced the threat of Nullification. Surely all would have felt that that threat had been drowned in blood in the 1860's. But after four score and ten years, as Lincoln would phrase it, the spectre rises from the tomb. Of course it is not called Nullification, as though it lost identity under an alias. It is called "massive resistance," "interposition," "evasion" and the like. But the wolf is discernible beneath the hide of the sheep.

Hear the voice of Old Hickory when, in 1832, South Carolina posed the issue:

Nullification was branded as an "impractical

absurdity." If this doctrine had been established at an earlier day the Union would have been dissolved in its infancy...Admit this doctrine and...every law...may be annulled. I consider, then, the power to annul a law of the United States, assumed by one state, incompatible with the existence of the Union, contradicted expressly by the letter of the Constitution, unauthorized by its spirit, inconsistent with every principle on which it was founded and destructive of the great object for which it was formed...The Constitution forms a government, not a league.

Virginia papers, please copy. Yes, Virginia, there is a government.

Jackson's ideas were recently put in homely vernacular by a kindred spirit, Carl Sandburg: "The United States *is*, not *are*. The Civil War was fought over a verb. Governor Faubus don't know this, but he goin' to learn."

As a sidelight upon the character of Andrew Jackson and as a model for any president disposed to be timid, we have Jackson's words to a South Carolina congressman:

Tell [the Nullifiers] from me that they can talk and write resolutions and print threats to their hearts' content. But if one drop of blood be shed there in defiance of the laws of the United States, I will hang the first man of them I can get my hands on to the first tree I can find.

When doubt was expressed that the President would go that far, one who heard him told a South Carolina senator: "I tell you, Hayne, when Jackson begins to talk about hanging, they can begin to look for the ropes."

So much for a little excursion into history. My apology is that what happened in the 1830's so closely parallels what is happening in the 1950's that refresher course may have some relevance to the present. Certainly the image of a strong man dealing with a Constitutional crisis should not be lost on these times.

Governor Faubus and Governor Almond and others of their type are subjecting us to the spectacle of rebellion without the dignity of formal secession.

Well, the Hermitage and anything associated with Andrew Jackson draws us to Tennessee. I am sure that such visitors are proudly received.

I hope that my conciliatory and placatory remarks may entitle me now to proceed on a slightly less saccharine note.

Tennessee has recently had guests from all parts of the nation. Many of these were only mildly interested in Jackson. They were all interested in a school—a bombed-out school. Millions of your guests did not come here at all, but in their living rooms and before their television sets they visited Tennessee. For a brief moment the name of Clinton was in the world's headlines.

Clinton had a real significance because it was there that the idea of resistance to law had its perfect and ultimate expression. If you cannot win your legal victories in a fair forum, then destroy the institution that forum has sought to preserve. For all Southern segregationists this was their finest hour, for here their philosophy came to full fruition. If you cannot bend civilization to your will, then blast its finest achievement.

Let me say at once that this state's reaction to that act of barbarism was magnificent. The universal and profound revulsion which the state publicly exhibited eloquently spelled out the isolation of the deed's perpetrators. So, if I refer to the incident it is only in order that we may draw lessons from it, that we may at least speculate upon its genesis. That we shall now undertake to do.

Following the Supreme Court decision there came from certain governors, senators, congressmen and others highly placed, declarations that their states would not observe the law. One law. The law relating to integration of the public schools. A new phrase crept into our speech—"massive resistance"—and two old ideas were resurrected after 100 years of quiet repose—"nullification" and "interposition." I wish to emphasize that the proponents of such views had in mind a purely limited objective, non-compliance with one single law, not public rebellion against all law. If we may liken their inflammatory utterances to a bomb, their pin-pointed target was integration of the public schools.

They employed all of their cunning to develop methods of preserving a segregated system—private schools with state subsidy, tuition grants, pupil assignment acts, re-districting and all the rest of a list of odorous maneuvers. One by one these devices come before the court and are branded as the transparent frauds they are.

Such was the pin-pointed objective and such were the methods of attaining it.

But, of course, basically, what they advocate is disrespect for law.

They choose to limit such advocacy to one law. But when you enter the area of disrespect there is no such thing as a limited infection. It spreads. What right have they to tell me what laws I shall observe? My right of choice is fully as good as theirs. They choose to flout school law. I may, with as much right, choose to flout the law which protects the life and property of a man who disagrees with me. They seek to get results by chicanery. Men less subtle and sophisticated may perforce get their results by violence.

The bomb is aimed at integration of the schools. But whither drifts the fall-out? It drifts in part into the mind and heart of the ignorant, the unlettered, the evilly disposed. When cunning and sly maneuvers have had their day, when all legal tactics are exhausted, when what passes for intelligence has failed—what is the *untutored* citizen to do? Well, he has his fists, doesn't he?

He has dynamite. He has torches. There rings in his ears the voice of authority telling him segregation must be preserved. So he uses the only tools he knows.

So we have proceeded inevitably from the rolling phrases of governors, through the subtleties of legislation, to repression, cross-burnings, assaults, bombings and murder. Through all these evil and sometimes bloody acts there runs the dark thread of connection. The official policy of resistance to one law was the bomb. Foul and dastardly deeds are the inevitable fall-out.

Then how crocodile are the tears of the segregationist public officials who weep at violence! Actually, there is blood on their hands....

Certain public officials are appalled at the wrecking of a single school. Who wouldn't be? But what shall be said of governors, legislators and school officials who wreck the entire school system of a state? Which offense is the more despicable?

Yet in certain states to the south of you, constitutional and statutory provisions carefully designed through the years to perfect systems of public instruction have undergone mayhem and emasculation in order to thwart the Court's decrees. Happily, Tennessee has not stooped to this folly. If I refer to it here, it is only that you may enjoy the feeling of superiority and reflect upon the responsibilities which go with leadership.

Of course, in this violence to organic and statutory law, the statement is never directly made by the perpetrators that "We are destroying our schools," or even that "We are evading a Supreme Court decision." Their action is put upon grounds more acceptable, more palatable. "We are preserving states' rights," or "We are preserving our Southern way of life."

I am sure you must have heard those phrases so often they they nauseate you as they do me. But perhaps it may be incumbent upon us to give them some clinical attention. We should like to see what lies behind their noble facades.

We have already observed that they are cloaks and shields for skullduggery, both official and private. Have you also observed that only when *civil* rights are involved does the issue of *states'* rights rears its head? There is complete willingness—even eagerness—on the part of Southern statesmen to accept every form of federal aid to the states, except aid which might help the desegregation process. They are present, hat in hand, when national funds are distributed. Their harsh strictures upon the federal government are strangely muted and stilled when Uncle Sam wears his Santa Claus costume. Have you ever heard of a Southern filibuster against federal aid to roads, waterways, ports, harbors, or post offices?

How sincere are they, anyhow? Last year the Congress had before it a bill prescribing humane procedures for the packing industry. Was there a filibuster directed to the point that how Chicago butchered its hogs was a matter of only local concern for exclusive consideration by the sovereign state of Illinois and that Southerners should keep their cotton pickin' hands off Illinois affairs?

The nation, with full Southern approval, enacted that law because of proper national abhorrence of cruelty. Even a hog has the right to die with a minimum of suffering. If a hog has the right so to die, has not a child the right so to live? If the national conscience is properly concerned with the rights of dying hogs, is it not equally concerned with the rights of living human beings?

Is there cruelty in the segregation system? Unfathomable, incalculable cruelty. In every waking moment the segregated black child has shouted at him with the somber eloquence of deeds "Unfit, unworthy, despised." The whole system tends to grind him down, to reduce and abase him.

Toward the end of the war with Germany there was much discussion of what form of punishment would fit Hitler's monstrous crimes. A Negro girl answered in a few words: "Paint him black and make him live in the South." A procedure probably in conflict with the Constitutional prohibition of cruel and inhuman punishment.

When an ancient prophet sought to express the ultimate in human woe and misery he turned to the plight of one "despised and rejected of men." Such a one is "a man of sorrows and acquainted with grief."

Segregation is a diabolical device to proclaim every hour on the hour that some millions of American citizens are despised and rejected by their fellows. They are no less citizens of the United States than they are citizens of Mississippi or South Carolina. Yet the states rights advocates claim that, in the area of segregation, American citizenship counts for naught.

And what of "our Southern way of life?"

Certainly there are many features of Southern life worth preserving—the tradition of hospitality, good manners, urbanity, mastery of parliamentary procedure; sense of international obligation and responsibility; appreciation of the leisurely and the informal, and a scale of values which minimizes the sharp commercial instinct. For all of those things I am sure we would all like to stand. Some of us might like to add fried chicken and grits and red-eye gravy to the list.

But when the segregationist uses the expression "our Southern way of life," he never seems to mean any of those things. He seems to mean only a system of caste legally enforced. Probably he doesn't intend to do it, but the image of the South he is fashioning and exhibiting to the rest of the world is of a region obsessed with the significance of pigment, with the preservation of a fixed and unchangeable status for some millions of Southerners, with holding on to a state of society in which he enjoys a secure and preferred position, with embalming a part of the dead eighteenth century within the living body of the twentieth.

I am sure that none of us here wish to stand for that kind of South.

So the Hermitage and Clinton have drawn visitors to Tennessee—compete for their attention. Is there not drama in the fact that within the borders of a single state these two symbols should exist? The one a symbol of a strong federal government; the other a symbol of anarchy. The Hermitage, where national concern for the rights of the humblest citizen received their finest expression, and Clinton, where a denial of such concern was spoken with dynamite.

No rational citizen of this state doubts for one moment that Jackson's was the authentic voice of the state and nation.

Stream of consciousness is, of course, a baffling thing. Somehow it has in my mind tied the Hermitage and Clinton to another of your focal points of interest. I refer to Oak Ridge, which always pops into consciousness when one thinks of Tennessee. There mankind took a long stride toward the development of the atomic bomb.

Who does not view that development with awe and fear? The reason for the bomb's creation was that it could obliterate a purely military objective as a fort or an arsenal. But we saw that with even a pint-sized bomb in Japan some thousands of civilians were also obliterated. And over the awesome shape of the hydrogen bomb there looms the dark and sinister shadow of fall-out, carrying devastation which renders relatively trivial and innocent the results of the searing and scalding flash.

Those thousands of miles away may be affected by the pollution and in future generations by grotesque and misshapen and bestial creatures having but faint resemblance to their human ancestors.

I hope it is no stretching of analogy beyond reasonable limits to liken such bombs and their somber consequences to resistance to a court's lawful decrees. With such resistance, too, the objective is immediate and specific. Defeat the application of one law, that directing desegregation of the schools. But we have already observed, as President Jackson foresaw, that resistance to one law leads to resistance to all law and anarchy. The road leads straight from legislative halls and governor's mansions to Clinton.

It is true, as has been proved in Tennessee's case, that fall-out drifts in from abroad. There is a geographical distribution which ignores state lines, or even national lines.

No doubt every governor and senator who champions the cause of rebellion feels that the effects of his action are limited to his own state. This is a naive faith in privacy. No longer is any official action taken in a dark corner. It is known and its effects felt throughout the world.

Those more philosophical than I have with alarm pointed out that the growth of scientific knowledge far exceeds man's spiritual development, that twentieth-century tools may be employed by eighteenth-century mentalities. Especially is this true in the field of communication. So we have the phenomenon of a governor or a senator whose words may leap across oceans and continents but whose moral perceptions can't leap across his back yard fence....

The evil that men do does, indeed, live after them. What is now being said in the heat and rancor of the moment, what is being done in anger and spite—the bitter word, the evil deed—these tragically, are assimilated by the very young, the babe in arms. They become a part of the mass of each child's experience, to be years later dredged up from the depths of the subconscious. They will enter into the attitudes and the conduct of the adult.

We are now rearing in many parts of the South a generation of white children who are being taught by words and deeds that the government of the United States is something foreign, alien, hostile. How will their loyalty to that government be later affected? And who is a subversive if it be not one who spreads the doctrine of disloyalty?

At the same time we are rearing a generation of Negro children who are being taught by what daily transpires about them that the states of which they are natives are cruel, repressive, vengeful, bent upon doling out to them second-class childhood. How will their loyalty to their respective states be later affected?

At the same time these Negro children are observing that the national government is their natural friend and protector, that the federal courts, the national congress, the national executive, stand between them and the raw tyranny of the states.

Much more than government is involved. The Negro child sees both major political parties on the national level standing firmly for his rights; the white child sees as his champions the small, dissident splinter groups which constantly threaten to bolt over the civil rights issue and actually, in a ludicrous moment, ran Senator Thurmond for the presidency.

The Negro sees the national press, radio and TV, with negligible exceptions, giving eloquent expression to his normal and legitimate aspirations; the white finds that Nordic or Aryan supremacy is upheld only by the communication media of community or region.

The cause of the Negro is endorsed and supported by such respected bodies as the World Federation of churches and all national religious groups, while the local church turns him away from its altar.

So, to what a paradox are we drifting! As the world shrinks in size and the significance of local boundary lines melts and dwindles, we are conditioning our white youth to the narrow, provincial and parochial approach to public affairs, and out Negro youth to the broader, vaster, more all-encompassing approach?

We are at that period in human affairs when world government is within man's dreams and not beyond his grasp. The segregationist would probably be the last to admit it—certainly the last to see it—but he is helping to withhold citizenship papers for tomorrow's brave new world from tomorrow's white citizens, while bestowing them freely upon tomorrow's Negro citizens. Thus does the sword of discrimination turn upon him who wields it.

We are being propelled, even hurtled, into an age when we shall have daily relationship and involvement with every human being on this now shrunken globe. Hurled by cosmic forces which no senator or governor may deflect by a hair. We shall have identity and common interest with every Chinese catching fish from his sampan, every Laplander herding reindeer on the tundra, every Egyptian tending his cotton fields on the mud flats of the Nile.

When the probing question comes "What preparation gave you for membership in the world community," what a dusty answer will be the reply that we taught white children that debasement came from learning that two times two equals four in company with colored children learning the same fact, that the Holy Grail of learning must be sought by separate routes, that the Pierian spring must be separately approached?

The policy of division of men into groups, orders and sub-orders could hardly commend itself to intelligent minds at any time. It seems particularly primitive in 1959. Man-made satellites hourly traverse the reaches of space above this continent. They send back their little beeps which men in laboratories record for the books. We may translate these beeps or we may not. It hardly seems important.

But these satellites say one thing in a language all may understand. Unite or perish. Not unite as Negro and white. But unite as human beings, bound together as equals by bonds of mutual respect. We must so unite, or

> *The cloud-capped towers, the gorgeous palaces, the solemn temples, the great globe itself. Yea, all which it inherit shall dissolve; And, like this insubstantial pageant faded, Leave not a rack behind.*

On May 14, 1959, Wright spoke before the Urban League of
Detroit. His thesis was that Northern cities were not safe from
the violence which segregationists had created in the South. At
the time he spoke Southern officials were invading the North in
an effort to enlist Northern support in efforts to limit the power
of the Supreme Court and to defeat civil rights legislation
pending in Congress. He urged resistance to Southern
blandishments and, on the contrary, support of liberals below
the Mason and Dixon line.

BY-PRODUCTS OF RESISTANCE

I am delighted that you have given me this opportunity to
visit your city and am especially pleased that we meet under the
auspices of the Urban League. No doubt I would have known
something of the League if I had never had connection with the
Southern Regional Council. But my work with the Council has
given me unusual opportunity to have some knowledge and
appreciation of your accomplishments. Those who seek to
establish a better social order in the South have long recognized
the superb contribution you are making to realization of that
goal....

Well, here I am, a man from the deep and rural South, before
a city audience in the industrial North. I am tempted to dilate
upon the contrasts in our situations. But surely no good can
come from accentuating differences. They tend to set us apart
from each other, whereas we are drawn together by things we
hold in common. As Mr. Attlee remarked in his graceful
birthday tribute to Mr. Churchill, "The things which unite us are
vastly more important than those which divide." Under the
enveloping mantle of American citizenship, my interests and
yours are identical.

If I may paraphrase the blunt and forthright language of a former head of General Motors—sometimes called "Bird dog Charlie"*—what is good for the South is good for the country.

And, of course, one of the startlingly obvious facts of the times is that the contrasts between our regions are rapidly disappearing.

Certain factors are inexorably at work. The most important of these is the movement of industry to the South. I shall not burden you with the figures. The pained cries you hear from New England mark the departure of textile mills to warmer climes. Steel, petroleum pulp—the story is the same everywhere—Southward, ho, is the cry. Birmingham, Atlanta, New Orleans, Houston and hosts of lesser cities and towns are new hives of industry. A citizen of Flint or Pontiac or Detroit could move there and fill his lungs with the old familiar smog.

Of course, the important fact is that what goes South is not machines but ideas. The plantation economy, with its semi-feudal system of share-croppers and tenants in thralldom to the owners, has gone forever. Under such a system segregation developed as a natural child of slavery. It has no place and will not long survive in an industrial society.

Therein lies one of the ironies of the present situation. Certain states are officially committed to preservation of their caste systems. Yet their governors and other state officials lead their safaris into the North stalking the mills, trying to bring them back alive. With every success they have they speed the doom of a segregated society. They must choose between segregation and industrialization. Thus far they have found no way to eat their Southern hot biscuits and have them, too.

Recent developments must have given them some concern. The Southward march of industry has ground to a halt in Arkansas and begun to stumble in Virginia—two states most noted for their insistence upon segregation. The conservative *Wall Street Journal* presents an imposing array of instances of

*Secretary of Defense Charles Wilson.

plants abandoning intention to move South because of the local segregation practices.

There has been, too, for two decades a pouring of Southern labor into your Northern cities. Farming has become increasingly precarious at a time when Northern wages were rapidly advancing. So the tenant farmer and share cropper of the South have moved in with you here in Flint and Pontiac and Detroit and are now full fledged citizens of Michigan. In every industry of this region there are strong personal bonds between substantial numbers of employees here and families in towns, villages and the countryside of the South.

These are facts of great significance for the nation. They mark the removal of sectional differentials. A nation in a strictly technical sense may be created by ratification of a constitution. But this is far removed from the organic entity of a people. That depends upon the existence of forces more unifying than a paper compact. First the steel rails, then the telephone and telegraph wires, then the long strips of macadam, and finally the airwaves themselves—means of moving people and goods and ideas—these are the forces which create the essential unity and indivisibility of a people. Because we have these instrumentalities and employ them liberally we are at that state where every section of this nation—the great city, the crossroads, the farm—has an abiding concern with the problems and the fate of every other section.

If I take the time to remind you of our common concern in each other's affairs, it is only because that fairly elementary truth seems recently to have come under violent attack. You should be aware of the attack and on guard against it.

The segregationists, as you no doubt know, have lost nearly all of their legal battles. It is quite evident that on the legal front all that they may now do is to fight rear guard actions. So they pitch their battles on new terrain. That terrain physically is here in the North. Intellectually and spiritually it is in the minds and hearts of Northerners. The present strategy of the white supremacists is, at a minimum, to neutralize Northern opinion; at a maximum, to enroll you under their banner....

I may only indicate to you the extent to which your benevolent neutrality or active partisanship is being sought.

Several Southern states maintain their propaganda bureaus out of tax funds—contributed in part by Negro taxpayers—which flood the North with slick and glossy literature proclaiming that desegregation is a Communist device and that the Supreme Court is a tool of Moscow.

The notorious White Citizens Council takes full page ads in such respectable Northern papers as the New York *Herald Tribune* to present a letter developing the thesis that Negro inferiority is scripturally established. Over a quarter million dollars has been spent in such advertising and distribution.

Extensive radio networks present what is called the Southern story.

Skilled and effective advocates of bigotry invade the North eschewing the term "white Supremacy," but nevertheless seeking your help in maintaining a social system of which a preferred status for whites is the core.

If thus far your city has been spared this pestilence from the South, don't congratulate yourselves prematurely. They have just not gotten around to you. Your time will come.

Now, when a pestilence may strike, wise medical practice is to publicize the symptoms. Thus may the endangered population be on guard, and hence, inoculated. Surely those of us in the human relations field may take a lesson from the doctors. This may be a rare chance to get free medical service.

Of course, if the white supremacist were quite frank with you, this medical exercise would be unnecessary. The segregationist would say to you openly and boldly, "We want your help in maintaining in our region a system by which people with white skins enjoy certain advantages over people with colored skins." That approach would, of course, not be recommended by Dale Carnegie. Whatever else the segregationist may be, he is a master of diplomacy. So he adopts finesse in his approach. He is oblique and indirect.

Since, according to his view, the Supreme Court is the author of all of his misfortunes, it is the object of his malevolent attentions. All of its decisions upholding the right of an accused to confront the witnesses against him, the right to freedom of travel, the right to privacy of association, the right to retain governmental employment unless removed for valid cause, the right of freedom from tapped telephone wires—all of these stern judgments will be paraded before you. Little, if anything, will be said about the school decisions. The impression will be subtly conveyed that here are nine men drunk with power and bent upon destroying the republic; hence, their authority must be curbed.

Historically, one of the conspicuous badges of tyranny is its antagonism for courts and established judicial process. From the banishment of Aristides, the Just, from Greece, through establishment of People's Courts by Hitler and Stalin to the creation of a special tribunal by Fidel Castro, that antagonism has found expression.

When limitation of judicial authority is now urged upon the rest of the nation by the segregationist, it is not unreasonable to infer that he seeks to throttle the one agency which protects the Negro citizen from the raw tyranny of the state.

Speaking of badges of tyranny, we must not overlook the fact that every tyrant rises to power or retains power by suspending constitutional guaranties. You may examine every one of history's more grisly chapters and there emerges a man or clique who have ruthlessly ignored or struck down constitutional provisions asserting rights of the citizen. A tyrant may be one or many acting in concert—a Hitler or a Stalin, or a governor or a school board. The right involved may be freedom of the press or attendance upon a school. When any right is denied by official action, there is tyranny.

I remind you of these disagreeable facts, not, I hope, because

I am morbid, but because you should know for what cause the segregationist seeks your aid. The cause is nothing less than the denial of a constitutional right. That is nothing less than tyranny.

Now, those of us on our side of this issue are by no means disinterested spectators in this struggle for the minds of the Northerners. We, too, seek your support. I am not above doing a little proselytizing of my own.

You will recall that Mr. Adlai Stevenson remarked that when a Republican turned Democratic, wisdom had been granted him but when a Democrat turned Republican, he had succumbed to treason.

Similarly, when the segregationist seeks your support, he is guilty of vile propagandizing; when we seek it, we are merely being reasonably persuasive.

First of all, let me get you to consider for a moment the plight of the Southern integrationist. (I must qualify that statement by conceding that conditions vary greatly in the South and that I intend no blanket indictment.)

What forces are against him?

There are against him his state and local governments. These have at their disposal tax funds, prestige, unrestricted and free access to television, radio and press. Time and space which would cost thousands of dollars are his for the asking, whereas the wisdom of men like Sandburg and Faulkner receives greatly curtailed presentation.

Usually, though with increasing exceptions, the press is strongly pro-segregation. The exceptions are occurring as it becomes evident that the hard choice is between integration and no public schools.

Adult public opinion, if given free choice, would overwhelmingly favor segregation. Hopefully, the youngsters are breaking with their parents on the issue.

Churches (on the local level), lodges, professional societies and private clubs are segregated—always with notable exceptions

The Southern integrationist then, must pit his strength against these impressive forces. Sometimes he must break with friends and family.

You can, I hope, begin to comprehend how vastly important to him are the favorable opinion, good will and moral support of those who live beyond the region. When every man's hand seems to be against him at home, there is balm in the thought that beyond an imaginary line bisecting the nation there are sympathy and understanding. If you should begin to weaken, his desolation would be complete.

The point which I should like to drive home is that your own destiny is bound up with the destiny of the Southern liberal. You may not weaken on him without weakening on yourselves. Liberalism cannot be divided into neat compartments labelled "Northern" and "Southern" with freedom to choose one and reject the other. Because this is one nation, indivisible, the fate of every citizen rides with the fate of every other. Thus, the liberal cause may not flourish in one section while it languishes in another.

I think that statement may be susceptible of proof.

You will recall that in the 1920's the Ku Klux Klan received a new birth in the South. It was ignored by the rest of the country as being a purely local phenomenon. With what result? It rose to great power in Indiana. It was a force to be reckoned with in many Northern states, and its sinister shadow fell across the Democratic convention which nominated Al Smith for President.

So, even now the anthropoid utterances of men like Senator Eastland and Governor Faubus have the power to stir the primitive in men, not only in Mississippi and in Arkansas, but in Michigan as well. Outcroppings of racial violence in New York, Chicago, even remote London, have been nurtured by the irresponsible mouthings of bigots in high places. Prejudices lie so close to the surface in even the most civilized and urbane of men that they may easily emerge from the subconscious into the conscious.

Hence, let no one deceive himself into believing that the Mason and Dixon Line is a rampart behind which he is secure or a kind of curtain which will inevitably deflect ideas and sentiments having Southern origin. Ideas nowadays are all-pervasive.

But, rather than have you think negatively and defensively about the pervasive quality of ideas, we much prefer that you think positively—if Dr. Norman Vincent Peale will pardon us—not so much about guarding against the bad idea as about wise and full use of the good. Surely every American city is under the moral compulsion, not merely to insulate itself against evil, but to aid right to triumph everywhere else.

You will see that we in the South don't want to settle for your neutrality. We want you actively on our side. We don't quite go along with Daniel Boone's prayer, "God help me, but, if you can't help me, don't help the bear."

To invite you to remain neutral does but little credit to your intelligence or your principles. It is to assume that you fail to perceive your self-interest in the integration issue, or that, perceiving such, you lack the spiritual urge to throw your weight into the struggle. When, therefore, the segregationist, flaunting the banner of State's Rights, accuses you of "outside interference" in a local matter—"meddling," I believe, is the exact term—you may, with complete propriety inform him that you have a stake in all that transpires anywhere in this nation, and that repression or denial of right is one infant industry you do not propose to protect. Or, if you prefer, you may tell him bluntly where he may go.

Neutrality assumes large proportions in segregationist thinking. He not only wants you, the Northern public, to remain neutral. He wants the Government of the United States to remain neutral. Neutral in what conflict and between what parties?

To answer that we have to go back a bit. The Court has held that a Negro child has a constitutional right to attend an integrated school. The child himself. He is denied admission. So a suit must be brought. In several states they have so-called anti-barratry statutes designed to inflict severe penalties on the NAACP if it should intervene.

Several senators and congressmen propose that the Attorney General be authorized to initiate a suit for the child, merely translating a paper right into an actuality, putting living flesh upon the bare bones of the court's decision. But the Southern bloc fought and continues to fight such a provision.

Their position is that the child, usually without funds or friends in high places, shall be left to match his feeble strength against the awesome power of his state; that the federal government shall remain a neutral and callous spectator of so unequal a conflict; that government, like Nero at the gladiatorial games, shall observe with indifference the outcome of a fateful issue.

I cannot believe that such is the sentiment of this nation. I am sure that all of us here wish the government we all support to interpose its majesty and power between the child and raw tyranny of the state.

More is involved than denial of the rights of a child. Consider, if you will, the by-products of such denial.

As the dark and bloody history of tyranny has revealed, one denial is not enough. The original felony must be compounded.

Governors, senators and others highly placed proclaim a holy war to preserve segregation. They are suave and sophisticated men. They propose to use legalistic and parliamentary strategems. But essentially what they advocate is disobedience to law. Some of their henchmen are not suave and sophisticated. They know nothing of such tools. But they have fists. They can easily learn the gentle art of dynamiting. So they use the only tools they know....

The segregationist asks you here in Michigan to regard with equanimity the condemning of millions of Southern children to relative or total ignorance and to turn your faces from lawlessness officially propagated.

The official weapons, as we have noted, are guile and

duplicity. They involve enactment of statutes and constitutional provisions which pretend to follow the court's mandate but actually are designed to thwart that mandate. This is a species of fraudulent misrepresentation which would be repudiated in an ordinary horse trade....

We say that a state *maintains* schools. Vastly more important than the school it *maintains* is the school the state *is*. Example is more powerful than precept. The example of a state resorting to subterfuge, evasion and misrepresentation will not be lost upon young minds. That example will effectively negate the noble maxims of the classroom.

Can you here in Michigan view with indifference a decay of public morals anywhere in the nation?

So, I am here in your city seeking your help. You do not need my help and there is little I could give you if you did. But those who fight for justice, for simple law observance, in the South desperately need your help.

You take just pride in your commercial primacy, in the long procession of automobiles that roll from your assembly lines, in the material products with which you flood the world. No one would detract for a moment from the significance of such achievements.

But it may not be amiss to remind ourselves occasionally that no one recalls the economic exports of Athens, of Judea or Alexandria. But the world still is moved by ideas and ideals which there found expression.

A secure place in history, a kind of urban immortality, is reserved for cities which fashion and show complete devotion to the highest principles of civic virtue.

Wright confessed to a meeting of the National Association of Intergroup Relations officials in Pittsburgh, Pennsylvania, that the white Southern liberal is "apt to be lonely." Moreover, because he often had to oppose the power of his state, his community, and even his friends and family, he was vulnerable and in need of the sympathy and aid which national, liberal groups might give. Aside from reporting the main outlines of the South's slow progress in desegregation of the schools, Wright warned of well-financed efforts on the part of segregationist groups to spread their views over the nation. He called it the "old story—Confederates capturing the Yankees."

INTEGRATION TRENDS IN THE SOUTH
(November 19, 1958)*

This experience has for me the spice of novelty. Those of us in the South who occasionally talk to Southern audiences have always the consciousness that, while the handful of people out front may approve, the community most assuredly does not. The walls hardly deflect the outer waves of hostility. One has to reflect upon the jeopardy of a tax-exempt status in which his words may place certain organizations. There is always the possibility that one or two grim and vengeful spies may be present to record and distort his more innocuous platitudes for the White Citizens Councils. It is, therefore, a relief to look over this happy and well fed group and see no face that could remotely be described as grim or vengeful.

I am not, however, so far carried away by this delightful circumstance that I omit a customary precaution. No representative of NAIRO or the Southern Regional Council or any other group has conspired or confederated with me in the preparation of these remarks or has any responsibility for them—"an ill-favored thing, Sir, but mine own."

*Reprinted in *The Crisis* (March, 1959) and in *Interracial Review* (January, 1959).

It is a further happy circumstance that the topic "Integration Trends in the South" calls for the talents of the observer or the historian rather than those of the prophet. About May 17, 1954, the date of the Decision, we were making predictions. These had to do with the strength of the opposition and the rate of speed. I hope none of you made book on our rosy estimates; if so, you took heavy losses. We sadly underestimated the opposition and overestimated the speed. So we have about gone out of the predicting business.

We were not wrong at all points. In common with the rest of the country, we felt that segregation would curl up at the edges; that the border states, having advantage of neighborly contact with integrated commonwealths, having relatively small Negro populations and no plantation background, would go first and easily. That prediction has stood up except in the case of Virginia which has thus far been held in line by the iron hand of the Byrd machine.

Since the May 17 decision there has been integration in degree ranging from the merely token to full and bona fide in the Southern states of Arkansas, Kentucky, Delaware, Maryland, Missouri, and Oklahoma and the District of Columbia. In terms of school districts the number integrated is some 800 out of a total of 2,890. And, in terms of Negro children in "integrated situations," as the phrase is, the number is 4,000 out of a total of 3,000,000. These figures, I am sure, are familiar to you but I like to recite them. They are evidences of solid progress and reassuring reminders that peaceful and statesmanlike procedures do not make headlines. "Happy the people whose annals are dull."

In passing, and in order to wring the last drop of comfort from the Southern situation, let us salute Florida which, in September, admitted the first Negro student to its law school, and Louisiana, which in the same month first admitted 59 Negroes as undergraduates in a white state college. Perhaps we should more appropriately salute the Federal Court which directed these admissions. But at least Florida and Louisiana have bowed gracefully to the inevitable. Grace in race relations is so rare as to deserve applause.

Apart from the public schools in the "hard core" states, desegregation is making, if not satisfactory, at least substantial, progress. It now appears, not only from what meets the eye, but from utterances of segregation leaders themselves, that, in practically all other areas except the public schools, segregation is withering with no impressive effort being made to keep it alive. Cities and states in most instances have taken lickings on golf courses, parks, transportation, and the like and have accepted the result. Of course, we hear of the golf course that is closed but a dozen others remain open to both races. There is nothing approaching "massive resistance" in those fringe areas of the segregation problem.

In their back-to-the-wall stand on integration of the public schools, the seven hard core states are now pursuing a new and significant strategy. The early effort of the segregationist leaders was to move and stir *Southern* opinion to the point of open opposition to the law. That was a thoroughly ignoble but fairly easy task. More recently they have embarked upon a much more ambitious enterprise—and I think you who live out of the South should be quite aware of it. They now seek to subvert the public opinion of North, East and West to the segregationist view. Of course, they don't call it that. They refer to it as education in states rights, limitation of judicial power, and other euphonious terms. But what they mean is the preservation of a caste system in the South. Under one name or another your aid—you non-Southerners—your aid is now being actively sought. It's an old story—Confederates capturing Yankees.

The movement to convert you is well financed and well organized. Certain states have their propaganda bureaus financed by public funds as well as by anti-labor money and reactionary subsidies. They pour out pamphlets by the hundreds of thousands. They send speakers on foreign missions. They flatter and fawn upon Northern papers or writers who abet their plan.

This effort should not be taken lightly. Already certain Northern columnists, magazines and newspapers follow the segregationist line. The effort to limit the jurisdiction of the Supreme Court failed by one vote in the Senate. And, the most unkind cut of all, the Chief Justices of the state supreme courts gave that effort their implied support.

There is something quite persuasive in this new Southern approach to the rest of the nation. In the first place, the rest of the nation hasn't perfectly solved its own integration problem. Our sense of generosity finds expression in the twin ideas "Who am I to tell you how to run your affairs?" and "I can appreciate fully what you are up against in the South." And, lamentably, there are many Americans in all sections of the country who are not democratic at heart. They listen with a sympathetic ear...

You who share the world's revulsion at the Russian treatment of Boris Pasternak will hardly remain indifferent to the stern fate of hundreds of lesser Pasternaks in the South who think and write and teach and preach and speak at their peril.

There is, then, this trend, this effort to sell the segregation cause to the non-Southerner. Beware of its soft seductions....

Acts of violence may often be dismissed as the impulsive and unthinking conduct of brutish men. But your legislative maneuverers—your private school men, your state subsidy, tuition grants, pupil assignment, local control, gerrymandering men—have no such claim upon our consideration. They are trained and skilled and cunning men. They plot their schemes, mull over them, debate them for weeks on end. There is malice aforethought, always more to be condemned than the impulsive act.

Bad as it may be, what is done by the poor devil who burns a cross or plants a bomb is his individual act, in no sense committing or involving his state. But what is done by men in Governors' mansions or legislative halls becomes State policy, carrying with it all the sanction and authority of a state. It seems almost blasphemous that men should use the sacred power of a state for such ignoble ends.

So the fall-out from the bomb of resistance to one law has borne in its train resistance to any law one does not like. Carried to its logical conclusion, the end result would be anarchy.

It was considerations such as these which motivated the Supreme Court decision in the recent Little Rock case. That decision means that there is to be no surrender to mob action, no compromise in the national effort to give an equal chance to every American child. More importantly, it made a point which should not be lost on every rebellious state. That is, that the court is not deceived by Southern evasive maneuvers. The hard core states now know they cannot win by subterfuge and evasion.

There is a moral aspect to such procedures. The legal qualities upon which the resisting states have relied have been cunning, slickness, shrewdness. (We have just witnessed the taming of the shrewd.) Such have been the qualities magnified in the public mind and held up as ideals before young lawyers and politicians. We now know they are no substitutes for brain, intelligence and character. The truly great lawyer or statesman is not slick; he is profound.

We may now return to our former conception of what are honorable courses for states to pursue.

Such is the meaning of the recent decision. Such is the handwriting on the wall. Those who can't read it should go to school—an integrated school, of course....

The books must now be purged and cleansed of all legal perversions written into them by bigotry. This is primarily the job of us in the South. The school laws; teacher's oaths; laws requiring that the NAACP bare its membership; anti-barratry laws aimed at the NAACP; laws setting up so-called anti-subversion committees the whole breed of repressive statutes—by last count 169—must be erased. That is largely a Southern job. And there are Southerners willing to undertake it.

In view of the former apathy of the administration and the solid phalanx presented by governments of the resisting states, it is remarkable that liberal voices should now be heard anywhere in the South. On the contrary, they are at this moment louder and clearer than ever. Those urging compliance with law are now more militant than ever. This is no mere rhetoric on a fall day. I give you the specifics.

In the first few weeks following the May 17, 1954 decision, journals of certain Southern university law schools carried scholarly articles by professors analyzing the proposed evasive schemes and condemning them all upon constitutional grounds. Their authors—men like Francis B. Nicholson, of South Carolina; Warren E. Guerke, of Emory; and Jay Murphy, of Alabama—exhibited not only scholarship but courage. They stood alone—eggheads.

But observe the effect of a good example. In Little Rock a few days ago 61 lawyers of that city signed a statement condemning as unconstitutional Governor Faubus' private school plan. Those men were not eggheads. They were run of the mine lawyers and they uttered the ancient and honored principles of the law.

Also, in those calm and reflective days of 1954, a few church bodies—synods, dioceses, conventions and the like—adopted supporting resolutions. They disturbed no one. They were far away and remote. They could do no harm. Let those men at the top resolve. But, observe in Arkansas and Virginia and elsewhere in the South within recent weeks ministers of all faiths, pastors of small churches in the very eye of the storm, have confronted governors and senators and denounced their wicked schemes. They uttered the ancient and honored principles of religion.

So your Parent-Teacher Associations of not too long ago might have been thought of as well-meaning and innocuous. But when the closing of public schools became a fact or imminent, the gentle folk who composed the associations were not over-awed or daunted by the entrenched power of a state. They challenged the prevailing lunacy.

I might go on. Concerned taxpayers. Public school children themselves—you have seen them on TV. Public opinion in favor of compliance with law is more militant today than at any time since the original decision. From being the view of a handful of so-called do-gooders, advocacy of compliance is now a grass roots phenomenon.

We may thank Governor Faubus and Governor Almond for that. So long as the fate of public education was a matter of idle speculation, those actually or potentially liberal were disposed to remain inactive, uncommitted. But when it became evident that the two states stood upon the very brink—to use a term from Mr. Dulles—when it appeared that the alternatives were to do complete justice on the one hand or to destroy public schools on the other, the silent became vocal, the hesitant became bold. There is also a national job and I appeal to you in NAIRO as being the one group preeminently qualified by training, experience and motivation to prod the national conscience and rouse the great giant which is America from its lethargy. Certainly, the demands of the moment cannot be met merely be a court. That is employing only one third of the national power and energy. The executive branch has its role. Congress has its role. For all three arms of the government there is good fighting all along the lines.

Consider with me for a moment the situation in stark and unvarnished terms, stripped of all its tawdry pretensions. The Supreme Court has held that racial segregation in public education is unconstitutional. But four years after the event it exists in seven Southern states which declare they will not obey the law. That is rebellion without the dignity of formal secession.

Certain school districts wish to comply with law. They are told in some instances if you do, state funds will be cut off, and in others, we will close your doors. That is blackmail by State action. No idle threat either, as Governor Faubus and Governor Almond have proven.

Negro children seek to exercise a constitutional right. They turn to the one great organization, the NAACP, qualified to help. That organization is beset with a series of state actions designed to cripple it or to force its suspension. That is sabotage of an honorable agency whose sole mission is to secure judicial determination of legal rights.

So, if we were morbid enough, we could run the entire gamut of repression.

Certainly, such activities are not matters of merely local concern. I say to you from North, East, and West that your own welfare, your own destiny, hang in the balance. The bright image of America as a land of equal opportunity, of concern for the rights of the individual, of the open door to merit and worth—that image is being marred and defaced. I know of no more serious indictment of a nation than that it permitted school doors to be slammed in the face of an aspiring child.

At the last session of the Congress, Senator Paul Douglas and associates introduced a bill which, if enacted, would have marshalled government's united power in aid of the liberal elements of the South. I have time only to point out, that, among other features, it provided federal funds for school districts whose state aid was cut off because of their compliance with law. What a different situation we might have in Arkansas and Virginia if such were the law!

While, admittedly, law will not solve everything, the Douglas, or some similar bill, must be enacted. A lone Negro child, seeking a right under the Constitution, a qualified person seeking to register to vote, a skilled and qualified workman seeking a job—these must not be left to pit their puny strength against the massed power of a state. The federal government should not be a callous spectator of such unequal conflicts.

Just a word as to what you beyond the South may do aid to aid the cause!

First, and negatively, don't succumb to the argument that you are outsiders meddling in other people's affairs. We must never overlook the dual nature of citizenship in this country. The Negro children knocking upon school doors may be citizens of South Carolina or Louisiana. They are no less citizens of the

United States of America. It is right under the *American* constitution they seek to assert. They do so as *your* fellow citizens. In that view, your concern is fully as acute as the concern of a native-born white citizen of South Carolina or Louisiana.

Keep always in mind that what is happening in certain areas of the South is a suspension of guaranties of the *American* constitution. That suspension is as real as if proclaimed by a formal edict of a dictator. Such a suspension, whether formally proclaimed or not, is an act of tyranny. No American citizen has the right to acquiesce in tyranny.

All rights guaranteed by the constitution are of equal sanctity. The right of school attendance is as sacred as freedom of the press. There is no moral difference between closing school doors and closing printing presses. One will lead to the other.

Finally, the white Southern liberal is acutely vulnerable. He bucks the truly formidable power of his state; quite often he bucks community, friends, family. He is apt to be lonely. Don't wash your hands of him. Let him at all times be sustained by the consciousness that, in those areas of this land where men are not so stirred by the passions of the moment, there are understanding and sympathy.

In the South, perhaps more than elsewhere in the country, the minister is a community figure of large importance, This seems to be particularly true of blacks. The position occupied by black preachers made their influence and leadership in the desegregation effort highly desirable.

In a speech before North Carolina Negro ministers at Greensboro, June 15, 1961, Wright sought to motivate them to assume active roles in that effort. The traditional evangelistic function with its emphasis on salvation, he stressed, must yield to the task of social reform. In his view the ethical issue involved in efforts to thwart the law as declared by the courts required all ministers to use their moral authority to secure compliance.

THE MINISTER AND THE STATE

I greatly appreciate the opportunity to participate with you in this meeting. All of my life I have been on the other side of the pulpit and have been lectured and preached at by scores of good men. I am not sure that it did me any good, but, at least, it kept me out of mischief while I was listening. Now I have a privilege which seldom comes to a layman, of lecturing you. Surely, preachers never get into mischief anyhow but, if they ever do, I will do my best for a while to keep you out of it.

It seems significant that you bring in a layman to talk to preachers. There was a long period in church history when the more orthodox among your predecessors felt that the church had little concern with lay affairs. Its mission was to prepare men for an eternal hereafter. Their entry into that blessed estate depended entirely upon their adherence to certain doctrinal beliefs. Under that view there was little, if anything, which the temporal world could say to the spiritual.

Well, men's minds have broadened with the centuries. The

accent today is not so much upon the hereafter as upon the here and now. The church has come to realize that, while man may not live by bread alone, he cannot live without it. One whose stomach is empty is in no condition to listen to any preaching, however profound and orthodox.

The idea may be illustrated by the difficult and pressing problem of juvenile delinquency. Carefully kept records confirm the conclusion that the city which provides parks, playgrounds, swimming pools, concerts—in short, opportunity for decent recreation—has gone far toward keeping the adolescent boy and girl from drifting into careers of crime.

Certainly, then, a church would be insensitive to its duty if it did not exert itself to the limit of its powers to see that decent recreation is provided. By the same token it would be insensitive to its duty if it did not involve itself with every activity of government which steers and tugs and pulls men and women this way or that, toward good or toward evil.

The idea which I am trying to advance has been far better expressed in *The Devil's Advocate*, a profound and moving book which I hope many of you have read. In that book an Italian bishop talks to a priest of the Roman Church:

> *I believe that the Church in this country is in drastic need of reform. I think we have too many saints and not enough catechisms, too many medals and not enough medicine, too many churches and not enough schools. We have three million workless men and three million women living by prostitution. We control the State through the Christian Democratic Party and the Vatican Bank; yet we countenance a dichotomy which gives prosperity to half the country and lets the other half rot in penury. Our clergy are undereducated and insecure and yet we rail against anticlericals and Communists. A tree is known by its fruits— and I believe that it's better to proclaim a new*

> *deal in social justice than a new attribute of the*
> *Blessed Virgin.*

Certainly, the church of the present day is concerned with social justice, if for no other reason because the kind of justice which we have in the world affects so profoundly the characters of men and women. To their fate the church cannot be indifferent. As George Bernard Shaw wrote, "The worst sin toward our fellow creatures is not to hate them, but to be indifferent to them: that's the essence of inhumanity."

The church is concerned with society because society is the great teacher. I do not speak in any figurative sense. The school, which impinges upon the child's life for a few hours a day for nine months of the year, tries to teach him correct English. But in his home he daily hears incorrect English used and certain radio and T.V. personalities, among his idols, butcher the language. How can you teach him to say *"as"* when almost every hour on the hour, in the form of a jingle, he is told "Winstons taste good *like* a cigarette should?" A world famous evangelist concludes his radio service by wishing that "God will keep you real good."

So there is then the omnipresent school of the state. As Justice Brandeis write some years ago:

> *In a government of laws existence of the*
> *government will be imperilled if it fails to observe the*
> *law scrupulously. Our government is the potent, the*
> *omnipresent, teacher. For good or for ill, it teaches*
> *the whole people by its example. Crime is contagious.*
> *If the government becomes a lawbreaker, it breeds*
> *contempt for law; it invites every man to become a*
> *law unto himself; it invites anarchy.*

Whatever the old-fashioned view may have been, there is no longer any doubt in the minds of rational men that the church is concerned with government. Since government, as Justice Brandeis observed, is the great teacher of men and since the church is concerned with men's lives, it cannot be indifferent to the lessons which government teaches. Depending upon the state's own observance of law, those lessons tend to make men law observers or law violaters.

You and I live in the State of North Carolina. For the moment let us focus our attention upon certain aspects of the law of our state.

Seven years ago the Supreme Court of the United States declared that public school segregation of pupils by race was a denial of constitutional rights. That was the unanimous decision of nine white justices interpreting a constitution written entirely by white men. Every public official of North Carolina is under oath faithfully to uphold that constitution.

Today only 1/50th of 1 percent of the Negro children of North Carolina enjoy a right the court declares is theirs. I spare you the details as to how this denial has been accomplished except to point out two facts about it:

There was enacted what was known as a Pupil Placement Act which makes every pretense of complying with the court's ruling while actually refusing to comply, and

It places upon every Negro child the emotional and financial burden of going into court to assert a right which is clearly his.

When he goes into court he has arrayed against him the massed legal and financial power of his state which unblushingly asserts that the child's race was not a factor in assigning him to a school.

We are here in the mixed field of law and morals. If ministers of the Gospel should feel that they are not concerned with law, surely no one of them will deny that he is concerned with morals. There is no minister in North Carolina, whatever his color may be, who is not under the heavy moral obligation to protest this infamy....

There have been episodes of Church history of which none of

us may feel proud. There have been occasions when the church danced attendance upon corrupt regimes, granted divorces to libertine monarchs, and, even in our own South, upheld the corrosive blight of slavery.

The image which we like to keep alive in our minds is that of stern and fearless men who challenged the corruption of their day and risked the stake and the cross in defense of their faith.

The church of today, by silence and inaction, by remaining supine, may condone, if not approve, an immoral policy.

If religion is actually to be a force in the lives of men, it cannot retreat when confronted by a moral crisis. To do so is to abdicate its authority in the field of ethics. When, later, it seeks to set up standards of conduct in other fields, it may be reminded of its failure in this particular area. More, it will be haunted and its effectiveness blunted by its own consciousness of failure....

The state, as Justice Brandeis observed, is a great teacher. Its lessons are not limited to laws. They embrace, also, the field of morals. The state is a teacher of morals.

In the bright lexicon of honor there is no such word as evasion, or misrepresentation. Yet, throughout the South, with noble exceptions here and there, laws have been enacted and official steps taken without a frank declaration of their real purpose. Their purpose has been to preserve a segregated society, but the assigned reason has been something quite different—public peace and tranquility, freedom of association, consideration of psychological factors, and all the rest—you know the jargon as well and I. The pupil, copying the ancient motto "Honesty is the best policy," may look out of the school window and observe his native state laughing at him for being so naive.

In the struggle between the wisdom of Benjamin Franklin and the lessons learned at Sunday School with the example of his state and the society about him, the betting odds are heavily against pure and noble ethics. Eminent men, whom he knows or of whom he has read, tell the pupil by deeds that the ancient moralists were wrong. What chance has pure morality against the examples of living men whom his state has exalted to high station?

The hope is that our young men and women may observe the monotonous regularity with which our slick, shrewd and cunning lawyers are rebuffed by courts above the level of parish magistrates, and how such politicians are silently ignored or publicly repudiated by both political parties. Minor successes in obscure forums may await the newcomer in law or politics who has heeded the admonition of his state; he will stretch forth his hands in vain for greater prizes.

It is to North Carolina's shame that it brought into common usage the expression "token integration." What the phrase implies is that the state will so conduct itself as to fool the court into believing that it has desegregated its schools, while, in sober fact, it has not. This is a form of obtaining credit by false pretenses. It is a species of ethics which would be repudiated in an ordinary horse trade. Surely there is not a minister in this state who feels content and undisturbed in the evolution of such a policy. Particularly is this true in view of the state's powerful example spread before all of its citizens.

Consider for a moment some logical extensions of the token integration idea. I will stop at only one red light out of ten, as a token of my obedience to law. I will pay one tenth of my income tax, and serve only one month of my enlistment in the army. Finally, as evidence of my devotion to honorable living, I will observe only one of the Ten Commandments.

Not merely ministers of the Gospel, but all North Carolinians, were taught that, if a man sues you at law and takes away your coat, you should give him your cloak also; and if he requires you to go with him one mile, you should go with him twain. Can people so taught be long content with the view that, if the law and good faith require the desegregation of a hundred pupils, we shall desegregate only one?

I address my remarks not to Negro ministers or white ministers, not even merely to Christians. There is not a religion anywhere on this globe which does not condemn such intolerable hypocrisy: And even men professing no religion—atheists or agnostics, if you please—have consciences and their consciences must reject such a policy.

Certainly, I hold no brief for the State of Virginia. But its policy of massive resistance was at least honest and forthright. And, when its inevitable failure occurred, Virginians began with much more sincerity than North Carolina to comply with law. The first year they integrated 100 Negro pupils and this fall, the third year, they will integrate 800. Meanwhile, after six years, North Carolina has integrated 60. Thus leadership in honesty slips from our own to our sister state.

My thesis is that ministers of the Gospel bear a special and heavy responsibility for trying to influence the moral tone of a state's policy. Its laws reflect only a part of policy. Its customs and manners have equal significance. . . .

Twenty-eight American states and an unknown but large number of cities now have laws which forbid discrimination in public accommodations. Such laws will be enacted here. When no one may guess. Until their enactment the Negro dilemma persists: Submission to personal indignity or non-violent resistance.

Why do I talk to ministers about these ancient discriminations? What special concern is it of theirs?

If religions have any mission on this earth, this mission is to refine and ennoble men, to make them just, generous and compassionate. The tenets and precepts of religions and the lives and examples of their founders heroic figures are set against harsh and brutal, or subtle and sophisticated, injury to any of God's creatures. Our segregation practices daily inflict such injury. Surely, no minister may ignore them and preserve his self-respect.

While enforcement of court decisions regarding desegregation of schools was, in the first instance, the responsibility of government, nevertheless the private citizen has an important role to play. By applause or censure of public officials for their conduct, by attending meetings of school boards and making their presence felt, by lending moral support to blacks exercising their newly declared rights, white Southerners could speed the process.

In an address delivered at Charlottesville and printed in *New South* of December, 1959, Wright sought to impress upon his hearers the significant contribution each of them could make in aiding the transition process.

THE CITIZEN'S RESPONSIBILITY

Dr. Edward Teller, one of the nation's better brains, recently made two somber predictions. He said flatly that within 10 years Russia would have outstripped this nation in all major fields of science, and that by the year 2000, Russian ideas would probably prevail throughout the world.

Whether it is good or bad for mankind as a whole to embrace Russian, rather than American, principles will not depend upon their national origin. Principles have no right to survive just because they are labelled "Made in America." The triumph of one set of principles, one view of the relationship of citizen and state, over another will depend in the long run upon relative merit.

All human progress, all of what we call civilization, has come about because of comparison of concepts, because of the ability of men to discriminate between what serves them well and what serves them ill. The life and growth of society has been not logic but experience.

In this competition between systems there is one goal for

which we may strive. It is the goal about which we hear most. It is to surpass the Russians. That is, I submit, a goal unworthy of a great nation. This implies that we are engaged in a kind of foot race for a blue ribbon as prize and that the race is worth the running so long as we come out first.

Are we not stirred by far more lofty motives if we conceive the national mission to be the development and dissemination of ideas and principles designed to improve the human lot? Under such a concept, the impelling force is not the fairly primitive urge to win but is the spiritual urge to lift all men an inch nearer to the stars.

So we must be concerned, first, with what our principles are, and next with how we exhibit them to the world. Under modern conditions, it is not enough to build a better mouse trap. The image of a nation which is exhibited to the rest of the world, rather that what it says about itself, determines its impact.

For example only, and merely scratching the surface of principles we proudly call American, there are equality of all men before the law; equality of opportunity; freedom from burdens or penalties because of race; the zeal of the law to protect the humblest man from despotic power; freedom of speech and all the other freedoms.

Certainly, those principles have given the nation character and direction. They have contributed to our nation's greatness. We have no intention of abandoning them or retreating one inch from them.

But we are concerned with the national image we exhibit. That image is not a composite of abstractions. If so, we would have an easy task. The Voice of America would beam the words of Thomas Jefferson and Abraham Lincoln and other noble spirits around the world. Of course, we would have to be selective in broadcasting even the words of our leaders—that is, we would have to choose our authors. For we must remember that men like Senator Eastland, Senator Thurmond, and Senator

McCarthy have also spoken on these fundamentals.

But we would be naive to assume that the world will judge us by the words of our leaders, good or bad. What counts is not words but deeds. If events negate claims, events will have the ear and attention of the rest of the world.

IMAGE EXHIBITED

This brings us to the matter of how we apply our principles. If they are correctly, fairly and honorably applied, the image we exhibit is one of consistency and resolution, of determination to put into practice the noble sentiments we have so proudly proclaimed.

This is peculiarly the field of the private citizen. The eloquent expression of a principle is the task of the political leader, or publicist, or intellectual. Translating these pronouncements into reality is the job of inconspicuous men and women who labor unnoticed at their thankless occupations. But by putting flesh upon the bare bones of principles, they perform a task essential to giving perspective to the picture of a nation.

A field for employment of the gifts of the private citizen is now opening in certain areas of the South.

STATE STATUTES

I am sure that few persons doubt that most of the legal devices contrived to defeat segregation of the public schools will be declared unconstitutional. In certain states, however, the statutes were held to be constitutional on their face. The court specifically held open the question of constitutionality in application.

The statutes in question grant to local school board authority to assign pupils upon the basis of certain factors. The word "race" is studiedly omitted from these factors, though, feel sure, anyone of us above the moronic level knows it is th controlling factor. Certainly, the officials know it since the have publicly patted their backs until raw over their cleverne in devising such a scheme.

We may be sure other resistant or reluctant states will no follow the examples of North Carolina and Alabama.

So the question of assignment of pupils under the acts is no a practical one. The question will be answered initially by th local school board. Normally such board members are known t residents of the district. To express to them an opinion as t their duty requires no trip away from home, no intermediary c advocate. Communication may be personal and direct.

These circumstances present to the local citizen the trul golden opportunity to strike a blow for liberty—and I don mean what you may be thinking of.

If he is fed up with evasion and subterfuge and does not wis to see the application of the statute attended by the hypocris which surrounded its enactment, he will take steps to place h views before the board.

Remember, the image we present of this nation will not b manufactured out of statutes which seem fair upon their face; will be manufactured out of events showing how the statute operate. When North Carolina, for example, uses the statute t admit only 11 Negro pupils into white schools, its conduct not reassuring as to its bona fides. It is conduct strikingly i contrast with the national claims.

So, as to the desegregation issue generally, we have, in th last five years, been living through the period of conflict ove strictly legal issues. Broadly stated, this was conflict ove principles of government. The Southern view was that a cast system is compatible with democracy. The view that prevaile was that the caste system is not compatible with democrati principles, and that, under the 14th amendment, no state may legally enforce such a system. A whole majestic series of decisions reveals the will and conscience of the court.

APPLICATION

For the next decade certainly, we will be living in the period of application of principle. In that field the will and conscience of the people, as distinguished from the court, will be revealed.

The rest of the world will not be content merely to read judicial opinions and conclude "This is America." It will read headlines, it will examine statistics, it will heed the voice of events, and conclude "This is America."

No one, of course, may legitimately disparage the profound importance of judicial opinions; but the opinions which will have impact upon mankind are fashioned by average men and women. They will reflect the thinking, the attitudes, the principles, of the anonymous citizen.

LITTLE ROCK

Some weeks ago, the Supreme Court declared unconstitutional the Louisiana statute forbidding boxing between opponents of different races. That was another judicial blow at discrimination and will be hailed by all Americans who are truly democratic.

On the same day the voters of Little Rock struck their own blow at discrimination—this time, in the field of public education. Theirs was the blow that will be felt around the world. In that election the average citizen of Little Rock put Southern politicians upon notice that the voter has his own principles which he will not forever forego. In that election, we heard the real voice of the nation.

So all individual concepts of principles will be tossed into the national hopper and from their blending the real national principles will emerge. Upon the quality of those composite principles will depend their survival in competition with rival ideologies.

So, then, the role of the private citizen is vastly enlarged. The contest is no longer between Thurgood Marshall and Senator Byrd. The struggle of the Titans is ended; the struggle of the Lilliputians begins.

I call your attention to a sharp reversal of our usual concepts of the functions of a leader. The view which Thomas Jefferson announced was that a political leader actually led; that he was ahead of the thinking of his day and, by force of intelligence, character and personality, he informed his constituency and elevated it to something approaching his own superior standards.

In a sentence, we may fairly dismiss the political leadership of most of the South on the desegregation issue with the comment that it was insensitive to the pressures and necessities of this age and was geared to the thinking of the 1860's.

With what results?

For sheer evil there was nothing in the annals of Reconstruction to equal the legislation spawned and concocted throughout the South for the sole purpose of depriving some millions of people of their constitutional rights. And this example from high official source has begotten the ugly brood of violence and bloodshed which have brought disgrace upon an entire region.

We have had in Virginia and elsewhere, a political leadership which not merely did not lead, but which actually retarded normal adjustment of the inevitable. In mechanical terms, what these leaders supplied was not motive power, but brakes; not sail, but anchor.

This bankruptcy of leadership forces upon us the reversal of our concepts to which I have referred. The impulse to progress, instead of moving from the leader to the citizen must now move from the citizen to the leader. The citizen, by force of his own intelligence, character, and personality, must now elevate the leader.

LEADERSHIP FAILURE

This failure of political leadership has occurred not merely upon the state level. If the leadership there has been vicious and depraved, it has, on the national level, been bumbling and inept.

The press conference is the president's most effective means of getting his views to the American people. Have you kept up with the reports of these conferences on the desegregation issue? Without regard to such trivia as grammar and syntax, subject and predicate, have you detected one word or note of strong moral leadership? When the nation has begged for bread what stones have been given it!

When repeatedly asked his opinion of the 1954 Supreme Court decision, the President's replies have run the gamut from it didn't matter what he thought—surely the very limit of abnegation—to the statement that he may have privately told friends that desegregation should proceed more slowly. That, at a time when seven states had not moved an inch in four years! To move more slowly than that you must go backward. How many times have we been treated to the inane platitude, delivered with an air of great profundity, that you can't legislate morals!

So, into this vacuum created by absence of state and national leadership the private citizen perforce must move. Perhaps this is not all bad. It revives and strengthens the conception that, in a democracy, he is the ultimate repository of power. Thereby it adds to his stature and dignity. It further accentuates the point that, while in the field of politics *per se*, the superior capacity

186

of experienced officials may be conceded, in the field of morals
each one of us carries his credentials in his heart.

The legal rights of Negro children are now established. The
period of quibbling and evasion, insofar as the law is concerned,
has run its course. With unparalleled faith in human nature, the
court has assumed that the pupil assignment statutes will be
fairly administered—that school officials will completely
disregard the color of children in determining to which school
they will be sent. The question now becomes one of good faith;
in other words, one of morals. Here John Doe and Mary Smith
may throw their weight around.

This shift of emphasis from law or politics to morals is one
of the striking phenomena of the times. Both law and politics
require special skills, special competence. That requirement
disqualified the layman from full participation in the making of
major decisions affecting the public schools. Necessarily he was
side-lined while the battle raged. But in the struggle's aftermath,
in the grassroots adjudication of the right of a neighbor's boy or
girl to go to a nearby school, no one of us is so insignificant
that he may not influence the result.

JUSTICE

Consider for a moment the import of such adjudications. The
school board of Charlottesville, for example, is an arm, or
agency, or creature, of the state. It exercises a fractional part of
the state's sovereign power. Its decisions, wise or unwise, good
or bad, will be regarded in this country as an expression, not of
the Charlottesville, but of the Virginia, sense of justice. And
abroad, no note will be taken of Charlottesville or Virginia.
There they will be regarded as an expression of American sense
of justice. What happened at Little Rock, for example, is not
used by Russians to discredit that city or Arkansas, but to
defame the United States.

NATIONAL PRESTIGE

, Such, then, is the momentous nature of every decision affecting a lone Negro youth seeking admittance to a white school. If there is a formerly white school near his home, but he is sent across the city or county to a Negro school, there is a stain upon the national honor. If, however, it should develop that assignment is made upon the basis of distance and other proper considerations, without regard to race, Virginia and national prestige are enhanced.

Lest it should be thought that foreign opinion of Virginia's fairness and sense of public honor should be over-emphasized—I doubt that it is possible to over-emphasize it—let us reflect for a moment upon the internal effect of decisions such as we have mentioned.

If experience should demonstrate that the Supreme Court's trust in fairness of administration of assignment statutes should be misplaced, what moral consequences would ensue?

Every Negro child improperly denied admission to a desegregated school knows in his heart of hearts that he has been betrayed by his state. What a reservoir of bitterness would be built up in the minds of future adults! Is widespread bitterness a good foundation upon which to rear a great state?

Every white child receiving special treatment and consideration because he is white tends to acquire the conviction that rewards are inherent in color and they they flow from sharp practice. Is a widespread attachment to such a standard of values a good foundation upon which to rear a great state?....

Now that certain states have gotten around to application of pupil assignment statutes, let us hope that the original felony will not be compounded and that the average citizen's sense of justice and fairness will set the state again upon an honorable course.

We have lived through five years of legislation, litigation and liquidation of much of our public school system. Who among us has not breathed a sigh of relief that, apparently, that sordid era draws to a close? We should be on guard that we do not enter upon another.

We are relieved because there now seems ground for hope that the tragic dissipation of the energies of state government may be at an end. I have no way of proving it, but I think you will agree that far more than half of the time, thought, effort and energy of our governors, legislators and public officials generally has been devoted to shoring up the shaky edifice of segregation. That item has been No. 1 on any political or legislative agenda. Education, science, the arts, the humanities—all of those functions of government which tend to improve the lot of the citizen—have been relegated to secondary position. What matters it that a man is poorly fed, or clothed or housed, or unemployed, or his children poorly educated, or justice poorly administered, in face of the dire threat that young people of both races shall together learn that two times two equals four?....

Surely with the legal issues settled for all time, the state governments may now cease frittering away their energies upon ignoble enterprises and apply them to legitimate and appropriate governmental concerns.

And what of you and me as individuals?

We, too, may now, at last, apply our own energies to constructive ends.

We may let school boards know that we expect them to deserve the faith expressed by the Supreme Court that they will disregard race in pupil assignments.

We may applaud them when fairness is evident and rebuke them when it is lacking.

OTHER DUTIES

We may let police officers know that they will be held to strict accountability for safety of Negro pupils and members of their families.

We may support teachers in maintaining discipline on the campus.

We may open Parent-Teacher Associations to Negro members, not as an act of grace, but as an act of simple justice.

We may, also as simple justice, secure Negro membership on school boards.

We may teach our children to receive the newcomers with warmth and cordiality and appreciation for the ordeals they have so nobly borne.

We may express to Negro parents our admiration for the ambition they have for their children and for their own spartan courage in braving the community's hostility.

PUBLIC INTEREST

In one sense these are but trivial acts. They will receive no headlines. The actors will remain anonymous. But, in these pendulous times, even the trivial deed is affected and charged with a public interest. Upon such deeds may hang the destiny of this nation, the fate of mankind.

The nation has been treated to few spectacles more thrilling than the recent assertion of the moral power of the private citizen. We may perhaps thank Governor Faubus and Senator Byrd for prodding the citizen into this self-revelation, into this calm assertion of his essential decency.

When those two characters made it apparent that the public schools may be closed, the silent became vocal, the hesitant became bold. Teachers, risking their careers, have challenged the prevailing lunacy. Ministers in the eye and vortex of the storm have confronted evil with the zeal of the ancient prophets. Editors risking circulation and income have denounced the destructive tendencies of the times. As you in Virginia well know, Parent-Teacher Associations have asserted their own profound convictions. Thus is demonstrated the inherent moral strength of the anonymous individual.

We have referred to the Supreme Court's faith in school boards. I hope it is not invidious to point out that a democracy rests upon a faith more sublime. It is a faith in the sense of honor, the decency, of the average man.

To the extent that those qualities are non-existent or anemic, democracy fails. To the extent that they are present and vital, democracy succeeds. The measure of its success is the zeal of the state to safeguard the rights of the weak.

The test of the honorable and decent citizen is his willingness to grant obedience to the unenforceable, to move in response to inner compulsions.

Nothing offers greater hope for the future of this commonwealth than proof that its men and women now act in response to such imperatives.

The Quakers have a long history of concern with rights of Negroes. Abolitionists and providers of the underground railroad for escaping slaves—their credentials in the field of human rights are unassailable.

On May 23, 1964, Wright addressed a meeting of Westtown School alumni, Westtown being a Quaker institution situated at Westtown, Pennsylvania. Civil Rights legislation was then before the Congress. Massive Northern support would be needed if the legislation should pass. The speech was an appeal for such help.

The theme, which recurs in many of his speeches, was that wise Northern self-interest dictated support of measures designed primarily to aid Southern blacks.

THE NEW FRATERNITY

I thank you for letting me come up to Westtown and join with you in the events of this day. This is a great privilege for a man from the Deep South. In my day the heated theological discussions raged around such matters as infant damnation, sprinkling versus dipping as a means of salvation, and, still later, evolution versus instant creation of the universe. Arguments were grim. Epithets were tossed about. All of that time the followers of George Fox and William Penn pursued their serene and untroubled way. I must say you missed a lot of excitement and good clean fun which were to be found in these theological Donnybrooks. While Abe Lincoln was splitting rails we were splitting hairs, a fine art still practiced by some of our filibusterers in the Senate.

In my youth all that I knew about the Friends was that Oliver Cromwell said of them: "I can see there is a people risen that I cannot win either with gifts, honors, offices or places; but all other sects and people I can." That had a fine and noble ring to it. I cherished it. That is, until its effect was marred by something related by Pat Malin, known, of couse, to all Swarthmore alumni and all members of the American Civil Liberties Union, which he served so ably as executive director.

Pat said that his grandfather was a firm and devout Friend, but his grandmother was not. (I am probably wrong about these relatives and have the uneasy feeling that some of Pat's kinfolk may be here today.) Anyhow, Pat said that, as a small boy, he asked his grandmother: "Grandma, what do Quakers believe in?" The old lady replied: "They believe in 99-year leases at the corner of Broad and Chestnut."

In later years I have had pleasant contacts with many members of the faith. These have tended to confirm the Malin impression of happy accommodation of the temporal and the spiritual. In my cynical way I have come to feel that the reason Oliver Cromwell couldn't buy them was that they didn't need the money. They could have come nearer buying Oliver Cromwell....

THE MEDDLING NORTHERNERS

In this trek of a Southerner to the North, I am no trailblazer. It began more than a century ago when Thomas Garrett, Harriet Tubman and hundreds of other Friends, with imagination and daring, organized the Underground Railroad over which thousands of slaves moved from bondage into light and freedom. Pennsylvania was studded with "stations," where refugees were housed, fed, clothed and given God-speed into a new life. I have no doubt that students and alumni of Westtown were parties to this enterprise. Here, in this state, almost for the first time in this nation's history, there was convincing evidence of widespread and deep concern with the status of oppressed people living beyond your borders. Here there was no complacent feeling that slavery is merely a concern of the South—"we'll let them work it out."

Now, I have not consulted the history books, but I will give you odds that down our way your impulsive activity was denounced as "outside meddling in our affairs." Slavery was our "peculiar institution" off which—as Mr. Churchill would not say—you should keep your cotton-picking fingers. This seems a safe bet since today men such as Senator Russell and Senator Thurmond are using these same words in a closely similar connection.

The trek to the North continues. The view as to outside meddling persists. Within recent months, Governor Barnett, of Mississippi, and Governor Wallace, of Alabama, have invaded Northern territory, traveling at the expense of taxpayers of their states, including Negro taxpayers, waving Confederate flags, and urging Northern hearers to join the Confederacy in its present-day rebellion against the Union....

One is reminded of Churchill's remark about the defection to Labor of a member of the Conservative party: "This is the first time in history when a rat has been seen swimming toward a sinking ship."

But we cannot lightly dismiss Governor Wallace's forays into Wisconsin, Indiana, and Maryland. When one whose only claim to national attention is that he stood in a schoolhouse door to bar the entry of children seeking an education receives substantial backing from the voters of those states, we are shockingly reminded how deep run the roots of bigotry and in what a diversity of soils it flourishes.

THE BATTLEGROUND IS IN THE NORTHERN MIND

The point worth emphasizing is that the mind of the North is now the battleground of the civil rights issue. In the South the lines between the segregationists and the integrationists are fairly well-established. In some instances these lines have been etched with gunpowder, drawn in blood. Few Southerners there are who are not committed. This is inevitable where the problem is acute and of long duration. Only recently has the civil rights issue in its uglier manifestations erupted in the North. You can no longer be objective, detached, neutral.

So, at this critical juncture, while the public opinion in the North is still plastic and malleable, and is being hammered into shape, you are being wooed.

Hence, Governors Barnett and Wallace conduct their raids into enemy territory, seeking prisoners. Hence, Mississippi, the poorest of our states, spends taxpayers' money by the thousands for ads in the New York *Times* and other Northern papers....

Between those raids and my visit there are wide differences of motivation. I believe it is being fair to state that the philosophy of the governors is the nullification expounded by John C. Calhoun. That nullification was political in nature—a state by political action defying federal policy. What we now have is the logical outgrowth of these first two phases. What is now sought is the nullification of the nation's intellectual and moral attitudes and convictions. What Governors Barnett and Wallace are saying is: Never, never, never shall the *national* enlightenment, the *national* culture, the *national* good will and sense of justice, be operative within our states. We have our own standards. One who seeks to alter them is an interloper who incurs our undying hostility.

Nullification in its legalistic or classical sense ended at Appomattox. The present aberrant species will, of course, come to its own ignoble end. There will be no single, plainly-marked historical event which will denote the end. Rather there will be the cumulative effect of countless editorials, sermons, broadcasts over radio and television, interpretive reporting, letters to the editor, books, private correspondence, heightened ethical business standards, travel between sections of the country and abroad—all of these and more will erode local prejudices, make a mockery of state lines. There can be no quarantine against an idea; no embargo on thought; no Chinese or Berlin wall or iron curtain which will prevent seepage of opinions and convictions and moral standards into every hinterland.

INJECT YOURSELVES IN OUR AFFAIRS

My plea to you is not to keep out of our affairs, but to inject yourselves more and more into them. They are your affairs also, as your affairs are ours. No state is an island, entire of itself. No longer is there "outside meddling" because there is no longer an outside. Less than a global view is pure provincialism. Mrs. Peabody—bless her stout New England heart—the "undesirable guest" of St. Augustine, summed it up in a few words: "We are not just Northerners. We are part of the United States of America. I was doing just what any American should be doing."

How reminiscent of Thoreau's question to Ralph Waldo Emerson from a Concord jail, placed there because of his civil disobedience. Emerson asked "Why are you here?" Thoreau retorted "Why aren't you here?"

Since the civil rights problem is now national in scope, there is evolving a new fraternity between liberals of North and South. The Southern liberal until this time has been a fairly lonely figure. In most areas he has had against him the force of government and the more corrosive and sinister force of public opinion. Repression, intimidation and violence have been his portion. I could overwhelm you with documentary proof. The loneliness of a man on a desert island is no more melancholy than the loneliness of one isolated from the sympathy of his fellows.

You will understand, then, how heartening it has been to some of us in the South to have gallant folk from the North—clergymen of all faiths, teachers, social workers, college students, inconspicuous private citizens like the mail carrier done to death on an Alabama highway—come down and share the pains and penalties inseparable from a social revolution. So, we are saying, we may be despised and rejected at home, but elsewhere there are those who share our indignation at injustice and discrimination. We are not alone. We are attuned to the national conscience and aspiration. We have a new sense of fraternity.

OUR PROBLEMS ARE YOUR PROBLEMS

This new awareness of the national solidarity rests upon a much broader base than civil rights. Civil rights have merely brought the point into sharper focus. National solidarity exists—to use concrete terms—because your Senator Scott makes laws for South Carolina and Senator Thurmond makes laws for Pennsylvania. Senator Douglas makes them for Mississippi and Senator Eastland makes them for Illinois. Then you in Pennsylvania and in Illinois have a concern with the kind of senators South Carolina and Mississippi elect. So you have a concern with qualifications of voters and every step of the electoral process.

It is technically inexact to refer to a filibuster conducted by Southern senators. They are *United States* senators, yours as well as mine. What they are doing affects, not just the South, but the entire nation.

In the early days of this republic families usually "stayed put." Ancestral homes and farms passed from one generation to another. Sons followed their fathers in law or medicine or in storekeeping or in such crafts as silver smithing, saddlery or cooperage—those are quaint terms to our modern ears. There was a certain fixity and permanence about life. Men were indigenous to the soil.

All of that is gone with the wind. The industrial revolution has introduced mobility, fluidity, into life. Better jobs, higher wages, have snapped the cords which bound men to land and home. The throat-clutch of a familiar green hillside or garnet stream in the meadow avails naught against the high pay and tingling excitement of Pittsburgh's blazing furnaces or the interminable assembly lines of Detroit. So men shift and scurry at the siren call of the dollar.

Every state is now a melting pot. The ingredients of the brew come from all other states. Each state is a spawning ground from which population flows ceaselessly to all the rest. The 22-year old organizer of the effort to disrupt the New York Fair had spent twenty of those years in his native South Carolina and only two in Brooklyn. What he experienced in South Carolina determined what he did in Brooklyn. Future citizens of Pennsylvania now are being molded into attitudes, furnished their sets of convictions and prejudices, given their scale of values, in South Carolina and every other American state.

Today's foreigner is tomorrow's nextdoor neighbor. The battle of Philadelphia may be won or lost on the playing fields of South Carolina.

Then how blind is the man who asserts that what happens in Alabama or Mississippi is none of your concern; that the area of your legitimate and proper interest is lines drawn on a map and marking the limits of a single state. Don't believe it for one minute. The fate of people in Pennsylvania hinges upon the circulation of books from public libraries, the quality of education, the level of literacy and the mores and folk-ways of Alabama, Mississippi and every other state. There is no longer an immunity from contamination. Hence, men of good will, North and South, are drawn magnetically to each other. They have a common cause. Theirs is not an academic interest, not even a purely philanthropic interest, but an enlightened self-interest in their own welfare.

I certainly don't intend to imply that the citizens we send

your way are invariably the South's problem children. Far from it. The inevitable effect of discrimination is that its victims seek new settings for their lives. Who knows that better than Quakers or Pilgrims? And where repression and intimidation throttle free expression of ideas, men of ideas move elsewhere to a more congenial atmosphere. Southern exports of genius and distinction have enriched the North and impoverished the South.

The population shift has not been all one way. Many Northerners move South—probably lured by climate and a more unhurried way of life, to say nothing of grits and Southern fried chicken. We trade you chicken for shoo-fly-pie. We are concerned with the mental baggage these Northerners bring with them.

CORPORATIONS HAVE OBLIGATIONS

Several weeks ago Mr. James Reston, in an article in the New York *Times*, named twelve men, who, he contended, could have saved Birmingham its orgy of violence and sudden death. Nearly all of them are repatriated Northerners or businessmen having bases in the North. One of them, a steel official from Pittsburgh, replied that a corporation would be acting impertinently to use its influence or position to change local customs, that neutrality was the proper role of a business or corporation in any clash of local opinion on community policy.

I should like to see some bright student of Westtown School—aren't they all bright?—write an essay on the moral responsibilities of the corporation. While we await this work we may as well timidly enter the field.

A corporation is a legal entity. It is domesticated within a state. It receives the benefit of all state services. It has many of the attributes of citizenship. Is it fair for it to avail itself of all of these and then renounce the duties and responsibilities of citizenship? Is it moral for a corporation to say: "The good citizen should risk community ostracism, liberty and even life for a good cause, but we will not risk profits or dividends?" Should capital be more timid than the human being? Must a corporation be characterless?

If the corporations which you send South are merely to adapt themselves to a new environment, take on the local coloration, merge neutrally into the established background, they will only constitute additional social liabilities. I am reminded of something Havelock Ellis wrote years ago:

> *Prosperity is not synonymous with civilization. The community which is suddenly glutted by an afflux of mills and wages is like the savage who is suddenly able to fill his belly with a rich find of decaying blubber. It is prosperity; it is not civilization.*"

Actually capital is not safe, profits are not safe, when the community teeters upon the brink of social disorder or revolution.

WHAT MEN OF GOOD WILL CAN DO

But we were talking about the new fraternity between Northern and Southern liberals. It doesn't have its only expression on the picket lines and in peaceful demonstrations. (Let us hope we have reached the point where these may soon cease.) Since these acts entail hardship and risk, they properly draw our attention and admiration. There are less spectacular but equally effective methods by which Northern concern may be exhibited.

Every Northern state or city which enacts a fair employment practices law, a fair housing law, a public accommodations law, and gives them honest administration, builds up the pressure which flows from a good example. Every church which throws its doors wide to all believers; every association which removes racial barriers, and every individual who welcomes all deserving men within the circle of his friendship—such give renewed courage and hope below the Mason and Dixon line.

The national problem, not one for the courts alone, is to develop methods by which minimal national standards of decency and rectitude may prevail in all the states. We have been long familiar with the distribution in one state of surplus electric power generated in another. TVA is an example. The Federal Reserve Banking System and the Federal Deposit Insurance Corporation make the assets of all banks available to weak members without regard to state lines. It should not be too great a tax upon our ingenuity to find means by which the intellectual and moral strength of the entire nation shall permeate our wastelands. The country at large constitutes a cultural reservoir. No mere state lines should prevent some siphoning of its contents into our more arid regions.

Now, I am painfully conscious that I have been uttering a Macedonian cry. But there is no record that the Macedonians were ashamed of their appeal to St. Paul. However, I am haunted by Pat Malin's remark about the Quaker sense of thrift, their desire to make a wise investment. Senator Barkley, seeking a constituent's vote, was asked: "What have you done for me *recently*?" So I would like to establish a quo for your quid.

In the first place, by some beneficent principle, when the strong bear the infirmities of the weak, they strengthen themselves. So, when you support the Southern liberal by your contributions to his institutions which have racial concerns, by your repudiation of racist demagogues, by setting your own governmental house in order and by letting the spirit of brotherhood dominate your own personal relations with your fellows—when you do these things you help all of us, North and South, and of whatever color.

When you urge your senator or congressman to support policies which guarantee fairness in the voting process and in employment and tend to bring educational standards and opportunities in the South up to the national norm, you are helping to provide a more literate electorate in the South which will insure wiser political choices. Don't forget that, when men like Senators Eastland and Thurmond are elected, the bell tolls for you, too.

Someone wrote: "Nothing great may be accomplished by a state which dwarfs its citizens." Culturally deprived citizens inevitably produce a culturally deprived state. By the seepage of moral and cultural values, the entire nation is infected. Thus racial violence, originating in the South, has spread to Philadelphia and San Francisco and New York. It originated and spread because of the spontaneous rebellion by some millions of American citizens against state policies which tended to make dwarfs of men.

Surely the converse is true. Every great thing is possible for the state which magnifies its citizens—which provides the environment, the atmosphere, the opportunity, the facilities and the incentive for the development of all of their latent capacities to their ultimate possible limit.

THE NEGRO POTENTIAL

Only in recent years, as the walls have come tumbling down, have we begun to get a glimpse of the Negro potential. In every field of human endeavor, as doors of opportunity have swung open, there has been a rush of Negro talent, skill, undreamed of capacity. They have immeasurably enriched American life. Such is the inevitable response when society ceases to dwarf its men and begins to provide growing space for their rich gifts.

These gifts are indigenous to Southern soil. Such is their original habitat. They should burgeon under our blue skies. In the genes of the Negro Southerner and in the harsh role which history has assigned him are found the stuff which destine him to lead this nation to new peaks of greatness and grandeur.

It is not learning, grace nor gear,
  Nor easy meat and drink,
But bitter pinch of pain and fear
  That makes creation think.

Such has been the Negro lot. Out of suffering have come our great religions, philosophies, arts, culture. Here is a vast, untapped natural resource. It is the antithesis of the commercialistic and mechanistic spirit of the times.

From his veins the Negro Southerner, if given the chance, will provide a redemptive transfusion for the nation.

If given the chance—there's the rub. No doubt may be entertained on the point that, so far as it can, government will give him the chance. His civil rights will be firmly established by the Congress, by the courts, by executive action. Such is the national will and purpose. It will not be thwarted.

But, vast as is the domain of the law, there are vaster areas beyond its reach. The walls which separate men may come tumblin' down, but men may still stand and glare at each other over the rubble. They may stand side by side on the assembly line, feed textile thread into the same machine, read under the same library light—do all of this and still be separated by an emotional gulf, dark and unfathomable.

MANNERS AND MORALS

We talk much of civil rights and civil liberties. These may be secured by law. But beyond the law's power to add or subtract, lies the vaster domain of the civilities. Here we are in the area of manners and morals. We complain, perhaps justly, that we are hedged about by law, that at every turn there is a law which says "Thou shalt" or "Thou shalt not." But our activities which are a matter of legal concern are infinitesimal compared with those where a man is on his own.

When there is no law to say yea or nay, when one makes the little decisions—to smile or frown; to extend or withold the hand of fellowship; to welcome or reject the newcomer to our block or our school or our church or synagogue or our Parent-Teacher Association; to exchange or not a friendly word with a fellow passenger on bus or train or plane—in these minor but significant trivia of conduct, in this unpoliced area of manners and morals, we show what virtue or grace we possess.

Probably being in Pennsylvania and on the campus of a Friends' institution induces thoughts such as these. The qualities which one associates with William Penn and those reared in the tradition of his faith are a social concern, urbanity, gentleness, a capacity for all-inclusive friendship. If such qualities do not pass with the genes, they must assuredly be strengthened by tradition, nurtured on campuses such as this.

Men and women of Westtown are under special obligation to bring balm and healing to the nation.

The sit-in movement started on February 1, 1960, less than six years after the momentous Supreme Court decision of May 17, 1954. Some Negro college students in Greensboro, North Carolina, quietly took seats at the for-whites-only lunch counter of a variety store and asked for coffee. Upon being refused service, the Negroes began their sit-in protest. The movement spread quickly across the South and led to widespread closing of lunch counters and frequent use of out-of-order signs. When the Negroes responded by boycotting those businesses which invited their patronage in all departments save that where food and refreshments were served, the economic loss was quickly felt by the stores. Many white college students participated in the picketing, and some whites joined the Negro community in the boycott of the stores.

Re-opened and desegregated lunch counters appeared quickly and widely throughout the upper South. Even in the deep South, as in Savannah, the for-whites-only signs and tradition began to crumble.

The sit-ins were merely the most striking development among many as the younger generation of Afro-Americans, usually college or even high school students, who moved for quickening of the New Reconstruction's pace. Inspired by the leadership of the Reverend Martin Luther King, Jr., the young blacks strikingly demonstrated their mastery of non-violent techniques. "Christ showed us the way," King declared, "and Mahatma Gandhi showed us it could work."

The sit-in movement was greatly strengthened by the position taken by the administrations of Presidents Truman and Johnson. Lyndon Johnson, in a moving address, told of the embarrassment suffered by himself, Mrs. Johnson and a Negro woman who had long been a member of their Texas household as they traveled together by automobile from Texas to Washington. Segregated lunch counters, motels and restrooms were constant and tragic reminders of the inferior status to which the Johnsons' friend and all other blacks were assigned.

President Truman was reportedly visited by the Commander of the Charleston Naval Yard, who sought advice on how to implement desegregation orders issued by the administration. The practical Harry Truman replied: "That's easy. Just get a brush and paint out the words 'white' and 'colored' wherever they appear."

While drastic action on the part of Afro-Americans was required to bring an end a practice of long standing in the South, there were many white merchants and innkeepers who welcomed the new order. The old artificial arrangement of separate services was expensive and not always easy to enforce. Such business people proceeded immediately to take down the demeaning racial signs as soon as the practice of integrated services became legal.

THE SIT-IN REVOLUTION

Sit-ins threw the entire region between the Potomac and the Gulf into mass tumult. The predominant segregationist element in the South gave an exhibition of coarseness and, in many instances, of brutality, in reaction to the non-violent assertion by blacks of a constitutional right. Northern cities in their racial patterns sometimes presented the same revolting picture.

On November 17, 1960, Marion Wright addressed a national leadership clinic at Detroit. His image was that America's self-image and the image it exhibited to the other nations was besmirched by legal and extra-legal efforts to thwart attempts by Negroes to enjoy equal treatment with whites in all publicly operated facilities. "A welter of private acts, fully as significantly as official edicts, determines our nation's place and acceptance in the forum of world opinions."

On motion of Senator Paul Douglas of Illinois the speech which is here reproduced was printed in the *Congressional Record* of March 24, 1961.

IMAGE OF THE UNITED STATES AT HOME AND ABROAD

In a Scottish village some time ago a 16-year-old boy was roughly handled by two policemen. His injuries were minor and superficial. From the viewpoints of force employed and damage inflicted, the incident was not one of gravity.

But, in the British view, the facts that any unnecessary force was employed and any damage was inflicted in themselves made the incident one of extreme public concern. The local Scottish authorities seemed to move slowly in imposing discipline upon the officers. Throughout the British Isles there developed a tide of public sentiment demanding that action be taken. Summit conferences, the cold war, the conquest of space, of course received a share of British attention. But they were secondary to one case of official mistreatment of a lone youth.

Debate erupted in the House of Commons. Prime Minister Macmillan turned his attention from cosmic matters long enough to make a statement on the floor. Government created a board of inquiry to learn the facts and recommend appropriate action. Traditional British justice found full expression.

Mr. Churchill upon another occasion, when the Empire stood in mortal peril from searing and scalding bombs, referred to that as being Britain's finest hour. Time will tell. But surely a profound national concern with the invasion of rights of a single Scottish boy reflects a quality in Englishmen no less praiseworthy than the physical courage with which they bore the ordeal from the skies.

What American did not receive a momentary lift of spirit from the incident? Who among us was not proud to have a relationship by blood, by tradition, or by nurture upon the same common law, with the people who employed the full resources of government to redress a trivial wrong?

I refer to this incident because we are concerned here tonight with national images. What happened in the case of the Scottish boy served to help create in our minds an image of Great Britain, more particularly, of British justice. One swallow doesn't make a summer and one incident doesn't make an image. But we can dredge up from depths of memory other incidents illustrating British concern with the civil rights of British subjects.

From a synthesis of these there emerges a conception of a nation resolute always that the full power of government shall be employed to maintain the rights of the humblest citizen.

National images arise, then, from acts of government. We have been through some weeks of debate of the national prestige. Is it an alltime high, an alltime low, or just middlin', as we say down my way? I listened to all of the debate, as I am sure you did. We heard much of missiles, of satellites, of nuclear-powered submarines, of the national economy. The assumption seemed to be that prestige could be statistically computed; it was largely a matter of warheads and stockpiles.

I don't want to resurrect that debate. Certainly, I don't want to get into a semantic question involving prestige and image. But, diffidently, I suggest to Mr. Nixon and Mr. Kennedy that, above all other, the image which we should strive to create abroad is of a nation deeply concerned with strict and literal enforcement of the rights of every citizen of this republic.

Of course, I do not limit that concern to the Federal Government. Any single American state can create a national image. Virginia, with its massive resistance; Arkansas, with its use of the National Guard to keep a few Negro pupils out of public schools; Louisiana, with its special legislative session; North Carolina, with its token integration; Mississippi, with its Emmet Till case; Georgia and Alabama, with their callous mistreatment of Dr. Martin Luther King; South Carolina, with its patrolmen turning firehoses on peaceful demonstrators—all of these and more besmirch the national image.

Foreign nationals do not think of individual states as perpetrators of these infamies. In view of the dual nature of our citizenship, they are merely practical when they attribute to the nation, as a whole, responsibility for such outrages.

A favorite phrase of southern politicians is "northern meddling in our affairs." The idea seems to be that Yankees should keep their cottonpicking hands off affairs that are none of their business. But, of course, they are your business. The persons against whom official persecution is directed are, of course, citizens of particular states. They are no less citizens of America. Indeed, they are, in a broader sense, citizens of the world. There will come a time when world government will concern itself with injustice done to any citizen of this globe.

Of course, one of the great differences between North and South is that, in the South there remains in constitutions and statute books a formidable array of laws designed to preserve segregation. I think it does not take an expert in constitutional law to declare that these laws will ultimately be struck down.

But much time will be required; meanwhile one violates them at his peril. Outside of the South, if I may risk the generalization, no such laws obtain. Hence, I will assume that there is not to be found here an actual exertion of state power to operate detrimentally against any member of a minority group.

I am not sure about your cities, because I do not know where the line is drawn between official municipal action and mere mass public pressure. But, I must say that we in the South occasionally read of serious resistance in New York, Detroit and elsewhere to integration of public schools and in housing. We read of exclusion from hotels and other forms of racial discrimination. Let me say to you quite frankly that such events are joyfully hailed by the southern segregationist. They bring him aid and comfort. They strengthen his hand.

But we are here concerned with national images. Such may be created by city action. I mention the names of certain cities—Little Rock, Arkansas; Clinton, Tennessee, Montgomery, Alabama; Poplarville, Mississippi; Tuscaloosa, Alabama. These may be lovely and charming cities, but their names evoke sordid memories. In all countries the names are familiar. They and the train of ideas of which they are the core contribute to the picture we present to the rest of the world. They help to create the national image.

Let no city, then, indulge the fiction that what it does—distinctions which it makes in the treatment of its citizens—have no extramural effect. Consequences of municipal action may develop in the world's remote corners. They help to create abroad, not merely an image of a city, but an image of this nation as well.

Activities of the nation, the state, and the city by no means complete the picture, tell the whole story. There remains the role of the private citizen, the largest role of all.

In more than a figurative sense, each one of us is an ambassador of his country. We represent, speak for it. The American abroad viewed by other nationals, carries with him a fraction of his country's essence. And, at home, seen in his native habitat by a foreigner, he is part of a composite embodiment of national aim and purpose.

All of us, of course, are not ugly Americans. But the species exists in sufficient number to have impact on world opinion. There, for example, is the hotel clerk determining what guests he will accept; the real estate broker deciding what people shall live in certain sections of a city; the lunch counter operator choosing the color of his customers; the ticket seller passing judgment on who shall see what shows and where he will sit; the taxi driver selecting his fares, and so on—in the keeping of these, in the decisions made by little men and women, rest the nation's name and fame.

Our Supreme Court, of course, announces vastly important decisions affecting men's relations with each other. No one would detract for one moment from the significance of such pronouncements. But they come from men who are no cross section of the country's thinking, who are aloof and scholarly, who write from chill and distant heights. We will not be wholly judged abroad by the decisions of such men.

But the American genius, the spirit and character of our people, is revealed in the day-to-day decisions of average men and women, their opinions, expressions, gestures, laughs and frowns—whatever discloses, consciously or subconsciously, their predilections, biases, prejudices, likes and dislikes, their attitudes toward their fellows.

But it is more than decisions themselves; it is in part the manner in which they are made and announced.

Recently I rode through North Carolina with a Negro friend whose son was one of a few non-whites attending a State university. My friend asked his son, "Why do you come home every weekend?" The reply was, "To get out of that icebox."

It seems that the boy's fellow students were punctilious in their relations and attitudes. But they withheld the warmth and informality of full friendship and acceptance.

The icily correct may wound as deeply as the vulgarly brutal.

So, then, the image of a nation is found in the conduct of its government—at all levels—and the manners of its citizens. Perhaps more in the manners. For, as Emerson observed, "Your manners are always under examination and by committees little suspected...but are awarding or denying you very high prizes when you least think of it."

A welter of private acts, fully as significantly as official edicts, determines our nation's place and acceptance in the forum of world opinion.

For example, no official act of President Theodore Roosevelt advanced the cause of civil rights half so effectively as his entertainment of Booker T. Washington at the White House; a purely private activity. I have in recent years, when some cities are selling their golf courses, rather than permit Negroes to play, and other cities are throwing Negro players into jail—I have thought how electric would have been the effect of the President's example if a Negro friend had been a member of his foursome out at Burning Tree.

The example of the private citizen, of course, carries no such weight. But he is not thereby relieved of responsibility to set the example. Examples are the stuff of which public policy is fashioned. And the sum total of the examples creates the image of the nation.

There is a further feature about example. The effect is not limited to the area of action in which it occurred. It invades other areas.

The White Citizens Councils of the South were formed for the sole purpose of "keeping the Negro in his place," of preserving racial segregation. They were not effectively rebuked. Many southern politicians nestled close to them. They achieved a certain respectability. But not too long a time elapsed until synagogues were bombed, and, in all of the area which they infest, in the recent political campaign religious bigotry was most intense and and virulent. Examples of racial intolerance move the suggestible to demonstrate intolerance in religion, and, indeed, in the whole realm of thought and conviction.

It was almost 200 years ago that Thomas Jefferson wrote that we must "have a decent regard to the opinion of mankind." The phrase has lain somewhat dormant in consciousness. Why have we so suddenly begun to appreciate its wisdom?

Is it not because of the present balance of power in the world and the competition between systems?

On a day in September, 13 new African nations became members of the United Nations. The nations of Africa and Asia now constitute almost 50 per cent of the membership. They are non-white members. Their destinies have heretofore been very largely in white hands. The converse could become true. I hope it will be more consistent with truth to say that the color of hands will not enter into the destiny of any nation, or any individual, for that matter, but that the combined wisdom of all men, distilled at the United Nations, will shape the destinies of us all.

But certainly the emergence of non-white peoples throughout the world, their new position of international authority, has a lesson for all of us. We need desperately to get along with these new fellow members in the family of nations. We need their sympathy and support, as, indeed, they need ours. Our attitude can be crucial in securing and holding sympathy and support.

Now, the civil rights movement in this country is designed to guarantee the constitutional rights of all people—including colored people. You may be sure that the peoples of Asia and Africa know what is happening to their brethren in this country. The Russian propaganda machine sees to that. So they are aware of the resistance movement in the South, aware of speeches made in Washington and in the state capitols, aware of the shabby and fraudulent tricks used to deny rights to people of color in the South, aware of burnings, boycotts and bombings, aware of resistance to school integration in Detroit.

Let us suppose that the colored citizens of Ghana were

simultaneously informed of certain facts. They were told that the U.S. Government had made a grant to Ghana for the purpose of building a dam. They were also told that a state had announced no Negro should attend its law school; or that Negroes must ride in the back end of buses in a certain city; or that another city sold its golf course rather than permit Negroes to play on it; or that a United States Senator gave active support to an organization set up to keep Negroes in their place. And so on indefinitely. Which kind of facts, do you suppose, would have the larger impact upon the minds of Ghana citizens? You and I know that the personal insult to men of color would far outweigh the national gesture.

So the bold and stirring program of aid to the new African nations which President Eisenhower presented to the United Nations may be completely nullified by the official policy of a lone state. The world may be plunged into chaos or holocaust, men by millions may be seared and pulverized, because Negroes are kept out of schools....

In a real sense the culminating drive against segregation had its birth at a lunch counter in Greensboro, North Carolina, on February 1, 1960, when some Negro college students ordered a cup of coffee.

The year 1960 may have interest to the historian for many reasons. Not the least of these will be because an idea emerged in the South—an idea which had application to the entire region.

You will note that I do not say the idea was then and there conceived. I say it emerged and it had application. For the idea itself—non-violent resistance to tyranny—was old when the pyramids were raised. Nebuchadnezzar made his great image of gold and set it up on the plains of Babylon. He issued his decree, directing that "at what time ye hear the sound of the cornet, flute, harp, sackbut, psalter, dulcimer, and all kinds of music, ye fall down and worship the golden image that Nebuchadnezzar the king hath set up."

But Shadrach, Meschach, and Abednego to his face told

Nebuchadnezzar "Be it known unto thee, O king, that we will not serve thy gods, nor worship the golden image thou hast set up."

And so they walked unscathed through the fiery furnace.

So on the plains of Babylon there was born an idea. Some centuries later, in the city of Jerusalem, it was expressed: "Render unto Caesar the things that are Caesar's and unto God the things that are God's." And so, by way of Walden Pond in the words of Thoreau, by way of India in the salt marches of Gandhi, by way of Montgomery, Alabama, in the person and example of Martin Luther King, the idea on February 1, 1960 entered a lunch counter in Greensboro, N.C.

There is epic drama in the emergence of such an idea at such a time and place. It emerged in the South in the year 1960. There is a jarring contrast between the gentle and humane philosophy of non-violence and the prevailing spirit and mood. A Sophocles or a Shakespeare would have arranged it thus.

Traditionally, the South is wedded to violence. It would be an exercise in morbidity to lead you through the maze of figures which indicate the southern tendency to rely upon guns and clubs and dynamite as substitutes for due process of law. It may be sufficient for our purposes to point out that, in the Southern states, the per capita rate for crimes of violence varies from one and a half to one and three-fourth times the national average. It is substantially higher than the rate of such uncivilized and benighted communities as Chicago and New York. More than incidentally, violence has often been the ready tool of some segregationists.

We hear much of our way of life. I am never sure what our friends mean, but it is the way of violence.

It was against this backdrop of raw, red violence, into this world of bared fangs and claws, that the idea of nonviolence entered a Greensboro lunchroom on February 1.

Here, then, for the resistant South, is a completely new concept, certainly a completely new tactic in securing social change.

It is an exclusively Negro conception. The movement that rocked the South was the product of brains of Negro boys in a college dormitory at Greensboro. Inevitably the insistent question will be asked throughout the South: If Negro brains can conceive and execute so unorthodox and masterly a campaign, could not such brains be profitably utilized in all other phases of southern life?

We are concerned with the national image. That image acquired new luster from the conduct of college boys and girls, calm, poised and resolute, who demonstrated that moral power alone, schooled, channeled and disciplined, is the inevitable and ultimate victor over oppression.

The initial reaction to demand for lunch-counter service was to close the counters. Mark the same reaction in other fields. Close the golf courses. Close the swimming pools. Close the parks. Close the libraries. Close the schools.

Now, if civilization does not inhere in such public instrumentalities, they are at least its expressions. Snip them off one by one, and, one step at a time, you withdraw from civilization. Finally, at the end of this somber process, you have attained complete savagery. Never before in human history have men openly advocated an inversion of the evolutionary process.

That is, not for human beings, I understand that a few scientists are crossbreeding horses in an effort to reproduce the dwarfed and stunted Eophippus, primal ancestor of the breed of present-day horses. The bunglers who propose to close schools and libraries would make cavemen of us all.

Few among us go that far. But those who seek to preserve segregation, in the South or in Detroit, retard, if they do not, reverse, the normal evolution of society into finer forms.

Men grow by experience, by contact, by absorption. Segregation limits the area of contact, the range of experience. Shut out from the lives of white and Negro alike has been the rich and rewarding experience of acquaintance with those who would bring to association and friendship a wealth of new background and social potential. Whites should realize that they, too, are victims of the order they have created.

Occasionally one reads of a demented parent who has for years kept his child secluded in some attic or basement, shut off from contact or association with other humans. The police find the child, undernourished, stunted, filled with fantasies and delusions, ridden with misconceptions and fears. Such life becomes when the world is shut out.

Members of both races, without awareness of it, have undergone an isolation differing only in degree from that of the unfortunate child. We, too, have lived without the mainstream of life. The circle of those whom we might have known, who might have enlarged the range of our sympathies and understanding, who might have enriched our lives by imparting into them a new breadth and depth—that circle has been racially constricted. We, too, have lived in a world of myth and fantasy and fear. We devise our own delusions of grandeur and of inferiority.

We begin now to tug at the bonds. We seek escape and exit into a brighter and better world. When, happily, full release has been achieved, we will laugh at the fears which so long possessed us and begin, at last, to devote our lives to noble purposes and happy ends.

Wright first spoke about the sit-in movement on March 18, 1960. He suggested to a meeting sponsored by the NAACP in Detroit, Michigan, that the Greensboro Coffee Party might loom as large in history as the Boston Tea Party. After analyzing the economic and moral bases for the new movement, Wright developed the idea that, "Legalized segregation would not long survive in the South if, elsewhere in the nation, all men, in their attitudes toward their fellows, rose above consciousness of race."

DOUGHNUTS AND DEMOCRACY (March 18, 1960)

It has often happened that those who lived through great events were unaware of their historical significance. Another generation with increased perspective begins to grasp their importance and, ultimately, to realize that they were milestones in human progress. What was merely an exciting episode to a participant may, upon later examination, turn out to have been one of the pivots upon which history turns.

A dozen or so citizens of Massachusetts clamber at night upon a ship at anchor in Boston harbor and throw some bags of tea overboard. As they slipped furtively back to their homes, probably not a man of them ever dreamed that his descendants would some day boast that Grandpa had taken part in the Boston Tea Party, or that his action had sparked the creation of a new nation. The determination of Bostonians to drink tea without paying a tax to the British crown, a few minutes of daring action—and History begins a fresh chapter.

Now, behold a parallel. On February 1, 1960, a few college students in Greensboro, North Carolina, enter, not a ship at anchor, but Woolworth's 5 and 10 cent Store. They do not throw tea out on the street; they order coffee to be drunk sitting down. (Instead of standing up for their rights, they sat down for them; in other words, they were sitting on their

Constitutional rights.) They were refused service. You know the result. The movement has spread electrically throughout the entire South, forcing every community to re-examine its segregation practices.

I play no favorites as between coffee and tea—I am a Bourbon and branch water man myself—but I suggest that in History's long view the Greensboro Coffee Party may loom as large as the Boston Tea Party. Lipton and Maxwell House may fight out that issue between themselves. Neither has given me any payola.*

If anything was inevitable, it was this strife over the lunch stools.

One thing to which the South has not yet fully adjusted is the Negro's increased purchasing power. So long as that power was insignificant, he could expect, and was reasonably content with, second class service. In all fairness, this discrimination was not entirely a matter of race. For example, I am sure that if Mr. Rockefeller and I, or, to keep politics out of it, Mr. Harriman and I, walked into Tiffany's at the same time, the clerks would knock themselves out waiting on either of them while I twiddled my thumbs. I would regard that as annoying but normal. But with my first hundred million, I would begin to pound on the counter and demand equal service.

The Negro has now reached that stage. His money is as good as anybody else's. When he may trade freely at all of the store's counters except the lunch counter, the calculated humiliation of him becomes obvious. It will no longer be endured.

But, transcending the economic reason, is a deeper motive. It involves the dissipation of the myth of white superiority. The older white and the older Negro had been reared on that myth. The white believed it firmly; the Negro, if only subconsciously, was at least half persuaded.

But in two or three decades the last shred and vestige of the

---

*Current slang for paying disc jockeys to use certain records.

myth have dissolved, leaving "not a rack behind." Jackie Robinson, Marian Anderson, Dr. Ralph Bunche and a galaxy of able and talented men and women have demonstrated conclusively that, in fair competition, the Negro stride for stride will match his white rival. No one now above the mental level of Senator Eastland ever even mentions white superiority. To tell the truth, if Secretary Benson will pardon the expression, there are times when I am disposed to settle for 90 per cent of parity.

The young people—particularly the college crowd—know this. They are not blind. It is "agin nature" to ask them to act as if they didn't know, as if they couldn't see. Knowing and seeing, they demand that they be treated as any other American citizen.

The demand confounds the segregationist. While it is at best specious reasoning, up until now the Southern white has indulged the fiction that the Negro Southerners were quite happy with their lot until misled by the NAACP, which capitalized upon ignorance. Here, however, we have a spontaneous movement among the most intelligent—college students, no less—erupting throughout the entire South.

And the confusion of the segregationist is further compounded by a fact of utmost importance. White college students of the South, in more than isolated instances, have stood loyally by the side of the protesting Negroes. The hecklers—who were they? Let the Richmond *News-Leader* answer:

> *Many a Virginian must have felt a tinge of wry regret at the state of things as they are, in reading of Saturday's "sitdowns" by Negro students in Richmond stores. Here were the colored students, in coats, white shirts, ties, and one of them was reading Goethe and one was taking notes from a biology text. And here, on the sidewalk outside, was a gang of white boys come to heckle, a ragtail rabble, slack-jawed, black-jacketed, grinning fit to kill, and some of them,*

> *God save the mark, were waving the proud and honored flag of the Southern states in the last war fought by gentlemen.* **Eheu***! It gives one pause.*

So, then, the issue is fairly and finally joined in the only way it should be joined. It is not Negro versus white. It is intelligence and decency of white and Negro versus ignorance and depravity.

The Negro people, during the past half dozen years, have given to the nation a host of brave and noble spirits who have endured martyrdom for a cause—Martin Luther King, Mrs. Daisy Bates, and a long star-studded scroll of the anonymous valiant. How often have I had occasion to praise them! Permit me now, as a white man, a brief moment of exultation that members of the race to which I happen to belong—students of Wake Forest College, Duke University and a score of other institutions—have conquered the tyranny of time and place to march with you, resolute and unafraid.

Don't forget, my friends, those students can sit and eat wherever they please. Can there be greater purity of motive than that which prompts courageous action to secure rights for another. All hail to them!

But, as is usually the case, action which has its principal justification upon high moral grounds is consistent with intelligent self-interest. We are concerned that the South shall get down off the dunce stool.

What an image we must present to the world! Conspiratorial and furtive planning how to thwart judicial decrees, massive resistance, gerrymandering, pupil placement acts, token desegregation, exclusion from the ballot, filibustering—all of these were and are bad enough. But they have about them a certain low cunning which bespeaks a kind of depraved intelligence. One might admire them as he would admire the artistry of the jackal or the crocodile.

But this lunchroom thing lacks even that dubious distinction.

Here are men in the year 1960 arrayed to defend a primitive taboo which might have flourished on a South Sea island 5,000 years ago. The whole majesty and might of states massed to see that certain people stand while they eat their peanut butter sandwiches! Where the rest of the world is not grieved by the tragedy, or amused by the folly, or shocked by the brutality, of state action, it must be appalled at its unfathomable stupidity.

Stupid, because this whole cause celebre, this fantastic and incredible episode, could end in five minutes if white Southerners would utter a phrase which they learned in childhood and have repeated ever since—"Sit down. Have a cup of coffee."

In other words, leaving law and morals aside, the situation would yield to ordinary good manners. And it is manners upon which the Southerner has always prided himself. Our politicians have led us into strange paths. They have, in our name, departed from established law, struck questionable compromises with principle. Manners are about all we have left. We shall be naked indeed if we surrender them.

But perhaps we have been unfair to our politicians. I have thought of them as having no concern about civil rights. I was wrong. There is one alleged civil right they seem determined to protect. It is the alleged right of a lunch counter operator to require a Negro customer to stand while eating.

I risk no legal opinion as to the existence of such right. But guessing as the future is a game all may play. So I give you my reading of the stars: This court, or a succeeding court, will hold that one who has a charter or franchise or license from a state to engage in business operates that business pursuant to exercise of state power, and that state power may not be used by a grantee to discriminate against customers because of race or religion.

There are certain inherent rights one enjoys merely as a human being. They grow in number as men's minds expand. They are not all found in certain amendments to a constitution.

Among them is the right not to be publicly humiliated on account of race by a policy of a business which exists under the aegis of a state.

The Greensboro Coffee Party may well establish that principle as a part of our organic law. It is doing much more than that. It is presenting the South with alternatives between which it must choose. There is no escape from definite and clear-cut decisions. Let us approach one of them a little bit obliquely.

The segregationists protest loudly against the Negroes' use of the boycott. In Montgomery, for example, scores were arrested for boycotting the buses. That in spite of the fact that use of the boycott against Negroes is blatantly advocated in the literature of the White Citizens Councils and that Negroes all over the South have felt the keen edge of that economic weapon. Let's not put it in such abstract terms. Thousands of Negro fathers, mothers and children have been driven from farm homes; thousands of Negro small merchants have been forced out of business, and thousands of Negro teachers and preachers thrown from their class rooms and pulpits—all for no other offense than that they acted as American citizens. But things have come to a pretty pass, the segregationist says, when the Negroes boycott a dime store.

How do they react? Virginia, birthplace of Thomas Jefferson, mother of presidents, and other Southern states rush through the legislature bills redefining trespass. Police are re-enforced, the National Guard alerted, stern warnings issued,—all to uphold the alleged civil right of a restaurant owner to require Negroes to stand while eating. Such the reaction against the Negro boycott.

But the white supremacists, without being aware of it, by the very nature of their acts, are themselves perpetrating a boycott of an entire region. By insistence upon preserving a caste system—engrafting a part of the dead eighteenth century upon the living body of the twentieth—they insulate the South against the intelligence and the superior moral force of the rest of the nation. Cultural and scientific groups, professional societies, religious organizations, refuse to hold their conventions in the South because they refuse to humiliate their Negro members. That is one phase of this self-imposed boycott.

There are others. Able Southern professors and ministers of the gospel—white men and women—have been expelled, sent into exile beyond the region, because they spoke out for truth and decency. Still others, suffocated by the local atmosphere, voluntarily leave for realms where they may live as free men.

Such, then, is the colossal intellectual boycott of a third of the land mass of this nation. Such the choice with which the segregationist is confronted. He may let people sit on lunchstools or he may make the South a Sahara of the mind and spirit.

I must interpolate that silver linings appear on the clouds. Perhaps for the first time, the Negro has widespread support from the South's intellectuals. I have referred to the white college students. The ferment has spread as well to faculties, who are becoming vocal. And ministers of all denominations now speak out against the prevailing infamy. Never in history has sheer brutality been a match for the still, small voice. It will not be now.

Do you here in Detroit have any stake in what is now transpiring in the South? I understand that your constitution and statutes require complete absence of racial discrimination. But may you for that reason wash your hands of us?

We live in a closely knit world—a fact of which the segregationist seems unaware. He talks eternally about something he calls states' rights, as though behind a river, or some line drawn on a map, citizens are free to conduct themselves as they please, without a "decent regard to the opinion of mankind." Someone should take him by the hand, lead him out back of the barn and tell him the facts of life. Among these facts is that this *is* one nation, indivisible.

Nothing may now be done anywhere in this nation without everywhere producing consequences and repercussions. Ideas spawned in South Carolina or Mississippi today may find lodgement in skulls in New York or Michigan tomorrow. The tools of science are sometimes invented before men have the spiritual qualification to use them wisely. Thus ideas may leap across continents and oceans before their authors may mentally leap across their backyard fences. The anthropoid utterances of Senator Eastland and Senator Thurmond may stir the primitive in men, not merely in Mississippi and South Carolina, but in Detroit and Chicago as well.

So, don't for one moment entertain the delusion that the Mason and Dixon line is a rampart behind which you are secure. Your own destiny is involved with the fate of the Southern liberal.

But, surely, it is a narrow and selfish view which prompts one merely to take steps for his own protection. That is negative virtue. A person of robust goodness wants to throw his weight around, to influence favorably the course of events beyond his community limits. So, what may be done by the private citizen of Detroit?

As I pointed out a moment ago, I understand in this state there is no discrimination based upon law. Now, I have complete recognition of the validity of the distinction between discrimination legally enforced and discrimination voluntarily practiced. But I think I should be evasive if I did not point out that voluntary discrimination in any section of this nation, Michigan, for example, strengthens legally enforced discrimination in the South. Discrimination, even if not legally sanctioned in one state, encourages the application of such sanctions elsewhere. This fact places upon the non-Southern private citizen the solemn duty of taking care that his individual and voluntary acts and attitudes are above reproach.

I carefully skirt the cliches about the power of the private citizen of which power we are constantly reminded. But we may profitably consider for a moment the expanding significance of private action.

There is a legal phrase to the effect that a certain business or enterprise is "affected with a public interest." The classic illustration would be a utility company holding a franchise to furnish electricity or transportation. It is a rapidly enlarging conception, even in corporate circles.

But, under conditions of the modern world, may we any longer limit the connotations of the term to corporate action of a commercial nature upon a large scale?

Dr. Ralph Bunche was recently denied membership in a tennis club because he is a Negro. It was a private club acting within its legal rights. But that action had repercussions around the world. In a hundred different translations it was blazoned before people of color whose friendship this nation needs desperately to win. The simple black-balling of an applicant for club membership was profoundly affected with a public interest.

So, every college fraternity, the American Legion, the Forty and Eight, the churches—every organization which makes color or race a qualification for membership—affects the safety and destiny of this republic.

In Charlotte, North Carolina, a year or so ago, a photographer snapped a picture of some people surrounding a poised and serene Negro girl on her way to a white school. There was a snarl on the faces of the menacing group. That picture, in addition to publication in this country, won an award in international competition at Amsterdam. It travelled around the world. The mere facial expressions of a handful of people were affected with a public interest.

So, without elaboration, whoever hires and promotes employees; whoever builds, leases and sells homes; whoever receives guests at a hotel; whoever sells tickets to shows; whoever deals with his fellow human beings—all with a vision which takes no note of color—such a one in only the narrowest sense engages in private action. In the widest and truest sense he contributes to national grandeur. Vastly more important, he strengthens the bonds which unite all human creatures into the family of man.

While it must at times seem to all of us that government is forever regulating our conduct, actually only a small percentage of our acts are regimented. Beyond the pale of law, beyond the reach of government, lies a vast domain of conduct, a kind of moral penumbra, where the citizen is free to act as he pleases. Here are no legal restraints or imperatives, no penalties or sanctions. Here passions and prejudices may be freely indulged, likes and dislikes freely expressed, without other than self-imposed limitation. Here the sovereign authority is not law, but conscience.

But let it not be supposed for one moment that, because the public, through government, does not invade this uncharted area, it is not concerned or involved with what there transpires. On the contrary, from this uninhibited welter of conduct are fashioned customs, institutions, a way of life, and, ultimately, even government itself.

The business of government, we say, is civil rights; that is, the preservation of privileges and immunities guaranteed by the Constitution. Outside of that field, as broad as it may be, lies a vaster domain. It is the field of the civilities. Here the citizen is on his own. Here his conceptions of right and decency and honor find full expression. Here such religion as he may have may come to full flower. It is one thing to grant grudging obedience to law; it is another and more important to do what is right, not because of law's command, but because of promptings which spring from the heart.

No one, of course, may legitimately disparage the profound importance of judicial opinions. But they come from men aloof and scholarly who are no cross section of American thinking. The opinions which will have impact upon mankind are fashioned by average men and women. They reflect the thinking, the principles, the attitude of the anonymous citizen.

So, what does this mean to the anonymous private citizen of Detroit? Simply this; you have a deep concern with the injustice and pain resulting from legalized segregation; if you are sickened by the violence, and shocked by the duplicity, which have attended efforts to preserve it; if you consider it a scourge and pestilence upon a fair land—then examine the secret places of your own heart. Legalized segregation would not long survive in the South if, elsewhere in the nation, all men, in their attitudes toward their fellows, rose above consciousness of race. The very means of communication which bring you the words of Eastland and Thurmond carry in exchange the soft persuasion of your own deeds and words and thoughts. To such persuasion no state would long be adamant.

In any community in a single day there are thousands or millions of private acts. There are millions of thoughts, ideas, emotions, expressions, gestures, postures, assertions, laughs, nods, frowns—all of the things which individuals do, consciously or unconsciously, to give outward expression to their inner selves, to indicate their reactions to events and their attitudes toward other individuals. The composite, the resultant, the synthesis, of these myriad and fleeting revelations of attitude is an awesome and potent force. It is the force of community pressure.

The destiny of the community is involved with that force. As an instrument of community development, the NAACP is involved with it. The attitude of the community may drive talent and skills and genius out, or it may retain and attract men and women of such qualifications.

If the community attitude is hostile to the new and novel; if it places limitation upon advancement; it it assigns fixed status to men and women, drawing lines beyond which one proceeds at his peril; if it exalts a way of life merely because it is venerable—if the community attitude does those things, men and women of spirit, initiative and enterprise will elsewhere seek a more congenial climate. The constrictive force of the community, like pressure which forces cream from a tube, will expel the superior and elite.

That same constrictive force will warp and twist those who

remain. Community pressure is a Procrustean bed which fits to its own dimensions those who yield themselves to its clutches. But, so insidious is its operation, its victims do not comprehend the extent to which they have been shaped and molded.

But if the community attitude encourages every creative activity, however novel; if it slams shut no door to human aspiration—men and women of genius will remain and others will come to join their gallant company.

Nor dare we believe that they who leave go only for better pay. Admittedly, many move in response to that lure. But your really superior man, your man of genius, who doesn't keep pace with his companions here, in Thoreau's phrase, moves "because he hears a different drummer." He wants to breathe an ampler air, have his being in a freer society. He will "step to the music he hears, however measured or far away."

For a state to have against it a balance of trade in commercial products and commodities is bad enough. To have against it a balance of trade in ideas is profoundly tragic.

No one knows or cares what products moved by boat or camel back from Athens or Judea or Alexandria. What matters it to us in 1960 that so many tons of olives, or so many hogsheads of wine, or so many bushels or rice, were loosed in the channels of trade 2,500 years ago? What *does* matter profoundly is that in Athens and Judea and Alexandria the foundations of science were laid and there were evolved ideas and principles of conduct and ethics, which, if they do not wholly govern us, at least have daily impact upon our lives. They evolved in a society in which every man was prodded to think, to express himself, to achieve up to the full limit of his powers.

So, in some dim and distant future, men will little note nor long remember what agricultural or commercial products flowed from Detroit in the 1960's. But the attention of men could be riveted to this city, and they could be exalted in spirit, if there were here produced ideas and principles of use and service to mankind.

A secure place in history, a kind of urban immortality, is reserved for those cities which, in the lives of their citizens, show complete devotion to the highest principles of civic virtue.

THE STUDENT'S NEW ROLE (August 19, 1960)

Dr. Howard Odum produced his monumental *Southern Regions* in the year 1936. In it he ably developed the point that the South, more than any other area of the nation, was in the grip of regional or sectional consciousness. New England, the East, the West and the Northwest had no comparable feeling of sectional integrity. Citizens there were oriented to the nation—indeed, to the world at large. But to the Southerner, the South was an entity, apart from and almost alien to, the rest of the country.

Only the historian is concerned with the factors which created this insular spirit. It existed in 1936. Perhaps to a lesser extent, it exists today. I hope you will not throw me out if I suggest that this meeting itself is evidence of the persistence of that spirit. This is a *Southern* student human relations seminar. By convening such a meeting—Southern students only—we attest to a regional consciousness, to our recognition that the South is a kind of entity with human relations problems peculiar to itself.

Having said so much, I call your attention to an amazing paradox.

One of the things of which we in the South may be most proud is that the leaders we have furnished to the nation have usually been internationally minded. The conception of the interdependence of nations, "one worldness," as Wendell Wilkie phrased it, emerged as the result of World War I. Woodrow Wilson first give it authentic expression. The League of Nations was its concrete embodiment.

The League was done to death by leaders from New England, the Midwest and the Far West—men like Henry Cabot Lodge from Massachusetts, William E. Borah from Idaho, and Hiram Johnson from California. Its staunchest defenders were men like Senator Carter Glass from Virginia, Senator Oscar W.

Underwood from Alabama and Congressman James F. Byrnes from South Carolina. In all the national debate of the era, Southern leaders were solidly behind Wilson.

That was no unique and exceptional performance. Whenever the issue of internationalism vs. isolationism has had congressional attention, Southerners almost to a man have stood for full discharge of our obligations as member of the family of nations. Support for United Nations, foreign aid, the Marshall Plan and all the rest has come most powerfully from the South. Senators George from Georgia, Sparkman and Hill from Alabama, Johnson from Texas and Fulbright from Arkansas, to mention only a few of an imposing company, have expressed the moral conviction of the country that we have a concern with the welfare of men and women everywhere. The South has produced no counterpart of Bridges, Knowland, or McCarthy.

Our representatives on the national scene, insofar as legislation in foreign affairs is concerned, have been citizens of the world at large and of the twentieth century. It seems safe to assume that we, their constituents, share their laudable sentiments.

So there is one stream of influence operating upon our leaders. They have nobly responded to the international demands of this age.

But there is another stream which also operates upon these same men. It is one of the dramas of the times that at the same time and before the same Congresses which debated the issue of internationalism vs. isolationism there was debated the issue of civil rights. The most modern and the most ancient of issues juxtaposed. The twentieth and eighteenth centuries competing for the loyalties of men's minds. One must record in sorrow that many of our leaders were loyal to both.

It would serve no useful purpose to catalog events since the segregation decisions of the Supreme Court—the series of inflammatory statements by Senators, Congressmen and Governors, the schemes and maneuvers devised to thwart the law, the shameful Manifesto, and all the rest. Of course, there were noble exceptions with whose names time will deal gently. But, in the main, our leaders have stood solidly in opposition to law. They resurrected the doctrines of Interposition and Nullification, which means·that their thinking is one with the thinking of more than a century ago.

I know of no paradox more amazing than that the mind which can be as modern as 1960 can be as antiquated as 1835.

So the minds of our leaders have been subjected to the tugs of two conflicting forces—they wish to be loyal to the world of the Sputnik age and, at the same time, loyal to the world of the age of John C. Calhoun. Ambivalence can be carried no further.

The task of the South is not to harmonize these conflicting forces—that is impossible—but to eradicate root and branch all lingering traces of attachment to antebellum conceptions of superiority based on race. Tidings from the battle fronts upon which that struggle rages give heart to us all.

From the political front the news is good. the present session of the Congress has seen the Southern senatorial bloc reduced to a position of relative futility. Only by the aid of Northern Republicans—that unholy alliance—were they able to maim, but not destroy, civil rights legislation. The four senators from Tennessee and Texas have defected. Among those who remain, only such characters as Eastland of Mississippi and Johnston and Thurmond of South Carolina may be said to be white supremacy advocates of the old school, to carry on the Bilbo, Tillman, Cole Blease and "Cotton Ed" Smith tradition.

Among those nominally members of the bloc are men of such attainments of Fulbright, Hill, Sparkman and Long who obviously gag and retch as they observe the tribal rituals.

So, as the recent Senate debate made clear, the obstructionists are fewer in number and weaker in conviction. Instead of inspiring awe or fear, they are now merely a little ridiculous, a little pathetic.

Both political conventions ran rough-shod over opponents of

civil rights. A few days later came Senator Kefauver's smashing victory in Tennessee. Earlier there was in North Carolina Terry Sanford's striking win over Dr. I. Beverly Lake, who beat the tom-toms for segregation.

As important as these political developments may be, they. are of minor significance when compared with a movement in which some of you may have had a hand. Certainly, I am sure the movement had your full sympathy. I refer, of course, to the battle over the lunch stools.

That battle began on February 1, 1960—less than seven months ago—when a few Negro college students in Greensboro, North Carolina, entered Woolworth's 5 and 10 cent store and ordered coffee. There have been few more significant events in Southern history. The movement spread with electrical swiftness all over the South. To indicate the explosive thrust, on August 7, the Southern Regional Council reported that twenty-seven cities and counties had opened lunch counters to all customers. Three days later, on August 10, the Attorney General announced that chain and variety stores operating in sixty-nine Southern cities had agreed to capitulate. Surely, the rest will follow suit. To all intents and purposes, the lunch stool battle is over. A social revolution of first magnitude has ended its initial phase.

It was a revolution led by college students. In so leading, they fulfilled the ancient and traditional role of students who are proverbially at the core of reform movements. But this movement was unique in student annals in that the leadership came, as it should have come, from Negro students, and had the loyal backing of white students and faculty members. Some went to jail for their temerity.

The whole controversy was, therefore, lifted from the status of a mere interracial brawl to a vastly higher plane. It became a struggle, not between white and Negro, but between intelligence and decency of whites and Negroes versus ignorance and depravity.

Surely this joint adventure in a noble cause is but a prelude of things to come.

The civil rights movement up to the lunch stool episode had been directed against law. The effort had been to secure repeal of laws which entrenched and buttressed segregation. Here, however, the adversary was not Law but Custom. The effort was a massive but peaceable assault upon community habits. The well-worn cliche of the gradualist—even the President has been known to use it—is that change of custom is a slow and tedious process. It takes twenty-one days to hatch an egg. Don't try to rush things, is the pontifical admonition.

Well, let them take a second look. A deeply rooted custom has withered in a few months. It has withered because Southern college students of both races were sickened at the indignity inseparable from segregation and resolved that it should perish.

I wonder if you agree with me that this was a student-led rebellion, not merely against custom, but also against the elders who manage our affairs. Here, for what it is worth, is my slant.

When the Southern college student surveys the passing scene what does he observe?

The political image of the South is created by the Southern bloc in Congress, the shabby group which holds its caucuses to devise strategy to defeat civil rights legislation; which conducts its obstructive filibusters, using lung, instead of brain, power; which files its minority reports to liberal political platforms; which threatens to bolt, and, in a moment of extreme lunacy, actually ran Strom Thurmond for the presidency; which investigates as subversive every liberal organization operating in the South; which resists attempts to look into voting registration practices; which fights organized labor, the minimum wage, the FEPC—and all the rest.

Such, with eminent exceptions, is the calibre of politician with which we have been saddled. His philosophy is light years removed from the philosophy of the Southern college student. So is the benighted theology which tolerates a segregated church. So is the state policy which, with flagrant dishonesty, seeks to evade a supreme court decision. So the editorial policy which gives its benediction to the prevailing mood of sullen resistance to the demands of the twentieth century.

Surely the Southern image created by the fusion of all these forces is not one to charm or beguile the college student. It is my thesis that he needed only the opportunity to declare, openly and boldly, that he wanted no part of such a South. The furor over the lunch stools provided the opportunity. At long last he could show the jaded and unimaginative men in control of our affairs that they were no longer his spokesmen or even the spokesmen for the true South.

The success of the lunch room sit-ins is a demonstration of power—the power of organized and determined Southern college students. This is the first flexing of your muscles. The question is now: What shall we do with the power?

Well, one swallow doesn't make a summer and one battle doesn't make a campaign. There are a variety of facets of the segregation problem—parks, playgrounds, golf courses, swimming pools, libraries, hospitals, transportation, the movies, public accommodation, employment—the list is inexhaustible. But rather than fragmentizing the problem, let us solidify it. The problem of the South is to see and appreciate human beings for what they intrinsically are, not as racial stereotypes.

I indulge in no idle flattery when I tell you that, in my opinion, you are and represent, better than any other group, the hope of the South.

A feature of the times is that youth is moving into control of public affairs. Two mere boys are battling it out for the presidency. Not a grey hair on either head. Governor Williams of Michigan, after four terms, looks like a halfback. You see them on TV—sleek, crew-cutted lads who are taking over. So the national trend is in your favor.

In the South, perhaps more than in any other section of the nation, the college group is an elite class. The student enjoys a prestige and exercises an influence arising from his relative scarcity. So he has two points in his favor—youth and preferred status.

Moreover, he functions in an area ripe for new leadership. The older leadership is spent, exhausted, sterile. In politics, it has concealed its intellectual bankruptcy by parading its only asset—parliamentary skill in depriving some millions of citizens of their constitutional rights. Insofar as the production of ideas is concerned, its contribution is limited to mechanical parroting about States Rights and cries of subversion about every liberal spirit of the region.

In theology, the picture is one of grim, bitter fundamentalism proclaimed to rigidly segregated congregations.

Even in education, with which you are concerned, certain faculty members who speak or write as civilized citizens of the twentieth century are shunted out of their jobs. Those who remain stifle and mute their consciences in order to conform.

Let me be quick to admit that I have stated the situation in its darkest colors. As Edmund Burke remarked, you cannot indict a people. Against this somber background, there have been silhouetted in momentary brilliance politicians of the Gore and Kefauver type—rare spirits in Southern legislatures who fought repressive measures. All over the South there have been in pulpits men who confronted their deacons and elders and stewards and congregations with the social responsibilities of the modern church. There have been editors and writers like Ralph McGill, William Faulkner, Harry Golden, P.D. East, Hodding Carter, Harry Ashmore, James Dabbs and Paul Green who have used their natural tools of reason, logic and persuasion to steer the South upon an honorable course.

The tide now runs in their favor. The South in its better mood and in the secret places of its heart responds to such leadership. From college students such as you must their ranks be expanded.

In one sense the college or university is a social laboratory.

Therein men and women are tested for the tasks which lie ahead. The campus is the state in microcosm. Habits and attitudes formed or expressed upon the campus come to full flower in the citizen.

It becomes, then, a matter of supreme importance to the democratic state that the spirit and atmosphere of the campus shall conduce to the development of liberal leaders. Negatively, there should not be on any campus organizations which restrict membership racially or religiously. There should be no discouragement, legal or otherwise, official or private, of any student seeking to enter. Positively, every student should so conduct himself that the worthy and aspiring of whatever race or creed shall feel that on the campus nothing is withheld from him because of the slant of his eyes, the shape of his nose or the color of his skin.

The Southern white college student should learn one lesson above all others: He has been victimized by segregation. Men grow by experience, by contact, by absorption. Segregation has limited the area of contact, the range of experience. Shut out from the life of the white student has been the rich and rewarding experience of acquaintance with those who would bring to association and friendship a wealth of new background and social potential. His college days are the last clear chance the white student will have in his formative years to make up for this imposed deficiency....

In the lunch room demonstrations the white student marched side by side with his Negro counterpart. It was a glorious adventure in a joint struggle for principle. Surely this comradeship of arms, crowned by victory, is but a prelude.

Other victories lie ahead. When all have been won, you will have put the Southern Students Human Relations Seminar out of business. The South will have rejoined the Union and have entered the mainstream of twentieth century civilization.

By 1961 lines of resistance to the desegregation movement had begun to crumble. The liberal forces, heretofore discreet and diplomatic, Wright now felt should become more forthright and aggressive. The sit-in movement had demonstrated not merely the moral resolve of Negroes but also their capacity for organization and leadership, qualities of which the South stood in need.

Hence, in a speech at Talladega College, Alabama, on February 4, 1961, Wright urged his fellow workers to abandon any apologetic or defensive attitude. They should instead, he urged, stress the positive gains which full recognition of Negro rights would bring. Excerpts follow.

THE POSITIVE APPROACH (1961)

The times have changed within the last year or so. Massive resistance has crumbled in Virginia and Georgia. Technically, only South Carolina, Alabama and Mississippi remain as die-hard and completely segregated states in the educational area. A whole series of court decisions and the reception greeting the sit-in demonstrators show the gathering force which is on our side of this question. We may now move, serene in the knowledge that the national power and the national conscience are with us, pointing up the utter futility of opposition.

Under such circumstances, if we have ever been disposed to be hesitant or apologetic, we may now abandon that mental attitude. I am sure that none of us has been consciously apologetic but it has been easy to urge no stronger view than that law should be observed and that integration will not be so bad, once we get used to it. If any of us have had that kind of spirit, I propose that we now throw it out of the window and adopt a more robust and aggressive attitude. In the words of a popular song, "Let us eliminate the negative, accentuate the positive."

Our position from this point on should be that the white South has paid a high price for the luxury of segregation and that integration, so far from being a status to be approached reluctantly, contains elements of positive value which may well regenerate the entire Southern region.

Even the most ardent segregationist who examines the relevant tables of statistics must admit that our section experiences a cultural lag when compared with the rest of the country. It is interesting to observe that this lag is greatest in the so-called hard-core states of the South.

I think it will be agreed by all students of the Southern region that the principal cause of this lag in cultural development is the attachment of our present leadership to what is called "our way of life."

The South has proven, what China proved centuries ago, that ancestor worship is the natural enemy of progress. We have been shackled by misguided loyalty to a fictitious entity known as the South. It has no corporate existence—has had none since Appomattox. Yet it is daily invoked by our politicians as if it had some political vitality. Always the rest of the country is supposed to be attacking the South, seducing it from ancient principles, ramming something down its throat.

The evil consequences of this sectional loyalty were foreseen as far back as 1882 by one of the South's enlightened spirits, George W. Cable, a Louisiana author. Speaking, of all places, at the University of Mississippi, he said:

> When the whole intellectual energy of the Southern states flew to the defense of that one institution (slavery) which made us the South, we broke with human progress. We broke with the world's thought. We have not entirely in all things joined hands with it again. When we have done so we shall know it by this—there will be no South. We shall be Virginians,

Texans, Louisianians, Mississippians, and we shall at the same time and over and above all be Americans. But we shall no more be Southerners than we shall be Northerners. The accidents of latitude shall be nothing to us. We shall be the proud disciples of every American alike who adds to the treasures of truth in American literature, and prouder still if his words reach the whole human heart and his lines of light run through the varied languages of the world. Let us hasten to be no longer a unique people. Let us search provincialism out of the land as the Hebrew housewife purged her dwelling of leaven on the eve of the Passover.

There is a newly-coined name that most agreeably tickles the fancy of the young citizen in our Southern states, but which I would gladly see met with somewhat of disrelish: The New South. It is a term only fit to indicate a transitionary condition. What we want—what we ought to have in view—is the No South! Does the word sound like annihilation? It is the farthest from it. It is enlargement. It is growth. It is a higher life.

Obviously, the up-coming young Negro leader does not share this unqualified devotion to a way of life which has served him and his people so ill....

There exists, therefore, in this potential new leadership an essential ingredient lacking in the old, such being devotion, not to a geographical section, but to a set of principles, which have universal appeal to the better elements of mankind.

The integration movement, then, has the possibility, if not the certainty, of introducing into Southern life a new type of leader, or a new element of leadership heretofore lacking and which the region sorely needs.

This is one of the positive boons flowing from integration

which you and I should recognize and frankly acclaim....

Not only will the Negro bring into Southern public affairs a lack of devotion to the worst features of "our way of life"; he also brings a demonstrated capacity to marshal and channel his moral strength to combat the raw violence sometimes employed against him....

We hear much of "our way of life." I am never sure what our friends mean, but it is the way of violence.

I am quite sure that it will be said all over the South, "Oh, yes, but a large part of that bad record is made by Negroes."

Let's examine that for a moment. Consider an analogy. Here is a child who, all his life, has had orange juice for breakfast, a balanced diet, cod liver oil and all the rest.

Here is another who has been reared on fat back and cornbread.

What right has the well-nourished child to say "You should be ashamed of yourself for being stunted and having rickets?"

Now, anyone who knows anything about crime knows that there are conditions which foster it. Slum neighborhoods, lack of parks, playgrounds, and swimming pools, exclusion from libraries, concerts and art galleries, inferior education and above all else, being branded as a second class citizen—these are among the ingredients of which crime is compounded.

The Negro in many parts of this country, not exclusively in the South, has lived under a regime of intellectual and cultural malnutrition. It comes with poor grace from those who have imposed the regime to disavow responsibility for its inevitable results....

So, then, we may positively proclaim undying hostility to the form of tyranny over the minds of men epitomized in the White Citizens Councils. So we may positively proclaim that the young Negro citizen will bring to Southern life this lack of attachment to its worst elements and the capacity to use non-violent means to secure his ends.

We may also proclaim the broader national and international

outlook which has been unwittingly forced upon our Negro citizen....

So the Negro college deals with youth attuned to the cosmos, conscious of his relationship with, and mutual dependence upon, all mankind. The age demands leaders so attuned, so conscious. One whose vision is merely national is no fit captain of the ship of state. One whose vision is merely regional—even the entire Southern region—is, in the truest sense, provincial. The fashioning of public policy must be in the keeping of those who feel united in interest with men everywhere, from Alaska to Rhodesia, from London to Calcutta.

On the campuses of Negro colleges may now be the men and women destined to preserve civilization and save mankind from mass destruction by nuclear weapons.

Such are among the qualities and attributes which the Negro has demonstrated he possesses. These are qualities and attributes which the white South should not greet grudgingly or reluctantly but which it should hail with enthusiasm as offering the best hope for the regeneration of our section.

I think we should proclaim quite boldly that the resisting Southern states are setting an example in wholesale lawbreaking. Some day those chickens will come home to roost.

"In a government of laws," wrote Mr. Justice Brandeis, "Existence of the government will be imperiled if it fails to observe the law scrupulously. Our government is the potent, the omnipresent, teacher. For good or for ill, it teaches the whole people by its example. Crime is contagious. If the government becomes a lawbreaker, it breeds contempt for law; it invites every man to become a law unto himself; it invites anarchy."

The lunchroom sit-ins were initiated by Negro brains. We may take pride that the sit-ins originated in the South and that white students and professors marched in the picket lines with the Negroes.

So the lunch counter struggle was lifted above the ruck of an interracial brawl. It was not whites versus Negroes; it was the decency of whites and Negroes versus indecency and injustice....

"What was once a legal question, as to which some doubts as to the rights of people may have existed, is now a moral question, a question of good faith in extending rights legally established and determined. In that field no one of us disqualified from participation." So Wright told the Institute of Race Relations at Fisk University in Nashville, Tennessee, July 2, 1963. At that time, nine years after Brown *v.* Topeka, some Southern political leaders were still urging resistance to segregation.

Wright pointed out that Southern liberals, black and white, now had the law on their side. The task now was to secure compliance with law. For the first time in American history a genuine comradeship between liberals of the two racial groups existed. Their solidarity, born in the sit-in movement, assured the success of the integration cause.

NEW ROLE OF THE SOUTHERN LIBERAL

I am grateful to you for letting me attend another Institute of Race Relations. I begin to feel at home here, probably because of the strong ties between Fisk and the Southern Regional Council. I sat on its board of directors with your Dr. Charles Johnson—the most persuasive man I ever encountered—and now sit on that board with his distinguished successor as Fisk President, Dr. Stephen Wright. (I hope that two Wrights don't make a wrong.) For many years Dr. John Hope was a consultant on the Council's staff until called to larger responsibilities in Washington. The director of this Institute, Dr. Herman Long, has been a valued contributor to our publications....

The story is told that years ago on the eastern edge of the great prairies a sign was erected to warn travelers. It read: "Choose your rut carefully. You will be in it for the next

500 miles." Darwin found on the Galapagos Islands ruts existing from prehistoric times along which the giant turtles moved to the sea. It seems to be a characteristic of ruts they they are difficult to leave. I take it we are here, not so much to choose a rut as to leave one we have used for a century and perhaps to decide upon a general direction.

We are to think about the new role of the liberal. There is one small difficulty—we would probably never be able to agree upon a definition of liberal. The word is attractive and nearly everybody likes to get into the act. I am sure that, by his definition, Senator Barry Goldwater considers himself a liberal. Who knows?—Governor Barnett* may do so. If the word means merely one who wants a better state of society, a better world order, every last one of us may huddle beneath that umbrella. The rub would come when we try to decide upon what would be a better state of society and the steps to be taken to achieve it. Probably the senator and the governor would have in mind a little more of what we now have—concentration of economic power in the one instance and intensified segregation in the other. Others of us—starry-eyed eggheads—might prefer a wider diffusion of economic power and an end to segregation.

But the matter of definition need not concern us too much. Since neither Senator Goldwater nor Governor Barnett is here—and, I hope, no spokesman for their points of view—we would probably not be challenged on the assertion that a liberal is one who advocates greater freedom of thought and action, who recognizes the imperfections of the world in which he lives and strives consciously and intelligently toward their elimination. Socrates referred to himself as gadfly of the state. Such is the role of the liberal—so to live and to conduct ourselves that the state is constantly stirred to revise and refine its policies in favor of greater freedom of thought and action. I say *constantly* stirred, being mindful of Nietzsche's observation that "Liberal institutions straightaway cease from being liberal the moment

*Of Mississippi.

they are soundly established: once this is attained no more grievous and more thorough enemies of freedom exist than liberal institutions."

So the liberal fights rigidity in institutions and frigidity in the minds and hearts of men.

But, if the role of the liberal in 1963 is the same as the role of Socrates in an era B.C. why *new* role? It is at least 20 centuries old. The role is constant, unchanging, the remorseless pressure for greater freedom of thought and action. The role doesn't change. Times change. Circumstances change. New occasions present new duties. And it is in that sense only that in 1963 the role of the liberal is new.

The South approaches the end of a distracting and enervating ordeal. Enervating because for a decade at least a vast amount of time, energy and brains went into a sordid pursuit. That pursuit was nothing less than an effort of some state governments to preserve a caste system in a democracy, to assign people to places or stations and keep them there—in their places, as we have been taught to say, as though in a democracy any man had a place from which all of his brains, talent, skill and industry could not extricate him.

During that decade Southern brains have been in cold storage. While other sections were moving forward in the happy and noble pursuit of getting children better educated; of providing parks, playgrounds and recreation generally; of rewarding merit with a fair and even hand; of holding wide the doors of opportunity and fostering skill and talent—too many in the South were trying to keep children out of school, closing down parks, selling swimming pools, in a word, stifling initiative and imagination, snuffing out talent and skill. It was the lost decade.

During this decade, with one lone exception, Southern political thought has moved not an inch in advance of the thinking of John C. Calhoun. The exception was the idea that new industries would usher in the millennium. So the frenzied effort to bring the mills to the South. No one doubts the wisdom of these exertions. We should keep in mind, however, something written by Havelock Ellis:

"There is a difference between prosperity and civilization. The community which is suddenly glutted with an afflux of mills and wages is like the savage who is suddenly able to fill his belly with a rich find of decaying blubber. It is prosperity; it is not civilization."

The task of the liberal is to see that new ideas move with the new machines and that the prosperity they bring is accessible equally to every citizen, white or black. A prosperity so shared may be a creative force in advancing civilization. If unshared, it may be a curse.

The Southern liberals in the last decade—and there were some in every state—even in Mississippi and Alabama—had their work cut out for them. It was to resist—by argument, persuasion and superior intelligence—the sheer horse power of this massive assault upon the Constitution and upon human decency. They were involved up to their necks—and, as Mr. Churchill would have said, some necks—in stemming the tide, restoring sanity.

Well, I think we may agree that we are approaching the end of one phase of that struggle. Surely, nowhere in the South is there a segregationist so blind that he cannot read the handwriting on the wall. What is written spells out the end of officially enforced or officially sanctioned segregation. Everywhere public officials begin to heed the still small voice of the Supreme Court and the Interstate Commerce Commission.

We now enter upon a new phase of the struggle. What we have been witnessing in this decade has been an epic legal battle waged on many fronts and composed of an imposing number of local engagements. They have now all been brought to a happy termination. Of course, there will be rear guard skirmishes to cover "disengagements," but the issue is no longer in doubt. Governors Barnett and Wallace may not know this, but, as Carl Sandburg says, "They are goin' to learn."

As long as the issue was legally contested, it was a struggle between lawyers. It required special competence or skill to participate. Hence from the legal conflict the liberal layman was excluded. There were other ways, of course, in which his concern could be manifested but these to no extent influenced the judicial decisions.

With the legal battles largely behind us, we in the South enter upon a phase of our history in which every liberal, lawyer, or layman, black or white, may play his part. This is because we have moved from the area of law to the area of morals. What was once a legal question, as to which some doubt as to rights of people may have existed, is now a moral question, a question of good faith in extending rights legally established and determined. In that field no one of us is disqualified from participation. Even the smallest and most inconspicuous among us may say to our governors, our legislators, our school boards, our park commissioners and all the rest: "You are my agent and representative. The courts have spoken. You have a clear duty to perform. If you perform it honestly, promptly, ungrudgingly, you may count on my vote and influence for you in the next election."

Certainly we have every right and the solemn duty to speak our minds. The fame, the repute, the good name of our city or state or nation are affected by our action. How the Greeks anticipated us on everything! Hesiod, writing in 720 B.C., said: "Often hath even a whole city reaped the evil fruit of one bad man." That 2700 years before Birmingham and Bull Conner.*

And Marcellenus, still B.C., wrote: "He that would live completely happy must before all things belong to a country that is of fair report."

Chief Justice Warren a while ago coined an interesting phrase when he said "Law floats in a sea of morals." Many of us were sidelined while law alone was the issue. In the sea of morals

*Police Chief of Birmingham.

every liberal is pilot and captain of the frail bark which is his life.

There is a little noted but profoundly significant development of the past decade. It is significant because it involves moral, rather than legal or political, considerations. With the rashness of one who is neither a psychologist nor a philosopher, I venture to touch upon it. To make the point clear I want to re-live a little history with you.

At the beginning of the decade there were, to be sure, Negro and white liberals in the South. They had respect for each other. They addressed each other respectfully but formally. There was—we may as well admit it—more than a dash of race consciousness in the relationship between them. These were the days of conventional bi-racial meetings, of adoption of resolutions, of issuance of statements. Certainly I do not denigrate such endeavors. While legal issues were being litigated there was little else that the Southern liberal, white or Negro, could do. These programs were of vast importance in keeping the flame of liberalism alive and in demonstrating that, upon the higher intellectual levels, men and women of different races held to the same principles....

The historian of the future, searching for Southern leaders of this period, will find their names on the police blotters of Birmingham, Jackson and dozens of other cities and towns. These demonstrators said to the Apostle Paul, John Bunyan, Thoreau and Gandhi "Move over; make room for me,"—and moved into jail and into immortality.

But the point which I wish to stress is that there was not merely this rebirth of nonviolent resistance; there was the initial birth—the first time on this continent—of a genuine partnership between Negro and white liberals. Pardon me if I get in a little plug for my race. White men and women—students, professors, ministers of the Gospel— were in the picket lines, languished in jails, received bullets and cracked skulls, even died on an Alabama highway carrying a message to Governor Barnett.

A better psychologist than I must explain this white conduct. I think three considerations enter into the explanation. There was obviously a sense of group guilt because the discriminations had been inflicted by whites. There was the dramatic opportunity to substitute action for inaction and frustration and thereby give proof of one's attachment to certain ideals. And there was the profound realization that this was not a conflict between Negroes and whites, but a conflict between law and anarchy, between right and wrong.

Again the Greeks throw their clear light upon the scene.

Aristides, the Just, wrote: "Not houses fully roofed or the stones of walls well builded, nay nor canals and dockyards, make the city, but men able to use their opportunity."

All over the South there were men who, solely because of color, were not able to use their opportunity. Against this white consciences began to revolt.

And Solon, when asked when there would be perfect justice in Athens, replied: "When those who have not suffered injustice are as indignant as those who have."

We have moved toward the millennium when those who can eat any lunch counter take up the cudgels for those who can't.

So much for my little plug for us white folks. Of course, the initiative and the direction were Negro in origin; he, far more than his white brothers, bore the heat and burden of the day.

The point of supreme significance is that, in this travail of blood and pain, was born a new and lasting partnership between Negro and white liberals. There is no longer a mere compact of association, with its little constitution and by-laws. There is now the lasting confraternity of men and women who have suffered together in a common cause. They were not drafted into service; they were volunteers, willing and eager comrades in arms. The first duty of the liberal of either race is to water and cultivate and tend the tender plant of this new partnership. We must never again go our separate ways.

We should take note of the fact that already forces are in motion which would dissolve this partnership of Negro and white liberals and divide them into two hostile camps. Surely we have not agonized together to destroy segregation only to revive it in another form. Surely we have not struggled to establish the principle that there is nothing in a Negro man's race to set him apart from other men only to have it asserted that, because of race, the white man must be thus set apart. The greatest enemy of his country is he who would drive lines of cleavage between groups of men. What we need is not walls to separate but bridges to unite.

With the emergence of this present and inspiring solidarity of Negro and white liberals, and somewhat related to it, is a drastic change of opinion on two fronts.

What the new partnership means is that liberals of both races realize that no problems are exclusively Negro or exclusively white. All are human problems with no ethnic subdivisions. By the same token the country has come to realize that there are no longer exclusively local or exclusively national problems. All problems, however local in origin, have repercussions and implications which are nationwide in effect. Hence, we hear the death rattle of "outside interference in local affairs." (What will Southern politicians do when that idea has been given decent burial?)

We must extract such comfort as we can from the conduct of wicked men. So let us give thanks to Senator Byrd, to Governor Faubus, to Governor Barnett and to Governor Wallace. What the Senator did in Prince Edward County, and what the Governors did in Little Rock, in Oxford and Birmingham awoke the nation into realization that these were no mere sideshows to which the nation could remain blind and indifferent. Those incidents affected *American* citizens entitled to *national* protection. They affected vital *national* interests. They were of profound *national* concern.

In that view there is no such thing as "outside interference" because there is no outside. National and local concerns are occluded and indistinguishable.

If I read the stars aright, we are merely at the beginning of this evidence of the national concern. Every child has the right to be educated. In certain states textbooks are altered to condemn United Nations. Mississippi requires the teaching of a pamphlet which holds that the Negro is inherently inferior to the white. Libraries are riddled to take certain books out of circulation and are stuffed with segregationist nonsense. I raise, and leave with you, the question: Has not the Federal Government the right and the duty to protect the future citizen from that kind of poisoning and infecting education?

So certain Neanderthal governors propel us into a new conception of state and federal relations. It took brutal police action and snarling dogs to drive home the point that, where justice to American citizens is involved, a state is not a water-tight compartment which the Federal Government dare not enter; it is not a sanctuary within which a police commonwealth may wreak its will upon its citizens. We came of age as a nation in Little Rock, in Oxford and in Birmingham, as France came of age at the Bastille. Who among us did not have increased devotion to our nation as we saw its will and purpose expressed in marching troops, and heard them expressed in our President's moving and eloquent words?*....

....We have long been familiar with the distribution in one state of surplus electric power generated in another. The Federal Reserve Banking system and the Federal Deposit Insurance system make the assets of all banks available to the weak members without regard to state lines. It should not be too great a tax upon our ingenuity to find means by which the intellectual and moral strength of the entire nation shall permeate our wastelands. The country at large constitutes a cultural reservoir. No mere state lines should prevent some

*The reference is to President Eisenhower's use of troops in Little Rock to uphold the court's order to admit black students into Central High School.

siphoning of its contents into our more arid regions. The liberal in the next decade will face no more challenging task.

While we are laying to rest the ancient nonsense of "outside interference" why not go a step farther and have a double funeral? There is another corpse awaiting interment—twin brother to the one just eulogized. I refer to "matters of purely internal concern." It occurs in international discussions and debates. We hear it often from South Africa when its apartheid policies are under attack. The relations of France and Algeria and of mother countries and their colonial or foreign possessions—these, it was said, were of purely internal concern, no business of the rest of the world.

The new role of the liberal will place him in the forefront of the movement to destroy the last vestige of that out-dated and stultifying notion. Injustice anywhere on this globe is of concern to every one of its inhabitants, wherever he may live. Like a deadly fall-out, it poisons the air we all must breathe. The liberal will strive to establish a world government which will afford redress and remedy for every human wrong.

We are 2,000 years from St. Paul. It has taken all those centuries for us to realize in national and international affairs the truth of his admonition to the Corinthians: "If one member suffers, all suffer together; if one member is honored, all rejoice together." Seventeen centuries later John Donne was to write: "No man is an island, entire of itself; every man is a piece of the continent, a part of the main."

The cornerstone of liberal thought and philosophy is some awareness of the interdependence, the intricate involvement, of men and nations with each other. Only the medieval mind thinks for a moment that human beings, or races or nations, may go their separate ways, oblivious, indifferent, unconcerned with another's woes or tribulations.

So we stand a-tiptoe upon the dawn of a new age. Legally enforced segregation is headed for the gallows. And following close behind are the constricting and blighting notions of

Federal unconcern with local injustices and international unconcern with national injustices. We grope toward establishment of a world order in which the acts of one individual may impregnate the tissue and galvanize the nerve system of society.

I hope it will not be considered unseemly haste if we turn from the funerals of certain unlamented ideas to espousal of a new cause. You remember Senator Barkley's* story of the gentlemen who, a few days after the loss of one wife, took a new bride. At night warm-hearted and jubilant friends with ten pans and drums, gathered at the home to serenade the couple. The groom appeared on the porch and told the crowd: "You ought to be ashamed of yourselves—making all this commotion around a house that has just had a funeral."

The liberal may soon employ elsewhere the energy spent in the civil rights crusade. The civil liberties effort beckons. It is an older struggle than the one for civil rights, and will never be fully won. It is in part the struggle over control of what men shall think, shall write, shall speak and how they shall worship.

Up until this point, so engrossed were Southern liberals with freedom of action and mobility, of rights of association and employment, of equal educational and recreational advantages, and all other *rights*, that there has been neglect of invasions of civil *liberties*. Fortunately, the American Civil Liberties Union has performed manfully in that field, fighting your battles and mine.

But in the South, as elsewhere in the country, these invasions of civil liberties have occurred, here on a massive scale. I will not harrow your feelings by reciting to you the list of discharged professors and teachers and ministers, the transplanted editors, the countless people hauled before committees headed by such men as Senator Eastland and the spate of state committees which branded as Communist anyone believing in fair and equal treatment of all citizens. A cloud of fear hovers over many areas of the South, causing men to

*Senator from Kentucky, later Vice-president.

become mute or to whisper their convictions; to write platitudes when scalding epigrams are demanded; to preach a diluted and filtered Gospel when its federal condemnations should be invoked.

There is nothing racial about these inquisitions and reprisals—black and white indiscriminately have been victims. So the grand alliance of liberals, formed on lunch stools and on picket lines and in filthy jails, has a natural target. Civil rights will never be secure unless civil liberties are everywhere enjoyed. Freedom to think and speak and write as one will subjects violations of rights to intelligent exposure and attack.

But, beyond law, beyond the realm of civil rights or civil liberties, lies the vastly larger domain of the civilities. Everyone of us is under inner compulsion to be civil.

So, we may look forward to a time when the last statute has been written and the last decision handed down and all men stand, at last, erect and free and equal in the eyes of the law. But the law is not all and the millennium will not be at hand until men stand erect and free and equal in the eyes of each other.

Men may read under the same light, or sit side by side in the same classroom, but be separated by a wide gulf. Men may feed the same thread into the machines of our textile mills, or, side by side, listen to the same opera or concert, and be completely walled apart from each other. The task of the liberal is to bridge gulfs and tear down walls. That the law cannot do. Beyond the reach of law lie emotions and attitudes and biases and prejudices and all of those things which move men to love or to hate. Law deals with the obvious and overt activities of men. Such is the part of the iceberg which floats above the surface. But beneath the surface, in the heart and in the subconscious, lie the factors which determine attitude.

Certainly since the days of the Greeks men have sought to probe the recesses of the heart. And here we are in 1963 probing outer space, the moon, Venus, Mars and all the rest, but none of us is yet so wise that he can know with certainty the mystery and enigma of the human heart. But eternally the liberal must try.

To return to our metaphor about the ruts. For 200 years the nation was in the rut which held that it was permissible and natural for one man, because of his race, to own another of different race, body and soul. That was slavery. We wrenched free of that rut with the Civil War and the Emancipation Proclamation. For the next hundred years in 17 Southern states we were in the rut which held that one man, because of his race, was entitled to a position of dominance over another man of a different race. That was segregation, offspring of slavery. Industrial development, the times and conscience have finally wrenched us out of that rut.

But, as Northern history convincingly proves, the end of segregation is only a step—a vastly important step, to be sure—toward a more perfect society. All legal barriers may be down but, through the breaches in the wall, men may still stand and glare sullenly at each other. Surely that is not the perfect society of which we have dreamed.

E.B. White wrote that he saw no particular virtue in disarmament if there still existed in the minds and hearts of men the fear and hate which had, in the first instance, caused men to arm. In the same way desegregation would be a hollow triumph if men still cherished the emotions which, in the first instance, had produced segregation.

We in the South are now selecting a new rut. If we choose wisely, select a course of something more than mere naked legal equality, a course marked by ungrudging mutual respect, undiluted good will, and unreserved admiration and reward for merit and worth; wherever found, we may follow that course resolutely and without deviation to the end of time.

Despite his emphasis on the moral approach, Wright was, and is, aware of the difficulties and complexities inherent in social change. This awareness was demonstrated in a speech which he made on January 20, 1961, at Johnson C. Smith University. Educational leaders from Southern Negro colleges were gathered at the Negro institution in Charlotte, North Carolina. Wright reminded them that training young blacks for leadership merely in Negro affairs would no longer suffice; the time had arrived, he argued, when Negroes must receive training for leadership in the broadest sense and for the entire community.

A member of the North Carolina Advisory Committee to the Commission on Civil Rights, Wright drew upon his knowledge of specific racial situations in the state to suggest research areas where Negro colleges might well go to work.

He concluded with the reminder that, "The Negro college, as the white college, is an anachronism."

THE IMPACT OF SOCIAL CHANGE ON THE
GOALS OF OUR COLLEGES

....If you have read the report of the President's Commission on National Goals, you will recall that it begins with the statement: "The paramount goal of the United States was set long ago. It is to guard the rights of the individual, to insure his development, and to enlarge his opportunity. It is set forth in the Declaration of Independence drafted by Thomas Jefferson."

These goals have not changed in almost two centuries. But the times have changed. Men have changed. Society has changed. Jefferson was properly concerned with ultimate goals. We are equally concerned with the attainable. The attainable in 1960, due to intervening decades of growth and social evolution, would have lain beyond Jefferson's dreams in 1776.

The educated man is no mythical ivory tower figure. He is a

part of society. That society impinges upon him and he impinges upon society. Education's value is measured, in large part, by the nature of this interaction. Therefore, education must perforce take account of the nature of the society, the environment in which one is to live. The Eskimo must be trained to capture seals in icy waters—training of no slight value to a dweller in the tropics.

Perhaps none of us is fully aware of the pressures of the times. The ideal man, we like to think, walks the earth in undeviating rectitude. He fashions his own standards and adheres to them—if you will pardon the expression—come hell or high water. The tides of folly or passion which engulf lesser mortals do not even lap at his feet. He lives, not merely above the battle, but above life itself, unseduced, unawed, unmolded by the world about him. No one may doubt the grandeur of the conception. But it is an empty dream. None of us is completely master of his fate. The world, always with us, intrudes into the subconscious, and, to greater or less degree, determines our attitudes and conduct.

So with the college. It, too, is never completely emancipated. It, too, in a measure, lives under the tyranny of time and place. It reflects the mores and folk-ways of the community in which it functions. The sources of its support and the demands of status impose an intolerable burden upon the spirit of independence.

I believe it would have been beyond mortal power for a college for Negro students in the South until this moment to have fulfilled one of the traditional functions of the college; that is, training for leadership in the broadest sense of that term. Let me elaborate.

With few, if any, exceptions, Southern graduates are trained in the expectation that they will live in the South. With few, if any, exceptions, leadership opportunities for Negroes in the South have been limited to leadership in Negro affairs. Possibility of Negro leadership of the community as a whole has

258

been almost nonexistent. Under such circumstances, it would have required rare faith in community reward for sheer excellence for the college to have trained leaders in the large and non-racial sense. Community or regional attitudes would have chilled, and, no doubt, did chill the college's normal devotion to the task of developing in its students the fullest capacity for leadership. Negro leaders, of course, but rare would have been the college with sights elevated to leadership of the total community.

The college has been merely realistic. Its policy has reflected awareness of regional employment practices.

The governors of all Southern states each year issue "Employ the Handicapped" proclamations. On October 5, 1959, in his proclamation, Governor Hodges said:

"As North Carolina moves ahead in its drive for economic prosperity, it will become increasingly important that the full productive potential of every citizen be utilized. The role of the handicapped worker in our development program should not be minimized, lest we lose the benefits to be derived from a sizeable, capable, and unusually dependable segment of our labor force."

Who is a handicapped worker?

I am afraid that what our governors have in mind is one who has lost a leg, or an arm, or an eye, through some accident—or misfortune. But this overlooks the most universal and cruel of all handicaps—the handicap of birth. I do not attempt to speak for other states but the case as to North Carolina may be rested upon two pieces of evidence.

In the state's National Guard there are 11,000 members who receive annually over $5,500,000. There is not a Negro member. A Negro who may become a general in the Army of the United States cannot become a private in the North Carolina National Guard. Talk about employing the handicapped!

The North Carolina Employment Security Commission has an annual budget of $5,500,000, every penny of which comes from the Federal Government. The announced Federal policy is employment of all persons upon the basis of merit, uninfluenced by race, color, or religion.

And yet — in the state headquarters at the Raleigh office there are only ten Negro employees, ranging from maid to janitor-messenger. Not a single Negro typist, stenographer, clerk, bookkeeper, accountant, or person in administrative capacity. In its operation throughout the entire state, in managerial and professional positions there are 651 white and 39 Negroes, a ratio of almost 20 to 1. In clerical positions there are 264 whites and only two Negroes. You figure the ratio on that one—my IBM machine doesn't deal in such minor figures.

Talk about employing the handicapped!

I refer to North Carolina, not because it is the worst of the Southern states—I believe it to be the best—but because I happen to be familiar with the local situation. Throughout the South I am sure the same situation prevails.

These are not pleasant facts. It is not diplomatic to refer to them. I do so only because there are signs that we soon may treat them by use of the past tense. The figures I have quoted were developed by the North Carolina Advisory Committee to the Commission on Civil Rights. The study is an indication of the Federal Government's concern with such inequities. More important, it was made and publicized by North Carolinians, a majority of them white. The national concern will not lessen; the local conscience will not harden. The fusion of those two forces spells the beginning of the end of discrimination.

What is the significance for the Negro college?

In its role as trainer for leadership, it may cease to function within racial limitations. The doors of opportunity which now begin to crack will soon swing wide. One hundred years of white leadership have not exalted the Southern states into a position of preeminent prestige. Mississippi, Georgia, South Carolina, Louisiana and Alabama—the hardcore states where white leadership has had a free hand—are hardly in the vanguard of

American states. The stern logic of events is that new hands be given a chance.

The Negro college, then, may raise its sights. It has larger incentive. It has greater confidence. Boys and girls now on campus may be called to high station in government, finance, science, education, medicine—in any career where superior excellence may take them. Every campus, therefore, should be stirred by these thrilling events. It is completely beyond my competence to translate this generalized statement of enlarged college vision into practical terms. But it may be safe to suggest that curricula, textbooks, libraries, personnel, campus publications—every influence upon the developing student—should be geared to the potentialities of the new day.

The Southern Negro college to this point has functioned in a society tolerant of racial discrimination. That view of life was in the bones of us all, Negro and white alike. While a few rare and bold spirits here and there struck out against the prevailing lunacy, such men were conspicuous because they stood alone. It is manifestly delicate to single out one for comment; but, as a native South Carolinian, I hope I may be pardoned for reminding us all that a white judge from Charleston rose above the claims of race and station to strike the most telling blows for justice and decency. I refer, of course, to Judge J. Waties Waring.

His, then, was a lone voice crying in the wilderness. Now what august company has rallied to his standard: the Supreme Court, the President, both political parties, national magazines and communications media—on down to little men and women of Main Street and the crossroads.

So, the college now functions in a society definitely committed to driving out every lingering trace of the stigma associated with race. Hence, the college has a freedom and flexibility long denied it under a segregation pattern. It and its faculty may at last enter upon their normal roles of critic, censor, or merely commentator, upon the passing scene.

The Negro college, then, in the future will no longer merely feel the impact of social change, as our subject suggests; the college will have impact upon society. It will help to *produce* social change. In that view, it now begins to fulfill in Southern life a role long withheld. I am, of course, aware that, through graduates and faculty, good influence has always been exerted. But the influence is now multiplied many times. There may now be candor and boldness in college programs and activities.

If the college is competently to fill its new role of critic and commentator, it will of course, not be merely strident and rasping. It will be factual and logical. It will proceed in the light of established truth. It seems to me this implies two imperative developments.

Research, particularly in the social sciences, must be stepped up; and extension service must be established or enlarged. The truth in every area of human relations must be learned; the public must be informed. Without, I hope, being captious, it may be pointed out that, with important admitted exceptions, research and extension have heretofore been the exclusive prerogative of the white colleges.

No one admits more cheerfully than I that certain Southern institutions of higher learning have performed conspicuous services in research in the field of human relations. But, to a great extent, that field still lies fallow. Particularly is this true insofar as Negro insights and experience are concerned.

I referred a moment ago to facts developed by the North Carolina Advisory Committee to the Civil Rights Commission. Those facts had to do with the National Guard in this state and with practices of the North Carolina Employment Commission. That is the kind of research a college might well undertake. The Advisory Committee is now attempting to establish the facts relating to discrimination in employment by all branches of the state goverment, by the Federal Government as it operates within this state, and by firms holding contracts with the Federal Government. The Committee operates in an admittedly amateurish way, devising questionnaires and using techniques with which it is unfamiliar.

There remain largely unexplored throughout the entire South such areas of discrimination as housing, recreation, hospitalization and medical services generally, libraries and public facilities. We, of course, *believe* such discrimination exists. But belief is no substitute for knowledge. Knowledge is established by careful, methodical research.

The development of such facts and their wide dissemination through extension services and otherwise is grist for the college mill.

If it should be objected that for the Negro college to focus its attention upon such matters is to preserve the idea of the Negro as a being apart, my answer is that a research vacuum must be filled and that the day when he will not be considered as a being apart will be speeded by demonstrating to the entire South the heavy cost it pays for the Negro's present isolation.

Legislation, public policy generally, responds to the pressure of facts. So what is here proposed may have the virtue of moving to action those who shape the nation's laws and practices. With a new administration in Washington, with both political parties firmly committed to full extension of civil rights, the times demand that some agency shall document existing inequities, spell out their financial and social cost.

I remind us of the educational aim as stated by Dr. John Dewey: "The development of all these capacities in the individual which will enable him to control his environment"....Not to adapt himself to his environment—in other words, conformity—but to adapt his environment to himself. The jelly fish and the oyster have admirably adapted themselves to their environments. It remains for educated men to make such studies.

A college may be comfortable and secure in the abstention from criticism. Risk may be involved in challenging the prevailing order. One pays a price to be free.

> *Some times when people pity me,*
> *I tell them with no rancor*
> *That for what it cost me to be free,*
> *I might have bought an anchor.*

A bold and independent college, then, will seek to refashion the world in which it functions....

Let me say, in closing, that only the necessity for clarity has caused me to use the expression "Negro college." I have had a feeling of guilt in doing so. Certainly, it is imperative that we cease thinking and talking in terms of color. The Negro college, as the white college, is an anachronism. We approach, perhaps with all deliberate speed but surely nevertheless, the day when both will have ceased to exist, when higher education will serve all qualified students of whatever race, and when students will seek out institutions whose excellence alone is the magnet which draws them.

In June, 1962, at Fisk University, Nashville, Tennessee, there was held an Institute on Negro Education. Participating were Negro college presidents and faculty members from throughout the South, as well as laymen who were knowledgeable in the field. The Institute followed the revolutionary sit-in movement which had profoundly altered the South's social structure. Obviously colleges for Negroes had to reassess their role in light of the larger significance of the black participation in government and public affairs.

Marion Wright delivered the keynote address which was, in part, a plea that Negro colleges not adopt standards and practices of white institutions but rather remain as conservators of the best features of the Negro tradition and culture. Notre Dame and Brandeis, while open to qualified students of any or no religious faith, had wisely remained respectively Catholic and Jewish in orientation. They had set policy which, he felt, institutions for black students should follow. Excerpts appear below.

MORE BRICKS WITH LESS STRAW

For as long as anyone here may be alive there will be in the South colleges for Negroes and colleges for whites.

I am a staunch advocate of desegregation. I have sufficient confidence in that cause to feel that all official barriers—whether of state or church or privately operated institutions—will soon come down. Indeed, they are doing so almost daily before our eyes. But it should now be apparent to us all that the lowering of official barriers doesn't mean complete integration. Custom, tradition, habit, group solidarity, what is called racial loyalty—all of these and more will for a long time to come preserve predominantly Negro and predominantly white institutions. Upon so much I am sure you and I will agree.

Where we may part company is over my contention that the preservation of colleges having racial overtones and patronage may have distinct advantages for the region. I hope this is no mere rationalization. Certainly I accept the fact that racial segregation is an evil thing; that institutions which practice it are engaged in evil conduct.

But I think there is a solid distinction between segregation compulsorily enforced or pursued as a desirable end on the one hand, and limited separateness developing normally and by choice of the parties, on the other. Freedom of choice—in government, in religion, in attendance upon college—is among the "unalienable" rights of the citizen. He should not be deprived of it by law or by artificially created pressures. Nor should the society be deprived of the richness which comes from differences among its people.

As communities, in this electronic age of mass communication, rub elbows they will in any case tend to lose their individual character. None will be able to preserve intact its tribal customs and rituals. The segregationist thinks he is fighting John Kennedy, Earl Warren, and the NAACP. Actually, he is fighting Marconi, Macadam, and Henry Ford. He is resisting the impact of twentieth-century world opinion. The outcome of that unequal struggle is not for a moment in doubt.

But the point I wish to make is that the obliteration of distinctive community characteristics is not in every case a desirable result. It is not sameness but infinite variety which age cannot wither nor custom stale.

So, while technically the day is almost at hand when there will be in the South, no all-white or all-Negro colleges, I feel there would be a distinct loss to society if the Negro colleges became mere replicas of white institutions, or vice versa. Notre Dame accepts non-Catholic students—did you ever read the roster of their football players?—and Brandeis accepts non-Jewish students. But one retains the best of the Catholic and the other the best of the Jewish tradition. The country is better off because they do. They contribute to variety and, hence, the spice, of life.

The world for which we should strive is one in which the individual retains an original bent of mind, the community its own local color, and the college its own distinctive character. Our goal should be, not absorption of culture of others and surrender of our own, but absorption of the best of others and surrender of the worst of our own.

The goal of the Negro college should be, not to become a little Harvard, but to become as great in its special way and for its generation and constituency as the noble institution in Massachusetts.

For its own generation and constituency—there's the rub. Therein does the task of the Negro college differ from that of the white. Essentially, of course, their purpose is the same—nowhere better stated than by John Dewey: "The development of all those capacities in the individual which will enable him to control his environment and fulfill his possibilities." The difference between the tasks of the two colleges is one of degree. Because of reasons wrapped up in their history and far beyond their control, there exists in the South a disproportionate mass of uneducated or under-educated Negroes.

According to the 1960 census, in the eleven southern states of the Confederacy there are 436,000 or 2.4%, of white persons 25 years of age and older who have had no schooling and 352,000, or 7.9% of non-white persons in the same category. Using the same age limit, 3,126,000, or 17.2%, of white persons have had at least one year of college as against 144,000, or 5.5%, of non-white persons.

Recognizing the arbitrary nature of definitions and statistics, there are, per capita, three times as many unschooled (we used to call them illiterate) Negro adults as whites in the South. And, per capita, only one third as many Negro as white adults have had as much as one year of college education. I think it reasonable to assert that, in the field of adult education, considering numbers alone, the task of the Negro college is three times as difficult as the task of its white counterpart. When, additionally, we consider that the Negro family has half the white income and that its library facilities and everything else which contributes to cultural growth is primitive by white standards, the job of the Negro college assumes staggering proportions.

Relatively inferior facilities, endowments, and income of the Negro college enlarge its already intolerable burden. It must make more bricks with less straw.

Such then is the condition of the Negro college, and the people whom it must reach and serve and elevate. We today are here concerned with the adult members of the Negro population. Since the impulses which flow from the campus cannot be neatly assorted and labeled, like medicine, "two for man and one for child," we will find it difficult to exclude the college student from consideration. What is good for the adult is good for the student on campus and vice versa. But we will take aim at the adult.

Indulge me in a little bit of over-statement, over-simplification. The adult Negro population of the South is being propelled into full citizenship. It is almost as though an emancipation proclamation were being written anew by a modern Lincoln. Voting, jury service, office-holding—these are privileges for the first time within the grasp of this generation. These are facts of tremendous significance for the Negro, for the South, for the nation, and the world.

I realize that good historians disagree on the lesson to be drawn from the Reconstruction Era. The Negro part in that epoch is a subject of controversy. But I hope we here may agree that there are grave dangers in placing the ballot in the hands of ignorant men. A pencil in the hands of an illiterate man in a voting booth may be as dangerous a weapon as an atom bomb. And someone correctly remarked that all of your constitution and statutes may be thrown out of the window by any twelve men in a jury box.

So there is a note of urgency in the task of the Negro college. All colleges, white or Negro, in this country seek to qualify men and women to be good citizens of a democracy. The white colleges have no easy job, as many election returns and jury verdicts will demonstrate. But the white colleges, from their creation, have worked at the job in the knowledge that their students would actually become full-fledged citizens, and the students have gone about their duties in the knowledge that they were preparing for the responsibilities of citizenship. Neither the Negro college nor the students have had that assurance and incentive. It is, I believe, merely being realistic to concede that, with many notable exceptions, the mass of Negro people approach the awesome responsibilities of full citizenship under the enormous handicap imposed by centuries of public neglect. The Negro college faces the job which generations of official indifference and apathy have placed upon it....

In the adult Negro population of the South there exists not only material for citizenship but material for leadership. It is peculiarly the task of the Negro college to discover and foster this unutilized potential.

In its role as trainer for leadership, it may cease to function within racial limitations. The doors of opportunity which now begin to crack will soon swing wide. One hundred years of white leadership have not exalted the Southern states into a position of pre-eminent prestige....

We have given some attention to the difficulties under which the Negro college labors. The picture however is not entirely bleak, and I believe the favorable factors may outweigh the unfavorable. They arise from the circumstances of the moment and qualities which a harsh society has forced the Negro to develop.

Let us approach the point somewhat obliquely. In Alaska the Eskimo has moved from dog team to travel by plane. There has been no fooling around with ox cart, horse and buggy, or even automobile. In transportation he telescoped some centuries of experimentation. He is the beneficiary of the white man's long period of trial and error. In a decade he has moved from Stone Age to Jet Age.

Similarly, Alaska and Hawaii, in laying the foundations of their new statehood, profit by the mistakes and experience of 48 older states. Logically they should have the greatest vision because they are mounted upon giant shoulders.

The Negro, moving at last into full citizenship, has centuries of white activity to draw upon. He should be the world's most modern citizen because his path is lighted by the clear flame of experience. Thus the rude and uncultured Englishman, profiting from tutelage by the Romans during the occupation, leaped centuries up the scale of civilization. He took Roman law, architecture and engineering, refined and bent them to his own uses....

Such are among the circumstances of the moment, factors of the times in which we live, that make society ripe for Negro leadership. His is the fresh approach to public affairs, an approach free of the strait-jacket of custom and convention.

But, in a sense, he has been conditioned. He has had a fairly harsh and tragic history. Poetry and all of the arts seem to flower in such a soil. Witness the Psalms and spirituals. Already, Negro authors and dramatists lay their moving indictments upon society's doorstep. They are the vanguard. From the great womb of Time there may issue a black Sophocles.

In a region peculiarly devoted to violence, he has taught the South that non-violence is the ultimate victor. From the plains of Babylon by way of Judea and Walden Pond and New Delhi the ideal of non-violent resistance to tyranny invaded a Greensboro lunch counter in 1960—and shook the South to its foundations. The South is sick with violence. From his own veins the Negro is prepared to cure that illness by a transfusion of the non-violent spirit.

The white South is being taught that the Federal government is something foreign, alien, hostile. The Negro is being taught that the Federal government is his shield and defender.

In some parts of the white South there is deep suspicion of the United Nations as a sinister agency, bent upon subjugating American citizens. The Negro looks to the charter of that organization and all of its momentous declarations as lending aid and support to his cause.

The Negro's aspirations are upheld by all national and international religious bodies while the local white church turns him away from its altar....

Such, then, are the circumstances of the moment and the age-long subterranean forces which push the Negro, whether he wills it or not, into leadership in the last half of the twentieth century.

Blessed is the college which has such promising material upon which to confer its ministrations.

Civil Liberties

Early in his career Wright became a member of the American Civil Liberties Union and, for many years, served on its National Committee. His interest in civil liberties was quickened by observing how closely they were related to civil rights. For example, the effort to desegregate schools and public facilities was met by official and individual acts in denial of rights to protest by marches, demonstrations and assembly. Editors, preachers and teachers suffered physically, financially and emotionally for exercising the civil liberty of freedom of expression.

He assisted in organizing the North Carolina chapter of the American Civil Liberties Union and in 1973 became its president. With the legal issues involved in civil rights having been largely settled by legislation and judicial action, Wright turned his attention to civil liberties, on which theme he wrote and spoke extensively.

As a former student editor himself, Wright spoke with a certain relish to a group of student editors attending the meeting of the United States National Student Association at the University of Minnesota. He analyzed the moral and historical significance of the Greensboro Coffee Party for his student audience. Admitting that the luncheon battle seemed already half won, he urged the editors to plunge in and deal with segregation in movie houses, on golf courses, or wherever "men have erected artificial barriers between themselves."

THE RIGHT TO KNOW: THE ROLE OF THE STUDENT PRESS
(August 19, 1960)

Some years ago Stephen Leacock wrote an essay on Oxford University which began by saying: "Ten years ago I spent a day on the Oxford campus. Recently I spent another day there. So the reader will understand that what I have to say about Oxford is based upon observation extending over a period of ten years."

Applying that formula, I may say that in 1913 I was editor of *The Gamecock*, student publication of the University of South Carolina. Recently I read a copy of *The Tarheel*, published at Chapel Hill. So you will see at once that anything I may say about the college press is based upon observation extending over a period of forty-seven years. That should put Mr. Leacock in his place....

Without, being able to document my position too strongly, I have the feeling that the college papers of today have greatly extended the range and scope of their interests. Occasionally—too rarely, I would say—you are quoted by your more commercial and professional brethren who operate beyond the limits of the campus. Putting aside for the moment those embarrassing occasions when the paper is in the doghouse because of its preoccupation with matters somewhat carnal in nature, you are usually quoted because of your position on public affairs. What makes you quotable, or newsworthy, is that your position is one in advance of the community press—indeed, in advance of the position of the commercial press itself.

My successor by some forty years as editor of *The Gamecock* recently made the daily South Carolina press. In addition to this editorship, he held some clerical position with the South Carolina legislature. He had the temerity, unalloyed by discretion, to write an editorial on integration of the public schools, an editorial which did not reflect the state's orthodox lunacy on that touchy subject. He was censured by the University authorities and fired from his legislative post. As we say down my way, "that'll learn him...."

The college editor functions in a scholastic atmosphere. Presumably—this may be a very charitable presumption—he is fresh from Plato, Aristotle, Hamilton, Jefferson, Lord Bryce and Montesquieu—great minds which have delved profoundly into affairs of state. Some smattering, at least, of their learning flows with the ink from his pen. His editorial counterpart beyond campus walls has probably long since divested himself of such impediments.

But above all, the college editor has the unpurchaseable asset of youth and this, of course is no new phenomenon.

In *Revolutions of 1848* Priscilla Robertson points out that in one year university students spear-headed uprisings in Austria, Prussia and Bavaria which altered the entire character of governments.

Students in the military and technical schools of the Ottoman Empire led the Young Turk movement in the years 1896 to 1908, a movement which compelled the Sultan to restore constitutional guaranties.

The nationalist movement in Germany in the early years of the nineteenth century, culminating in the War of the Liberation, has its origin in the student bodies of Berlin and Breslau.

So with the Cuban revolution of 1933 and the abortive 1956

uprisings in Poland and Hungary. The list is long and honorable.

But one does not have to thumb the pages of history, or leave American shores to document student leadership of revolutionary movement.

Revolutions are not always characterized by gunpowder, blood and barricades in the streets. Perhaps the more profound and lasting revolutions have had not had any of those features. Revolution, minus its violent manifestations, seeks the overthrow of custom—a much more difficult task than overthrow of law. Physical force only is required to overthrow government. Intellectual and moral force, the force of reason and persuasion, is required to overthrow custom. We in the South have been witnessing the application of such force in a social revolution of first magnitude....

If you ask me what is the role of the college press, I answer that it is to support with all of its strength every effort to remove the stigma attached to race wherever it appears. The lunch room battle seems half won already. Other good fighting for an aroused and intelligent editor lies ahead—swimming pools, golf courses, picture shows, public accommodations—in whatever field men have erected artificial barriers between themselves.

To Southern editors particularly I venture these suggestions:

The most maligned and misrepresented organization in this country is the National Association for the Advancement of Colored People. Throughout the South it is the victim of official and non-official persecution. For what purpose? To put it out of business with the result that a lone Negro child must pit his puny strength against the awesome power of his native state.

Expose the infamy. Inform the college community of the thrilling and epic story of this organization.

Turn your attention to employment—by the institution which you attend, by the community in which your institution is located, by your state. Few, if any, off-campus papers have touched this story. The field is fallow.

North Carolina, I am sure, is no worse than other Southern

states. In the central office of the Employment Security Commission, there are only ten Negro employees, ranging from maid to janitor-messenger. Throughout all of the system there are 264 whites and only 2 Negroes in clerical positions. Every dollar in the budget comes from the Federal Government whose announced policy is one of fair employment and non-discrimination.

Our governors every year issue employ-the-handicapped proclamations. These seem to relate to those who have lost a leg or an eye by accident or misfortune. But they ignore the thousands who have suffered the most ancient and universal of all accidents—the accident of birth. We set men and women with M.A. and Ph.D. degrees to driving trucks or waiting on tables. Expose that infamy.

In all of the efforts to preserve a segregated society there arises a question of morals. Literacy tests, gerrymandering, pupil placement laws and all the rest never state frankly and honestly their real intention. They are framed by skilled and cunning men to accomplish evasion of judicial decrees. But that purpose is latent and undisclosed. So we have the sacred power of government exercised for ignoble—indeed, unlawful—ends. Some day those chickens will come home to roost....

The college press, functioning at the site of training of such young men and women—an integral part of such training—is under the duty to counteract the corrosive moral effect of state policy and example.

If it seems to you that I have emphasized too greatly the impact of the college press upon affairs beyond the campus, my apology is that no longer may the two worlds be delimited. The line between them is blurred and wavy. The two interact. Whatever transpires in one world by osmosis impinges upon the other. Neither is, therefore, unconcerned with the other.

Woodrow Wilson was of the opinion that college communities tended to become smug and complacent, to entertain delusions of superiority. He felt—here I quote his biographer, Josephus

Daniels—"That the air of superiority assumed by college graduates, which often blocked their way to service, was the result of a lack of democratic practice in the colleges and universities."

We are quite disposed to compare ourselves favorably with others. We read of ill-trained children who use spitballs and taunts to torment those admitted. We are shocked and resentful. But let us indulge in no vainglory. . . .

The college or university which has a racial or religious quota plan of admission and the fraternity which similarly limits its membership have no moral vantage point from which to survey the conduct of those who defend their lunch stools from undesired occupancy.

Those on any campus who exclude from the circle of friendship any person because of his color or his religious practice, subscribe to the philosophy of the unregenerate segregationist.

If such practices exist, and to the extent they do exist, there is grist for the mill of the college editor.

We have remarked upon our inability any longer to delimit campus and the world beyond. There exists a vast occluded area where function and interest merge and overlap—where it is impossible to say campus stops and society begins, where identity is lost, where the ivory tower is at the end of the corn rows.

The campus is the nation in microcosm. It is the national boast that we are the world's melting pot. All races and creeds have here found sanctuary, we say. Certainly, in a physical sense, that is literally true. The nation, in its better mood, gropes toward a social order where national origin, race and creed do not keep men asunder.

The campus is a melting pot. To it there come, or should come, all varieties of men and women, all shades of color and belief, all heritages and backgrounds. This diversity of opinion and attitude is a great scholastic asset. Many men, many minds is the ideal.

But a melting pot, in the nation or on the campus, is not created by mere physical propinquity. A vast gulf may lie between men who work at the same lathe, or at the same desk, or behind the same counter, or who sit side by side in the same classroom, or share a common light in the same library. Between such there may still be the unopened door which Tom Wolfe lamented.

The door is the feeling that, somehow, the other fellow is odd or alien because of the slant of his eyes, or the shape of his nose, or the color of his skin. There can be no genuine fusion of culture, no productive exchange of ideas, no mutual growth, until the door swings wide.

The battle of Waterloo was won on the playing fields of Eton. The battle of democracy will be won on the campuses of colleges and universities. In the heat and thick of that battle, the college press is the vanguard.

On March 22, 1964, Wright spoke at the Unitarian-Universalist Fellowship in Columbia, South Carolina, at a meeting called to consider formation of a state chapter of American Civil Liberties Union. He exercised the privilege of a native son by recounting for his hearers a list of acts of violence, intimidation and repression committed against blacks and their white companions arising from desegregation efforts.

In such an atmosphere it was essential, he asserted, that those opposing official and private acts of the kind described unite in order to be effective. The American Civil Liberties Union was the appropriate organization through which to operate.

The speech enumerates a few of the celebrated cases conducted by the Union and sets forth its philosophy.

SOUTH CAROLINA AND CIVIL LIBERTIES

South Carolinians in the past have demonstrated a notable capacity for tolerance of what Pascal calls "self analysis and self-reproach." You will remember that, many years ago, Mr. Robert Latham wrote in the Charleston *News and Courier* an editorial on "The Plight of the South"—an editorial which won him the Pulitzer Prize. It was frankly critical of some features of Southern life. I quote a paragraph.

> *At the root of the South's present plight lies the fact that it has today virtually no national program and virtually no national leadership. Is it strange that it should be treated by the rest of the country as such a negligible factor? What is it contributing today in the way of political thought? What political leaders has it who possess weight or authority beyond their own states? What constructive policies are its people ready to fight for with the brains and zeal that made them a power in the old days?*

That was written on November 5, 1924. Would it be necessary to change a word of it on March 22, 1964?

Of even greater significance than the Pulitzer Prize was the fact that Mr. Latham's editorial was received with equanimity and approval by the South Carolina public. Surely that capacity for tolerance is still latent here. I trust it is not idle or foolish to hope that his enlightened spirit, long muted and suppressed, may again pervade the sanctum he honored.

The keynote of the editorial, and, indeed, the distinguishing feature of Mr. Latham's career, was tolerance of the opposing view. He deserved the tribute which one great South Carolina teacher expressed about another. Dr. Patterson Wardlaw, "Old Pat" to generations of Carolina men, said of Dr. Lewis Parke Chamberlayne: "Though he contended strongly for his opinions, he always realized that his opponent, too, might be a gentleman."

It is with this right of the unpopular position to be heard with respect and with suspended judgment that we here are today concerned. It is the most valuable right the citizen of a democracy may have. Upon it all of his other rights depend.

Such is the broad area of our interest. Our narrower purpose is to reflect upon the need in South Carolina for an organization whose purpose is to preserve the right of an unpopular thought to be uttered and heard; to secure, in Justice Holmes' memorable phrase, "freedom not merely for the thought with which we agree, but freedom for the thought we hate"; to strive to bring about that state of our society in which a man's rights are to no degree enlarged or diminished because he is a member of a majority or minority or has a certain color or slant of eyes or profile or hair texture. More specifically, our purpose is to consider the advisability of setting up here a chapter affiliate of the American Civil Liberties Union.

I hope you will agree with me that it is no waste of our time to reflect upon certain episodes in our recent history and the present state of our society. For out of these the need for such an organization arises.

We live in an age when civil rights are uppermost in the minds of us all—rights to vote, to serve on juries, to travel freely and without restrictions, to enjoy all publicly provided facilities upon the same terms as every other citizen—in short, to move among one's fellows without artificially imposed impediments or limitations or distinctions—such is the avowed national goal and ideal. With them I am sure none of us here disagrees. Those are among the "unalienable" civil rights of our Declaration of Independence.

Not merely eternal vigilance but also eternal struggle is necessary to preserve and maintain them. For their preservation and maintenance there must be a favorable public opinion. To form that public opinion men must be free to think, to write, to speak, to petition, to organize, to strive by every legitimate means to persuade, to win converts for their cause. Such are civil liberties. At their bosom are civil rights nurtured. Without the enjoyment of civil liberties there will be no civil rights.

Let us revert for a moment to Mr. Latham's editorial, written, as I have stated in 1924—some 40 years ago. What he was doing was stating in effect to the South Carolina public: Your leadership is bankrupt. For more than a generation you have not produced an original idea in the realm of government. You have shown no skill except in wielding a stone-age weapon, the filibuster. Your national representatives are a little ridiculous, a little pathetic.

(Being a Charlestonian, with the Charleston regard for manners, of course he did not put it quite that brutally. But that is what he meant. It must have been a white haired old lady from Charleston who remarked that she could tolerate cannibalism if the cannibals would only use knives and forks.)

The point of real significance is that 40 years ago the *News and Courier* could and did say such things without reprisal; that is, without loss of subscribers or advertisers. This is a great tribute to the state of the public mind at that time.

What have the intervening 40 years done to us?

Come with me on an excursion into some events occurring in outh Carolina in the past ten years. You are probably familiar ith them all. Nevertheless, if we are to consider the need for n organization to insure freedom of opinion and expression, we ust have fresh in our minds some evidence of the extent, if ny, to which such freedom has been curtailed, its exercise enalized.

Will you listen for a moment to an item about events ccurring in 1956, as related in *Intimidation, Reprisal and iolence in the South's Racial Crisis:* *

After two years of threats and pressure, the Florence *Morning ews*, which had repeatedly appealed for moderation and good ill in solving segregation problems, banned the subject from its ditorial page. For its views, the *News* had drawn violent abuse, ader complaints, circulation losses. The city editor struck while overing a Klan meeting; the church editor, a minister, had his res slashed and two cars had tried to run him off the road. ditor John H. O'Dowd had been threatened and chased at ight by a car. Finally, O'Dowd announced a "retreat from ason" and wrote, "We have....sought men of good will....but en seeking the fair solution have not, in two years, come rward."

(As a footnote to a morbid episode, Mr. O'Dowd left lorence to take up newspaper work in the North. South arolina is the poorer for his going.)

By way of further buttressing the position that, since Mr. atham's day, South Carolina writers at their peril express onest opinions on a controversial theme, I cull three incidents om a much greater number.

In March, 1956, a 23-year-old English major was fired as a gislative telephone page after writing an article in the *amecock*, student weekly at the University of South Carolina. is article said the State Senate was "intent on circumventing"

ssued by the Southern Regional Council.

282

integration and that Southern legislators and governors were "embarrassing sound trucks for the South."

In November, 1957, the home of a white physician in Gaffney, whose wife wrote an article urging a moderate approach to integration, was bombed. The article, which proposed gradual desegregation of South Carolina schools, had appeared in "South Carolinians Speak."* Five men identified by police as KKK members were charged with the bombing; only two of the five were brought to trial, however, and they were acquitted.

In December, 1959, following the publication of a letter from his wife to the editor of the Sumter *Item* criticizing segregation policies in the Sumter community, Major Walter J. Williams, of Shaw Field Air Force Base, was informed by a superior officer that Mrs. Williams' actions, if continued, would lead to his removal. Mrs. Williams was also a member of the Sumter Council on Human Relations.

Such are the reprisals for written dissent on the segregation issue. That issue arises from the Negro's long deferred insistence upon his civil *rights*. Securing those rights involves the free exercise of the civil *liberty* to disagree openly with majority opinion.

A graver peril attends the dissenting teacher in these post-Latham days. Because of the limitations of time I must here curtail the number and greatly abridge the gloomy recital, being sure that you are more familiar than I with the events in question.

In November, 1955, Dr. Chester C. Travelstead, dean of the school of education of the University of South Carolina, disclosed he had been dismissed "in the best interest of the university" after making a speech calling for an end to public school segregation.

In August, 1955, three Negro teachers said they were not rehired by the Summerton School District of Clarendon County

*Issued by the South Carolina Council on Human Relations.

because their father and the husband of one signed an integration petition.

In 1957 and 1958 three persons were released from the faculty of Allen University following repeated charges by then Governor George Bell Timmerman, Jr., that they were linked to communist-connected organizations. In 1962, a new Allen University President, Dr. Howard E. Wright, said the dismissal of the three had been "unjustifiable and disreputable in manner" and that they would be given "preferential consideration" if they were to seek employment again at Allen.

In July, 1956, twenty-four Negro school teachers in the Elloree School District either resigned or their contracts were not renewed for refusal to execute a statement inquiring into NAACP membership.

In May, 1958, three white professors at Benedict College for Negroes were told they would not be rehired. One of them, Lewis Smith, chairman of the Humanities Department, told reporters, "This is a capitulation to the Dixiecrat forces that have been persecuting the white professors because of their pro-integration stand."

In October, 1963, Mrs. Gloria Rackley, a third-grade teacher, was formally relieved of her duties by the Orangeburg school board because of her participation in racial protests. Mrs. Rackley had been arrested two years earlier in the courthouse in Orangeburg while attempting to use white washroom facilities.

Such are the perils confronting teachers in our state.

You are aware that I have merely skimmed the surface. Ministers, white and Negro, officials of the NAACP, those exercising the constitutional rights of petition and demonstration—against such has bigotry marshalled its vindictive forces. I have used names and places because we must not forget that it is people, human beings, who have endured this torment. But, to the statistically minded, it may be stated that, in the four years from January 1, 1955, to January 1,1959, there were in South Carolina 34 cases of intimidation, reprisal and violence arising from the segregation issue of sufficient gravity to be reported in the daily press. One may only guess how many more there were—lost jobs, withdrawn credit, foreclosed mortgages, ended tenancies, whispered threats, nocturnal visitations—which were denied the poor boon of publicity.

If we may go back for a moment, our effort has been to show that four decades ago the South Carolina public was prepared to accept without resentment the view that for a generation or more the South had produced not a single constructive idea in the field of government; that this implied a tolerance of temperate criticism which must still be latent in the state; that the emerging race issue has turned that tolerance into bitter intolerance; that the issue has arisen because of the Negro's legitimate and proper insistence upon his civil rights, and, finally, that the attainment of civil rights is dependent upon exercise of the civil liberties of freedom of discussion by the spoken or written word, by petition or protest or demonstration of any other legal means. So we come by a very round-about way to the American Civil Liberties Union.

Society must provide antidotes for its poisons. Where there exists in a state the Ku Klux Klan, the White Citizens Council, the John Birch Society, or the spirit which those organizations reflect and engender, and unless we are to resign ourselves to mass retreat from democracy and civilization, the state must have an agency to combat such organizations and such spirit. As Mackenzie King pointed out, "Government in the last analysis, is organized opinion." So the kind of government under which we live depends ultimately upon the effectiveness with which our opinions are expressed. The labor unions have taught us that the individual is ineffective against corporate opposition, but that when organized, he must be reckoned with.

Since it was formed in 1920 ACLU has been the one clear national voice lifted in opposition to "every form of tyranny over the minds of men," to use a memorable phrase from Jefferson. I should like, if time permitted, to discuss with you some of the dramatic cases in which it has participated, always espousing the unpopular, befriending the oppressed. As it is, I may only try to trigger in your minds some recollection of knowledge you may have of these crucial legal struggles.

There was opposition to the mass deportation of aliens conducted by Attorney General Mitchell Palmer as a part of the post-war hysteria in the 1920's. There was the Scopes case in Tennessee in which Clarence Darrow and William Jennings Bryan fought out in a country courthouse the great issue of freedom to teach evolution. There was the Sacco and Vanzetti case in which two poor men were finally put to death but secured imperishable fame. Let me digress to bring to you Vanzetti's farewell:

> *If it had not been for this thing, I might have lived out my life talking at street corners to scorning men. I might have died unmarked, unknown, a failure. Now we are not a failure. This is our career and our triumph. Never in our full life could we hope to do such work for tolerance, for justice, for man's understanding of man as we now do by accident. Our words—our lives—our pains: nothing! The taking of our lives—lives of a good shoemaker and a poor fish peddler—all! That last moment belongs to us—that agony is our triumph!*

There were the Scottsboro case from Alabama; the "Ulysses" case, involving the right to print and distribute a novel by that name; the case involving rights of Jehovah's Witnesses children to fail to salute the flag; the case establishing the right of Negroes to vote in the Texas Democratic primary, news of which was received with minimum enthusiasm in this state; a spate of cases combatting the investigative tyranny of the McCarthy days, and the school desegregation cases, probably praised even less hereabout than the white primary case. The tepid enthusiam greeting the school cases calls to mind the story carried by a New York newspaper on the nomination of a certain candidate for the presidency: "The Democrats yesterday nominated Judge Alton B. Parker for president. Judge Parker is a nice man who weighs 175 pounds."

Such are among the more celebrated causes with which ACLU has been identified. There are literally hundreds of others involving issues of equal gravity but attaining less national celebrity.

ACLU's activities have resulted from its attachment to certain fixed beliefs. Among these is the belief that, where the use of written or printed words does not create a clear and present incitement to illegal action, or otherwise endanger the public safety, the Constitution protects such use.

Thus, the ACLU opposes all prior censorship of what people may see, read, or hear.

The ACLU battles against laws and legislative committees that, under the guise of national security, punish "advocacy" and "teaching" of revolutionary philosophy rather than overt acts of violence.

The ACLU protects the right of individuals to associate and assemble.

The ACLU defends the right of religious belief, any, or none at all—no matter what community pressures attack that belief.

The ACLU resists invasions of teachers' and students' academic freedom, realizing that a flow of unfettered ideas in the classroom speeds the nation's intellectual growth.

Thus, the ACLU agrees with the dissenting opinion of Supreme Court Justice Hugo Black in the Barenblatt case: "...the real interest...of the people [is] in being able to join organizations, advocate causes and make political 'mistakes' without later being subjected to governmental penalties for having dared to think for themselves. It is this right, the right to err politically, which keeps us strong as a Nation."

ACLU is committed to upholding due process of law, which

merely means observance by government of all rights of every citizen in government's treatment of the citizen. This requires that the treatment shall not be arbitrary or capricious or dictated by the whim of one or many. It means that the police power shall not be employed to limit action merely because the action is distasteful to those in authority or even to the majority.

It is as opposed to the use of cattle prods and dogs to break up legitimate demonstrations in Birmingham, Alabama, as it is to use fire hoses in Orangeburg, S.C. for the same purpose.

These tenets of faith have involved it in cases in all sections of the country and affecting persons of all social and economic levels. Neither their purse nor their color has marked the limits of ACLU's concern.

In addition, in Washington and, through state chapters, in various states, it has opposed measures it felt would infringe upon personal liberty and advocated others designed to make that liberty secure.

It is, I think, no idle claim to assert that, since the year 1920, no substantial issue of civil liberties or civil rights has been fought out in this country without the active participation of ACLU. Its record prompted President Kennedy on the organization's 43rd birthday to write:

> *Your voice has always been raised clearly and sharply when our liberties have been threatened. America is a stronger nation for your uncompromising efforts.*

Surely in South Carolina there is need for a strong advocate of the minority view, an organization which does not ask "Is it popular?" but only "Is it right?"

I hope, in old Sam Johnson's phrase, "it is no mere cynical asperity" which prompts me to assert that civil rights and civil liberties in South Carolina have been lost by default. As Al

Smith would say, let us look at the record.

In the days immediately following the school decision, Professor Nicholson, writing in the University of South Carolina Law Journal, analyzed all of the evasive schemes proposed by cunning but shallow men. He demolished them all. But what were Professor Nicholson's philosophic views worth as compared with the intuitions and sly cogitations of our politicians?

One by one the schemes were tried. One by one the courts have struck them down. They might not have been tried, mayhem might not have been committed on our school system, if the intelligence and good will existent in the state had been organized and vocal. So we might have been spared the orgy of persecution of the NAACP—which fights, not the Negro's battle, but the battle of every last one of us—spared the tragic nonsense of closing our parks or limiting their services, and all the rest—spared these if we had been properly organized.

No one discounts the efforts of individuals and the *ad hoc* or temporary committees of able and dedicated men and women. But these are no substitute for the daily, steady, persistent endeavors of a permanently organized group. Those persecuted for such exercises as singing on the state house steps, or other proper expressions of the right of protest, would have been warmed and cheered if such an organization had stood with them. In South Carolina there is grist for our mill.

Few more poignant sentences have been written than the one by Editor O'Dowd: "We have...sought men of good will...but men seeking the fair solution have not, in two years, come forward." The loneliness of a man on a desert isle is no more melancholy than the loneliness of a man of noble spirit isolated from his fellows. It would have been comforting and heartening to Mr. O'Dowd, to Professor Travelstead and all the rest who have felt the keen edge of public obloquy to have had the assurance that organized men of good will endured their Gethsemane with them.

O'Dowd and Travelstead are gone and the state is

impoverished by their departure. How many more men and women of brains and talent have we lost? Who knows? Who can tell? But we may say with assurance that the state which does not provide the atmosphere for the free expression of opinion is following the course which will ultimately render it barren of genius. When Dr. Frank Graham* is censured by the South Carolina legislature for completely parliamentary remarks made at Winthrop College, honest and able men are officially warned to keep their mouths shut.

Justice Holmes said:

> *Since life is action and passion, one must share the action and passion of his time upon peril of being thought not to have lived.*

We live in a time of social upheaval. The winds of change blow through the South. No man of spirit, determined to live life to the brim, will remain unembroiled, neutral. He will seek to ally himself with other forward-looking men pledged to give free play to the intellect and free expression of conviction.

> *The mountains look on Marathon*
> *And Marathon looks on the sea;*
> *And musing there an hour alone,*
> *I dreamed that Greece might still be free.*

Surely there are elements in our past and qualities in our genes which inspire the confidence that organized and dedicated sons of this state may achieve for her the eminence and distinction which inevitably accompany the actions of untrammelled minds in a free and literate society.

*President of the University of North Carolina.

Impressed with the use by the Nixon administration of surveillance techniques in spying upon activities of citizens, and its advocacy of laws eroding rights of privacy and freedom from unreasonable search and seizure, Wright saw a strong resemblance in such activities to classic examples of tyranny. He developed that thesis in an essay entitled "Anatomy of Tyranny" which was published by the North Carolina Coalition in its November, 1972, Report which is reprinted below.

ANATOMY OF TYRANNY

Plato, whose writings were both timely and timeless, said of tyrants:

The people have always some champion whom they set over themselves and nurse into greatness...This, and no other, is the root from which a tyrant springs; when he first appears he is a protector.

When those words were written there was relatively little recorded history from which conclusions might be drawn. But 2,500 added years of experience, far from modifying Plato's judgment, have given it solid support. The tyrant, destroyer of liberty, first sets himself up in business as its defender. The transition from one role to the other is so artfully accomplished that eye witnesses have often been deceived.

Since, if mankind is lucky and moves quickly enough, the career of the incipient tyrant may by lighted before he enters his second and more harmful phase, it is important to make an early diagnosis. The loyal public servant is actually a defender of liberty; the demagogue pretends to be. The public task it to penetrate the disguise, to expose the imposter. It is by no means an easy job, as is attested by annals bristling with names and exploits of those who escaped early detection and rode herd upon humanity.

But there are badges of tyranny, as there are badges of fraud. They are aids to diagnosis. In the history and literature of despotism two of these occur with such frequency and inevitablilty as to permit infallible detection. When they occur prudent men will take stock of their liberties and adopt appropriate steps to give them safeguard.

The first of these badges is that tyranny establishes or maintains itself by suspension of legal or constitutional guarantees. It does so for the basic reason of self-preservation. It cannot exist where such guarantees are in full vigor. As William Pitt remarked, "Where law ends, tyranny begins." The tyrant or dictator wishes to impose his own will upon mankind but there stands the law, shining and undissuadable, between him and the citizen. So the law must first be struck down.

(It must be borne in mind that the tyrant, while classically an individual, may be a group acting in concert, may be government in whatever form, or may even be public opinion itself. Indeed, Herbert Spencer observed that "The tyranny of Mrs. Grendy is worse than any other tyranny we suffer under.") Limiting our concern for the moment to tyranny in a governmental sense, the record is studded with instances of suspension of legal or constitutional rights.

In England, in the period from November 23 to December 29, 1819, parliament passed six measures introduced by the government. They are historically known as "The Six Acts." In five weeks parliament stripped British citizens of their rights to engage in military drills; to bear arms; to be free of searches without warrants; to hold public meetings without approval and to publish criticisms of the government. All of these were traditional and prized rights of Englishmen. This happened in a land where those rights had received their most eloquent expression.

By coincidence in the same year, 1819, under the leadership

of Chancellor Metternich, a confederation of Germanic States adopted what are known as the Carlsbad Decrees. These were aimed at professors and students of colleges and universities. The confederated governments pledged themselves to remove professors who "deviated from their duty"..."excelled the limits of their functions"..."abused their influence over youthful minds"..."propogated harmful doctrines...subversive of existing governmental institutions"...and "proved their unfitness for the important office entrusted to them." Secret societies upon campuses were outlawed and certain types of publications forbidden to to go press without governmental approval.

In France in 1793 the National Assembly adopted a decree punishing by death the writers or printers of articles proposing the re-establishment of royalty and, by imprisonment, those who distributed such writings. Thus early was the Revolution's bright vision of liberty marred by events.

Tyranny moved into high gear in Germany in 1933 under Hitler. On February 4 of that year there was issued an emergency decree banning political meetings without prior police permission. If at such meetings government officials were abused, the police were authorized to intervene. Newspapers could be suppressed for similar reason.

On February 28 there was a further decree suspending seven constitutional guarantees, relating to freedom of speech and press; freedom of association and assembly; secrecy of postal, telegraph and telephone service; confiscation of property and search without a warrant.

And on March 23 the Reichstag adopted measures which transferred almost unlimited power to Hitler.

The same story is told in Italy under Mussolini. Labor unions were placed under police surveillance with power of dissolution. Later all associations were required to reveal names of members and officers to the police and to give any other information required. The result was that all organizations opposed to the regime were throttled. Mussolini was able to announce on

November 11, 1926, "All political parties, all anti-Fascist political organizations and others of a suspected character have been dissolved." Opposition to dictatorship had evaporated.

Under Russia's Fundamental Law (corresponding to our constitution)there are broad guarantees of freedom of speech, press, assembly and holding of demonstrations. But such guarantees are whittled away by later enactments limiting such privileges and membership in the all-powerful Communist Party to "toilers." The party and government have exercised rigid control over non-party members.

There might be infinite multiplication of instances of dictatorships created or maintained by suspension or revocation of rights guaranteed by constitutions. Illustrations leap out from every one of history's more unsavory and grisly chapters. Indeed, the generalization might be ventured that no dictatorship or tyranny is ever created except by first striking down the constitutional safeguards which surround the citizen. For the suppression of individual rights is of the essence of tyranny. It is impossible to imagine tyranny without suppression; conversely, it is impossible to imagine suppression without tyranny.

It is of interest to note the reasons given for suspension of constitutional rights. Aesop observed that "Any excuse will serve a tyrant." But tyrants have always been careful to couch their usurpations in attractive terms. After all, the people have some attachment for their liberties. They have been taught to revere their constitutions. If they are to surrender any part of rights guaranteed by constitutions, the reasons must appear plausible; the penalties must seem to fall only upon hateful and dangerous minorities.

So the unfailing recourse of the tyrant is the plea of necessity. Milton phrased it "And with necessity, the tyrant's plea excused his devilish deeds." The same thought was advanced by William Pitt: ,"Necessity, which knows no law, is therefore, the logical reason for destroying the law."

In 1794, George III pushed through parliament an act

suspending in certain cases the writ of habeas corpus. The reasons assigned were the formation of a traitorous and detestable conspiracy for subverting the existing laws and constitution and "securing the peace and laws and liberties of this Kingdom." Because of the grave perils of the moment it was necessary to discard normal procedures.

The act which gave Hitler dictatorial power had, as its ostensible purpose, "the reduction of the misery of the Nation and Reich," which could not be overcome under existing constitutional provisions.

The average man was led to believe that a handful of conspirators menaced the state; they had made the suspension necessary. Hitler beguiled the Germans with tales of Jewish perfidy; the Jews had made the suspension necessary.

Well, other occasions, other bogeymen.

There is a second badge of tyranny which is, in fact, but another facet of the one we have just considered. It is the hostility which tyranny feels for established and respected courts and judicial process. (We must keep in mind that tyranny may mark the conduct of an individual, a group or government itself.)

What stands between the tyrant and the citizen, as we have noted, is law, usually the constitution. The instrument through which law or constitution speaks is the court. The Law, conceived of as a real existence dwelling apart and alone, speaks through the voice of the court. The Law impinges upon mankind, not more because it exists than because the court has given it voice. The will of the dictator is thwarted, if at all, because of what the court has declared the law to be. In its final analysis, the inevitable clash is not between two abstractions, Dictatorship and Law, but between Dictatorship personified in an individual or group and Law personified in the court.

So, the character, composition and powers of courts are matters of profound and unholy concern to dictators. An independent judiciary, able, learned, and incorruptible, is anathema to the dictator. To him the court alone may say "Thus far and no farther shall you go." In his hot quest of power, in his trampling upon human rights, the sole agency to challenge the dictator's will is these interpreters of the law. So upon them war is declared.

The tactics of this warfare have been varied and nefarious. In earlier times there was direct action, such as chopping off the head of the judge or sending him into exile, as was done with Aristides, the Just. There have been, among other devices, impeachment, transfer of jurisdiction from civilian to military tribunals, limitation of authority, setting up of "people's courts," and change in method of appointment of judges. Whatever the method, the inspiration has been the judge's assertion of individual rights against autocratic will. The object has been to secure compliant tribunals.

Perhaps the most dastardly of all tactics is the sapping and undermining of public confidence in the court. This is a form of judicial character assassination which hardly attains to the dignity of slander. To be effective, properly to discharge his function, the judge must enjoy public confidence and respect. Whatever tends to deprive him of either tends to render him impotent and to make his labors futile. To the extent that the righteous judge is lowered from the pedestal upon which mankind has placed him he becomes valueless to society. Since, more than any other, he personifies the law, the creation of disrespect for him and for the judicial office creates disrespect for law.

The public, taught such disrespect by its leaders, is ripe for rebellion against law. Hence, the demagogue, aggrieved by a judicial decision asserting the rights of a minority, for example, first attacks the court which rendered the decision, inflames the people against the court, and then leads them in resistance to the decision. Thus, personal abuse is the prelude to anarchy. Thus, rights guaranteed by a constitution are nullified.

Such, then, historically, are the methods of tyrants or

demagogues. (The terms may be used interchangeably.) The formula is simple: By decree or legislative act strike down constitutional guarantees; and undermine confidence in courts to the point that their decrees have no public acceptance. Either alone would probably be effective. Taken together they inevitably insure the temporary success of tyranny, whether it be the tyranny of an individual, a clique or a majority. Under such a regime the rights of a minority are doomed.

Uses of those methods are the badges of tyranny or dictatorship. We may see that clearly by the backward view. We see it much more clearly than those who lived through the usurpation of power. When Hitler, for example, rushed his decrees through the Reichstag, millions of patriotic Germans gave assent without realizing for a moment that they were surrendering their liberties to his lust for power. Greater vision is required to discern the pattern of dictatorship in events to which one is party. In the capacity to discern, we are more likely to be affected with presbyopia than with myopia.

We have been concerned thus far only with affirmative action to destroy constitutional rights, best typified by the decree, the edict or the legislative act. But such rights may also be negatively destroyed. Here the procedure is relatively simple: Merely fail to support or uphold the rights. The results are identical in either case; individuals have been denied rights which the constitution and courts have said are theirs. There is no difference in morals or in practical effect between suspension of constitutional right by formal decree, on the one hand, and by non-enforcement, on the other. The individual whose home has been searched without a warrant, whose printing presses have been stopped, or who has been kept out of a school is hardly concerned with the precise method used to deprive him of a right the constitution and court have said were his. All that concerns him is that he has been the victim of despotic power.

One struck by lightning is only academically interested in whether the bolt which hit him is positive or negative electricity.

The states of the Southern Confederacy are classic examples of both kinds of tyranny...positive and negative. From their creation as colonies until 1865 slavery was part of their organic law. Slavery, of course, is the ultimate in tyranny. After a brief interregnum, segregation, slavery's twin, became embedded in law. So, until the Supreme Court in the Brown School Case and others, struck down the segregation laws, the governmental power of the Southern states was exerted to enforce an inferior status upon millions of blacks. That was bald, naked, legal tyranny, positive in nature.

The South did not take the decisions supinely. Little men in high stations began to pick such brains as they had in efforts to evade the consequences of the court's decrees. Even short memories will be triggered by such terms as "interposition," "freedom of choice," "the Pearsall Plan," "massive resistance"—a host of slimy devices concocted to preserve the region's caste system. Impeach Earl Warren billboards became a feature of the landscape. Official and editorial abuse of judges was some of the mental pabulum which was fed to Southern whites. Non-enforcement of legally established rights of blacks, while waning, is still part of Southern public policy. Non-enforcement of a legal right is negative tyranny.

Among architects of this Southern strategy were such men as Wallace of Alabama, Faubus of Arkansas, Byrd of Virginia, Byrnes and Thurmond of South Carolina, Hodges of North Carolina, Eastland of Mississippi and Talmadge of Georgia. Their creation was tyranny. How will history characterize the creators?

A blurred and wavy line separates civil rights from civil liberties. In the latter area at the moment there are portents which may well alarm the American citizen and prod him to vigilance. There are palpable threats to his liberties.

The classic pattern emerged. Attacks on the courts varying in tone from subtle to strident, are part of the administration strategy. President Nixon, for example, during his campaign, repeatedly stated: "Some of the courts have gone too far to weaken the peace forces as against the criminal forces."

In his secret session with Southern delegates at the Miami convention, the candidate promised that, if elected, he would find a Chief Justice who would "interpret the law...and not make it." He stated that "The federal government has got to set an example. But instead of setting an example of law enforcement, we have been setting an example of law softness."

Attorney General Mitchell, testifying before the Senate Criminal Laws Sub-Committee, spoke of his "great disappointment" at the Supreme Court "bugging ruling" requiring that transcripts of illegal electronic eavesdropping must be turned over to the defendant. And, before the International Association of Chiefs of Police in Miami in 1969 he asserted "There has been a tendency to ignore the law enforcement community in favor of social scientists."

The Washington *Post* of May 9, 1970, reported that FBI Director, J. Edgar Hoover, accused judges in Washington state, Missouri, Virginia, Detroit, Philadelphia and the District of Columbia of being too lenient with offenders.

If exile were still in vogue, as in the days of Athens, there seems little doubt that judges deemed liberal by the administration would have joined Aristides, the Just.

Harking back to Chancellor Metternich and the Carlsbad Decrees, mentioned earlier, the attack upon professors and students who dissent from administration policy appears in full swing. In administration eyes they too have "propagated harmful doctrines...subversive of existing governmental institutions" a term synonymous with "critical of foreign and domestic policy."

Candidate Nixon set the tone in an attack upon New Jersey Governor Richard J. Hughes, a Democrat. Governor Hughes has sustained the right of Professor Genovese* of Rutgers University to speak openly and critically of this nation's role in the Vietnam War. Characteristically, Mr. Nixon used the approach designed to stir latent prejudices when he said:

*Eugene Genovese.

I do not raise the question of Professor Genovese's right to be for segregation or integration, for free love or celibacy, for communism or anarchy, or anything else...in peace time. But the United States is at war...Leadership requires that the governor step in and put the security of the nation above the security of the individual.

The following nuggets taken from various Agnew speeches:

Speaking to students who heckled him at Towson State College, he opined "Mao supplies the philosophy while Daddy supplies the money."

In another campaign speech referring to the campus dissenters, Agnew said, "I think a lot of them are connected with foreign powers and have received instruction from active Communist leaders of the world."

At a Republican fund raising dinner at Hollywood Beach, Florida, in April, 1970, referring to disorders on the Yale campus, Agnew said:

I can well understand the attitude of the majority of the student body at Yale University when most of the Yale faculty votes to endorse a strike in support of members of an organization dedicated to criminal violence, anarchy, and the destruction of the United States of America...it is clearly time for the alumni of that fine old college to demand that it be headed by a more mature and responsible person. (Referring to President Brewster)

At Houston, Texas, at another Republican fund raising dinner in May, 1970, Mr. Agnew referred to a "small hardcore of hell-raisers" on campus:

It is my honest opinion that this hardcore of faculty

and students should be identified and dismissed from the otherwise healthy body of the college community; lest they, like a cancer, destroy it.

And at Citizen's Testimonial Dinner in New Orleans, Agnew declared

Education is being redefined at the demand of the uneducated to suit the ideas of the uneducated...A spirit of national masochism prevails, encouraged by an effete corps of impudent snobs who characterize themselves as intellectuals.

Mr. Agnew had the support of Attorney General Mitchell who, early in his term of office, told Sarah McClendon, a reporter, that "These campus riot leaders make it easy for foreign governments to make dupes of us."

Mr. Hoover also did his bit:

Increased campus disorders involving black students pose a definite threat to the nation's stability and security and indicate need for increase in both quality and quantity of intelligence information.

In support of the legislation of the "No-Knock" and "Preventive Detention" variety the Attorney General has uttered some startling legal contentions. For example:

The government merely contends that when the President, through the Attorney General, determines that the use of electronic surveillance is necessary to gather intelligence information needed to protect the national security, the resulting search and infringement of constitutional rights is not 'unreasonable'.

gain Mr. Mitchell:

In view of the enormous increase in reported crime, the limitation of pre-trial detention to capital offenses makes no sense at all...I believe that danger to the community must be made a significant consideration in the ultimate decision to release a suspect.

But Mr. Mitchell was outdone by Deputy Attorney General ichard Kleindienst:

You can't divide subversion into two parts...domestic and foreign. It would be silly to say that an American citizen, because he is an American, could subvert the Government by actions of violence and revolution and be immune from first, identification, and second, persecution.

he speech from which this quotation is taken was in defense of overnmental eavesdropping.

The views expressed by Nixon, Agnew, Mitchell and Hoover o not constitute idle oratory. They represent settled convic- ions as to the right of government to curtail traditional liberties f American citizens. Their views have flowered into actual or roposed legislation.

Already Congress has enacted the District of Columbia Court Reform and Criminal Procedure Act. This contains the notorious o knock and preventive detention features. The former permits olice to burst into a home or an apartment without identifying hemselves or knocking. The latter permits confinement in jail or 60 days without bail or other charge than that the incarce- ated person is "dangerous." So far as is known, "danger- usness" is an entirely new crime in American jurisprudence.

In the Senate a bill (S-2600) is pending to make preventive etention a feature of federal practice in all states.

As to "defense facilities," there are strict legal limitation upon conduct, no doubt necessary as precautions agains' sabotage. However, House Bill 14864 changes the definition o' defense facility so as to bring public utilities, schools and practi cally all factories within the meaning of the term.

A Senate bill (S-3976) authorizes the government or indivi duals to obtain an injunction in federal court against possibl heckling at public gatherings. No gift of prophecy is required t foresee the gagging of stockholders who might ask embarrassin questions of management, or voters who seek to punctur pretensions of demagogues.

Senate bill 3563 seeks to nullify Supreme Court decisions a to arrest and detention. If the bill becomes a law, a person ma be arrested and detained without a showing of probable cause The bill's purpose is to give the public time to take action forbidden by a series of Supreme Court decisons holding tha such police actions could not be taken until charges were file and arraignment completed. These actions include fingerprintin and securing samples of handwriting, blood and urine.

Each of these vicious legislative proposals represents a encroachment upon historic liberties of the citizen. Governmen intrudes upon areas heretofore deemed privileged and sacred Repression of liberties is tyranny.

The tyrant, as we have heretofore seen, may be, not a individual, but government itself. But individuals steer govern ment to adopt policies. to pursue courses. Their technique, a we have also seen, is to create fear of imminent public peril an to represent the proposed repressive actions as necessary for th public safety.

Government in the instant case speaks through Presiden Nixon, Vice-President Agnew and Attorney General Mitchell They create the fear; they propose the policies; they fill th ancient roles of public savior.

Not decay of our cities, not poverty, not unemployment, no massive accumulations of wealth in a few hands, not pollutior

f our environment...not these or any of them, but the
Communists, the militant blacks and the disgruntled college
students pose the genuine, the real threats to our security. Thus
say the administrative spokesmen.

Desperate diseases require desperate remedies. So...wire-
tapping, bugging, government surveillance, police dossiers, paid
informers, spies at public meetings, infiltration of campuses, and
all the rest are justified. In face of such somber perils, individual
rights must be abridged or stifled. So runs the argument. Hitler,
Mussolini and Stalin used the same line.

How right was Plato! Tyranny develops by planting in men's
minds the belief of vast national peril. To avert it men are
persuaded to surrender cherished personal liberties. Such
surrender is necessary if the republic is to survive. So reads the
script...from Nero to Nixon.

What we now behold is the ugly image of tyranny. Dress it
up in all the pretty words in the dictionary, it is still tyranny. It
follows the historic pattern. It uses the tools. Its leaders strike
the poses. It seeks the same ends. Unchecked, it will run the
same course.

IT NOT ONLY *CAN* HAPPEN HERE. IT *IS* HAPPENING
HERE!

Excerpts from an address by Wright on March 23, 1972, T. C. Robertson High School, Asheville, North Carolina.

THE STUDENT AND CIVIL LIBERTIES

In the memory of most of you, in the South there we statutes and ordinances requiring that people of different rac sit in different sections of grandstands or theaters, atter separate schools, play on separate golf courses and the like. Th was a shameful chapter in our history, now happily behind u One of the principal reasons it is behind us is because your people of both races exercised the right, guaranteed by the Fir Amendment, of assembly and protest. There were sit-in marches, public street corner meetings, all to condemn th senseless effort to drive a wedge between our people. For college boys in Greensboro began it all by going into restaurant and ordering a cup of coffee. If the Boston Tea Par began the American political revolution, the Greensboro Coff Party began the Southern social revolution. There should be monument for these four brave boys.

If there had been no First Amendment, those boys mig possibly still be in jail. Many were jailed for marching in th protest. But, in every case where marches and demonstration were conducted peaceably, the First Amendment secured the release.

Such, then, are civil liberties—the liberty to think, to spea to hear, to read, to worship or not, and peaceably to assemb and protest any policy of government with which we disagre The rebel, the dissenter, the freethinker—all are protected i giving vent and expression to any idea, however it may clas with prevailing opinion....

Our national permission to the citizen to exercise all of h civil liberties has been proven by time to be the wisest policy c

vernment. We enjoy religious liberty and our religious bodies
e at peace with each other. But elsewhere—Buddhists fight
tholics in Vietnam, Catholics fight Protestants in North
eland, Jews fight Moslems in the near East, Moslems fight
ndus in India.

Our national government has survived and prospered for 196
ars. Survey the world—Russia has had its revolution; monarchy
s perished in Germany, Austria, Hungary, Spain, Italy, and
ewhere throughout the world. Apparently only those
untries which grant to their citizens liberties such as are found
re—in England and the Scandinavian countries, for example—
n no risk of overthrow.

ROLE OF AMERICAN CIVIL LIBERTIES UNION

These liberties have not survived unnourished and unattended.
ternal vigilance is the price of liberty." For 50 years the
nerican Civil Liberties Union has been the guardian and watch-
g of our intellectual freedom. It has been, and is, waging war
ainst "every form of tyranny over the minds of men," to use
nomas Jefferson's memorable phrase. In the millennium when
victories have been won, government will no longer concern
elf with the tastes, the manners, the private morals of men
d women, the way they dress, or wear their hair, or criticize
eir government, or pray publicly, or salute the flag. In short,
vernment will keep its cotton picking fingers off the citizen
less his conduct presents a real and present threat to others or
government itself.

Some of our politicians are forever seeking to preserve some-
ing they call "our Southern way of life." A way of life that is
zen or static is not worth preserving. The only way of life
rth preserving is one which is constantly changing. Change is
oduced, not by merely tolerating, but by actually encouraging,

diversity of opinion and action. Thus we will prove the truth o
Plato's dictum that, "Democracy is a charming form of govern
ment, full of variety and disorder."

FEAR OF THE OUTSIDER

I hope an early casualty of this new freedom will be th
phrase "outside interference." Daily our leaders tell us about i
Always somebody up North is trying to "ram something dow
our throats."

No state can engage in a more fruitless enterprise than th
effort to exclude ideas from finding lodgement in the minds o
its citizens, whether on the campus of a state university or in
country crossroads store. Only a year or so ago our own stat
tried by law to prevent people holding certain views from
speaking at state institutions. Through the efforts of th
American Civil Liberties Union the courts throttled, at birth
this excursion into thought control....

The constant effort, indeed the passion, of the civil liber
tarian is to release *all* of man's creative energy, not merely s
much as society pleases. It is beyond the competence of govern
ment to proscribe or limit what the citizen shall read, or write
or hear, or print, or see, or wear, or with whom he sha
associate or for what purposes he shall meet with his fellows
Our purpose is, in short, to allow every man to make a fool o
himself if he wants to. Because only in such an atmosphere, ca
every man also become a genius if he makes up his mind to it
Democracy must take its risks.

Surely there is nothing in human history to support the belie
that, in the private life of the citizen, his morals, his philosophy
his religion, in the vast empire of his thoughts or acts which d
not present an immediate threat to public safety governmen
should for a moment intrude. Those are sacred preserves, int

which the entry of government is a form of profanation.

The eternal quest is for freedom. If thwarted at home, genius withers or seeks a more congenial clime. Witness the exodus of writers, artists, poets, philosophers, and scientists from Germany under Hitler and from Russia under a succession of despotic regimes.

Only in an atmosphere of complete freedom may the arts and graces of life come to full flower, may men be encouraged to become artists, poets, philosophers, capable critics of the world in which they live.

The end result of all that the civil libertarian undertakes to do is to produce a society in which conformity is not the chief end and aim of man; in which the goal of the individual is not respectable, but worthy; in which a man is free to march to a different drummer and to follow his own star, wherever it may lead. In the congenial sunlight and warmth of that kind of world, in a truly free society, spirits soar and the latent talents of men wax and burgeon....

The tools of the civil liberties efforts are, of course, law books and cases and decisions. But the aim is far more than winning a case, or even protecting the rights of some wretch in the prisoner's dock. It is nothing less than the emancipation of the human spirit and enabling all men to breath the free air of a diverse society.

This address was given by Marion A. Wright before th
Boone, North Carolina chapter of the North Carolina Civ
Liberties Union, on February 10, 1976.

CIVIL LIBERTIES AND A DIVERSE SOCIETY

I was brought up with the view, as I am sure you were, tha
whatever was written by the ancients packed a great deal c
wisdom. It has taken me a long time to outgrow that belief, t
come to feel that even the ancients had their share of simpletor
or merely mistaken men, probably no more and no less than w
have them today. Horace wrote that "Homer himself hath bee
observed to nod." No doubt Horace occasionally snoozed an
lesser Greeks and Romans had longer lapses into forgetfulne:
and error.

What has started me on this train of reflection is something
read a day or so ago. It was written about 2600 B.C. by a
Egyptian named Ptahhotep. (I am sure my pronunciation
wrong.) But this man wrote: "To resist him that is set i
authority is evil."

Now, I know nothing of Ptahhotep, but of some things I ar
sure: he had nothing in common with Shadrach, Meshack an
Abenego. He did not influence Moses who led his people out c
the house of bondage. So, he was fairly well discredited in h
own country. Abroad his doctrine fell upon the deaf ears c
such men as Martin Luther, Voltaire, Tom Paine, Thoreau
George Washington, and that later Martin Luther, whose la:
name is King. Finally, we may be sure he was not a member c
the Egyptian Civil Liberties Union.

Indeed, from Egyptian days to the present, many of history'
more lustrous chapters have recorded man's resistance to unjus
authority. The ages which grip and move us are not those c
supine acceptance of tyranny. They are the colorful and flashin

and militant periods when men turned at last upon the oppressor, confronted him at Runnymede, at Concord, at Wittenberg, at the Bastille, and in hundreds of other demonstrations of man's determination to be free.

We may be thankful that relatively few of these demonstrations were military in nature. The vast majority were in the civil domain, where the courage required is moral, rather than physical. The action was by one man, unpropped, unbuttressed, unsupported by the congenial and comforting presence of others sharing his ordeal. They were such men as John Peter Zenger, who dared to print the truth in his New York paper; Roger Williams, banished from Massachusetts for advocating separation of church and state; Mrs. Anne Hutchinson, who pleaded for freedom in all matters of religion; and unnumbered Quakers, Jews, Catholics, Moravians, Abolitionists, Freemasons, evolutionists, pacifists and integrationists, right on down to the present day.

Not to go beyond our own shores, the long and honorable company stretching from John Peter Zenger to the present day has not heeded the voice of Ptahhotep, saying that resistance to authority is evil. Rather have they harkened to Thomas Jefferson: "I have sworn on the altar of Almighty God eternal hostility to every form of tyranny over the mind of man."

The Civil Liberties Union is a confirmed protester. When there exist such groups as the John Birch Society, or the Ku Klux Klan, or the White Citizens Council, or there is to be found the spirit which they engender, there is grist for the ACLU mill. It usually appears in court as *amicus curiae*, or friend of the court.

The phrase *"amicus curiae"* has always seemed to me to be a misnomer. ACLU is not primarily a friend of the court. (If you doubt that, ask several Southern judges whose names I can supply.) It is, in only a narrow sense, friend of the poor devil who stands before the court. It is his friend in the sense that the right he asserts is one of common concern to all mankind. Its role might be more appropriately described by another Latin phrase—"*amicus humani generis*"—friend of the human race. (I like to use a Latin phrase now and then for the same reason Winston Churchill said he occasionally drank water—just to show you I can.)

In the profoundest sense those who assert with vigor the right of protest are the true friends of the state. It may not so appear to the aggressive state whose over-zealous investigative committees are sometimes thwarted; whose policemen are held to restrictive standards of decency, or whose prosecuting attorneys are denied the privilege of wire-tapping. But such methods tend to belittle and denigrate the citizen... The truly wise state will display zeal in protecting the rights of its citizens even against itself. Such a policy tends to develop and enlarge the citizen, to give him a deserved sense of his dignity and intrinsic worth. With such a citizenship every great thing may be accomplished by the state.

How have our states measured up to that standard?

Let us turn now to a lesson we may draw from medicine. The difficulty in performing a transplant of a kidney or heart is rejection by the host of the new organ. The old body tends to reject the new, even though rejection means death and adoption may mean life.

Unfortunately, that phenomenon is not limited to medicine. It seems to be a law of life. One of the significant current cliches is the expression "alien and hostile." It reveals much. Whatever is foreign is inimical. Whatever is alien is hostile. Some of us view with suspicion all ideas not developed by the home folks.

Consider names of a few of our diseases and pests: Spanish influenza, German measles, Asiatic cholera. Dutch elm blight, Mexican boll weevil, Mediterranean fruit fly, English sparrow—all evil imports. Who ever heard of Carolina pine beetle or Southern malaria?

So with ideas. The first impulse of government is to reject

any ideas not indigenous to this soil. Social security and the office of ombudsman originated in Scandinavia a century ago. Social security was not adopted here until the Great Depression of the Thirties drove us to it. The ombudsman idea here is now in its embryonic stage. You may still strangle at birth any idea by describing it as Communistic.

The ACLU exists in recognition of this official tendency to reject whatever threatens to disturb the status quo. Its primary purpose is to see that any idea—however hostile to the existing order it may be—shall have a forum, the right to test itself in the market place. Hence, its eternal quest is to allow men and women to think and believe what they please, to speak, to write, to print, to exhort, to petition, to protest, to their heart's content.

Society must develop antidotes for its poisons. Hence every state needs chapters of the Civil Liberties Union. They are curbs and restraints upon the tendency of government to abuse its raw power. Government is concerned with self-preservation. When small men control that power they regard as a threat any idea or movement which seeks to change the status quo.

One must assert with shame that, perhaps as much as in any other American state, this narrow view of governments' role is now evident in North Carolina.

Rev. W.W. Finlator, of Raleigh, known affectionately to many of us here as Bill, recently wrote in the Raleigh *News and Observer*:

> *Let me say it as kindly, as directly and as painlessly as possible: North Carolina, which for many years enjoyed the reputation of the most open, most progressive, most freedom loving state in the South, has now, in our day, become in the eyes of the world the most regressive state in the Union.*

Bill Finlator is a long time Baptist minister in Raleigh. He is chairman of the North Carolina Advisory Committee to the Commission on Civil Rights. He knows what he is talking about.

So does Tom Wicker, native of this state, long a writer for the Winston-Salem papers and now columnist for the New York *Times*. Sadly his conclusion parallels Finlator's.

What are some items in this somber indictment?

The bloody assault on Gastonia strikers; the prosecution of Julius Scales arising from his Communist beliefs or associations; the persecution of Boyd Payton of Charlotte for leadership of a strike in the textile industry; the relentless crack-down on draft-resisters and conscientious objectors; the unattainable bail required and tragically long sentences imposed upon black activists; the relentless hounding of a black dentist of Monroe on a kidnapping charge, finally dropped, because he allegedly detained a white couple for two hours during a violent racial disturbance, and finally the enactment of the "speaker ban" law, designed to deprive students at state institutions from hearing unorthodox ideas.

Throughout history men have tried to protect themselves by walls. The Chinese Wall, the Maginot Line, and more recently the Berlin Wall. All have been failures. All prove what Robert Frost said years ago, "Something there is which doesn't love a wall, that wants it down."

But the most absurd of all endeavors is to try to erect a wall against ideas. The Iron Curtain, the last great experiment in that field, leaks like a sieve. You cannot quarantine against an idea. You cannot place an embargo on thought.

No state can engage in a more fruitless enterprise than the effort to exclude ideas from finding lodgement in the minds of its citizens, whether on the campus of a state university or in a country crossroads store.

As charming and as nearly perfect as we Americans may be, surely none of us will deny that there is an advantage in cross-fertilization of ideas and standards of value. The introduction of a foreign element, an element from the outside, has been the factor which has enabled all forms of life, plant and animal, to evolve into richer, newer and more beautiful expressions of creation.

We have heard it said, not so much in recent years as formerly, that a section of this country was made great by its pure white, Anglo-Saxon population, and by its deep attachment to fundamentalist religion. I belive that, in the consideration of the recent immigration bill, a Senator from North Carolina uttered some such sentiments. Let us test that for just a moment.

You and I live in what is known as Appalachia. In the mountain counties of the Appalachian Range I presume that there exists the highest percentage of white, Protestant, fundamentalist, Anglo-Saxon population to be found anywhere on this continent. It has been there since the early settlers first moved into these hills and valleys. The North and the East had their waves of migration by the Irish, the Italian, the Puerto Rican, and every other race and conditions of men. They brought with them differing ideas, differing cultures, differing religions. Meanwhile, we of the Appalachian region continued largely unaffected by these tides of migration. Unaffected, while the northwest and central west were receiving hordes of Germans, Swedes, Norwegians, Chinese, Japanese and the like.

What is the result? What do we find? The North, the East and the West have vastly outstripped the South. It is being merely mathematically accurate to point out that in any table of statistics reflecting the degree of civilization of states, the region between the Potomac and the Gulf ranks at the bottom.

And, while this may be painful to some of us, it is only fair to point out that the region known as Appalachia, with its monolithic white, Anglo-Saxon, Protestant, fundamentalist components, is the section of the country recognized by the federal government and by the nation as a whole as being in such desperate plight that billions have to be poured into the task of bringing our citizenship up to the national level.

If any lesson is to be found in this, I think it is that there is value in variety—variety of races, variety of cultures, variety of religions, variety of ideas and variety of a scale of values. Variety is not merely the spice of life; it is almost the secret of life. And infinite variety, as the poet assures us, is the factor which prevents custom from staling and age from withering.

Erasmus wrote some centuries ago: "England is a country of one religion and fifty desserts. I would rather have a country of fifty religions and one dessert."

So, by a round-about way, I come back to my thesis. There are beauty and life in a diverse society, as a great tapestry exhibits vari-colored strands, or a great symphonic orchestra contains instruments of varying tone and timbers. Dullness and drabness characterize the society in which all seem to think alike. And, where all *seem* to think alike, no one is *actually* thinking at all.

As Richard Jefferies wrote in *The Story of My Heart*: "Let me exhort everyone to do his utmost to think outside and beyond our present circle of ideas. For every idea gained is a hundred years of slavery remitted."

A native of this state, a man of great distinction, Walter Hines Page, while ambassador to England, writing to President Woodrow Wilson in the year 1915, referring to certain segments of North Carolina society said this: "These men held the country and all the people back in almost the same economic and social state in which slavery left them. There was no hope for the future under their domination. There would be no broadening of thought because only old thoughts were acceptable. No change in society because society's chief concern was to tolerate no change."

Even if that picture may be overdrawn and even if it applied to a situation which existed five decades ago, at least we may draw from this utterance the conclusion that what is not needed in North Carolina is a temper and an atmosphere which are hostile to change. And there is at least no crying need for the type of mentality which is concerned only with economic progress.

What is needed, therefore, is a new type of citizen. We need men and women who are more concerned with the arts, the humanities and the social betterment of all mankind. We need men and women who are concerned about the art of living—living as an art. As Paul Green, the Chapel Hill playwright, wrote sometime ago: "There is more to existence than the creation of foods and services, of barter and trade, of growing crops and selling them. In every man there burns a primal impulse, an urge to the making of a more pleasing and beautiful world."

All of the arts—literature, poetry, music, drama, architecture, philosophy, cirticism, painting, sculpture, dancing—all of these are the glory our lives and the essential virtues of a civilization.

What does all of this have to do with civil liberties?

The germ of civilization is chilled by a repressive society. It flowers in a society in which there are no artificial limits upon man's self-expression in thought, in the arts, in aesthetics. It is no mere coincidence that the world's greatest works of art and its noblest philosophy were produced in one small city-state, Athens, where and when the purest democracy was developed. On the contrary, the present day dictatorship in Russia demands that all of the arts must be handmaidens of the state, serve state policy. Pasternak and Solzhenitsyn, acclaimed by all free societies, are condemned at home. No one knows how many more Russian geniuses were throttled by the infecting and corrosive fingers of the state.

When one thinks of the Civil Liberties Union the pictures his mind conjures up are of law books, court rooms and lawyers defending some poor devil who has paraded without a permit, or who has said a kind word about Communism, or let his hair grow beyond prescribed lengths....

When one joins and supports this Union he demonstrates his determination that everywhere in America, here in North Carolina, we shall have a part in the eternal struggle toward a humane and civilized society.

Death Penalty and Prison Reform

While a high school boy, living in Trenton, South Carolina, Wright had as a neighbor United States Senator Benjamin Ryan (Pitchfork Ben) Tillman, one of the earliest and certainly the ablest of the Southern politicians who rode to national prominence on the race issue.

The Senator, who was a self-educated scholar, maintained an excellent private library which Wright used extensively. Among his favorite volumes was one entitled something like *Modern Eloquence*, a collection of speeches and essays on a variety of topics. One of the speeches was an argument against the death penalty. By present-day standards it would probably be considered florid and over-blown. Wright had no such reservations. From age 16 he was dedicated to the abolition of capital punishment.

At that age he became a freshman at the University of South Carolina. From his sophomore year, 1910-1911, until he finished law school in 1919, he was from time to time a reporter and finally city editor of the Columbia, South Carolina *Record*. In 1912, South Carolina abolished the gallows and substituted the electric chair. As the youngest and lowest paid man on the staff Wright was assigned the job of reporting the first electrocution. It was the first of sixteen such sombre assignments. His academic objections to the death penalty, formed in Senator Tillman's library, became a visceral revulsion. To paraphrase Jefferson, he swore on the altar of Almighty God eternal hostility to legalized murder.

Constantly he wrote and spoke against the penalty. After retiring from the practice of law in 1947, he moved to North Carolina. Here he assisted in organizing, and became the first president of North Carolinians Against the Death Penalty.

Wright's early concern with the death penalty and prison reform found expression in June 1925, in a speech made before the Alumni Association of the University of South Carolina from which the following excerpts are taken.

EXCERPTS FROM SPEECH BEFORE THE ALUMNI ASSOCIATION OF THE UNIVERSITY OF SOUTH CAROLINA

For many, many years the psychologists have been demonstrating that no two memories have exactly the same power of retention; that men unconsciously remember what they want to remember and forget what they want to forget—conscientious men, mind you. Yet the law smugly assumes that if two men are honest and witness the same occurrence they will see, hear and relate exactly the same version of what happened. In other words the courts accept as an axiom what science has demonstrated to be untrue.

But it is in the treatment of the criminal that the law perpetrates its grossest absurdities. We send men to the penitentiary—why? For one reason, we are told, to reform them, so that when they are released they may become useful members of society. And in order to reform the criminal we give him as his only associates during the reformative process scores of other men who the law has said are anti-social in their tendencies. We throw him with those who can only teach him more crime, who can only fill his head with bitterness toward the law and the state, and at the end of, say, five years, five years of confinement behind steel bars like some wild animal, five years under the rifle of the guard, five years of bowing and smirking and scraping in the presence of authority, five years of shaved heads and prison garbs, five years of elbow rubbing with depravity, we pronounce him reformed and ready to take his place in society. Yet how inconsistent we are! Let some crime be committed later and the ex-convict whom the State has reformed is the first suspect of the police. And when he is tried the prosecuting attorney usually manages to let it be known that the man in the dock has served a term in jail so that the jury will understand that the law of probabilities is against him. Reform him—where is the man who believes it? Yet we continue to mouth about punishment as a means of reformation.

In South Carolina there seems to be little difference of opinion on the point that prisons and chain gangs as now managed are necessary institutions and that an effort to humanize them is trying to coddle the criminal. Ancient institutions, they must be treated with proper respect. The old rut again.

In taking into consideration the factors of heredity and environment as causes of crime—the ABC of criminology—nothing has been done. Of course, the far subtler matters of the influence of seasons on conduct, and of predisposing mental states short of positive insanity—why, the very suggestion is irreverent. One hears no question raised as to the efficacy of capital punishment to deter men from crime. There is not a whisper anywhere that the State should not set an example in murder.

The opening shot in Wright's effort to abolish the death penalty in North Carolina was fired at the Linville Falls, N.C. Community Church on August 5, 1964. His speech on that occasion was printed in the October 1964, issue of *New South*. The speech follows.

CAPITAL PUNISHMENT

Capital punishment is the penalty of death inflicted by law. The life of a man, convicted of crime, is snuffed out by the state. What is the creature whom society exterminates? One answer is given by the Psalmist:

> *When I consider thy heavens, the work of thy fingers; the moon and the stars, which thou hast ordained;*
> *What is man, that thou art mindful of him? and the son of man, that thou visitest him?*
> *For thou hast made him a little lower than the angels, and hast crowned him with a glory and honour.*
> *Thou madest him to have dominion over the works of thy hands; thou hast put all things under his feet...*

So it is a creation of God, one made a little lower than the angels, that society destroys, as you or I would crush a spider or a worm under our heels. It is as though one took a sledge hammer and smashed to bits a masterpiece of Michelangelo or slashed to ribbons Leonardo da Vinci's *Mona Lisa*.

Captial punishment is an ancient, if not an honorable, institution. It was prescribed for certain crimes in the celebrated Code of Hammurabi, who ruled over Babylon from 2067 to 2025 B.C. There are frequent references to it in the Old

Testament and in Roman law in the times of Justinian. So it has survived for four or five thousand years. But, as the centuries have unfolded, punishment by death has undergone profound changes in the crimes for which it has been inflicted, in the method of execution and in the circumstances under which sentences have been carried out.

From certain passages in Leviticus, and Exodus, Deuteronomy and Numbers we learn that in those times, the death penalty was inflicted for adultery, bestiality, blasphemy, cursing father or mother, idolatry, incest, rape, sabbath breaking, unchastity, and witchcraft.

Under Roman law it was inflicted for treason, adultery, sodomy, murder, forgery by slaves, corruption, kidnapping under certain circumstances, seduction, and rape.

From this beginning as punishment for relatively few crimes, in England the number of crimes skyrocketed to the point that more than 200 offenses carried the penalty. Among them during the reign of George III were: shoplifting to the amount of five shillings; consorting a year with gypsies; breaking the head of a fish pond; cutting down an ornamental tree in a park; coining, sheep stealing; horse poisoning; forgery; damaging Putney, London or Westminister bridges; stealing apples from an orchard; stealing in a dwelling house; being found armed and disguised in a park at night; highway robbery; stealing geese from a commons; bigamy; sacrilege; damaging the rail or chain or a turnpike gate; rick burning; cultivating the tobacco plant in England; and smuggling.

Under the grim mood of the time of George III—the period of the American Revolution—small boys were actually hanged for stealing apples from an orchard. How many of us would be alive today if that practice were still followed?

In England, it is now inflicted for only four crimes—willful murder, treason, piracy and arson. And every year parliament comes closer and closer to its complete abolition. The story is the same everywhere else in the civilized world—the list of capital crimes is steadily reduced or it is entirely abolished.

The idea seemed at one time to be to make death as bitter and cruel as man's savage ingenuity could make it. At one time or another, pursuant to law, men were torn to pieces by horses attached to arms and legs of the victim. They were broken on slowly revolving wheels. They were skinned alive. They were burned at the stake. Their flesh was ripped from them by the cat-o-nine-tails. A screw applied to the back of the neck was slowly turned until the spinal cord was severed. They perished on the cross. These tortures were not inspirations of some sadistic executioner acting on his own; they were methods prescribed by law. No man has ever been more cruel than an impersonal state or church. Many of these victims were put to death by ecclesiastical courts. The methods of execution now in use seem most generally to be the firing squad in some countries, the guillotine in France, hanging, electrocution and the gas chamber in others.

There has been an equally notable change in the circumstances under which men have been put to death. Anyone who has read *A Tale of Two Cities* will neve forget the circumstances in England and in France at the time of the French Revolution— Madame LaFarge, as a member of a multitude, knitting away as heads were chopped off by the flashing blade in Paris; and throngs of the curious—men, women and children—watching in fascination in London while the black cap was affixed, the noose adjusted and the trap sprung. There were public spectacles, attended as the Roman attended the gladiatorial games.

Now, there is no public exhibition. A few official witnesses are let into a small room. The final drama is enacted in awesome silence before a handful of pale and shaken observers. It is as though society were ashamed of the dirty business in which it is engaged and wanted no spectators of its shame.

So the trend is steadily toward fewer crimes, more humane method and less public display. You may almost measure the advance in civilization by these developments. As men slowly move upward from barbarism they legally snuff out human life with greater reluctance, with greater humanity and with greater appreciation of the fearful solemnity of the act.

It seems entirely proper to assume the final inevitable step is the abolition of the death penalty for any crime. Reason and religion may operate feebly but they do operate upon law and custom. That operation will ultimately cause mankind to regard the electric chair and the gas chamber, along with the rack, the thumb screw and the stake, as relics of barbarity and as proof that men do ever move upward toward the stars.

Indeed, this final step has been taken by eight American states: Minnesota, North Dakota, Alaska, Hawaii, Maine, Rhode Island, Michigan and Wisconsin; in six South American countries; in the Queensland province of Australia; in Austria, Denmark, Finland, West Germany, Greenland, Iceland, Italy, Mexico, Norway, the Netherlands, New Zealand, Portugal, Republic of San Marino, Sweden and Switzerland. There are a number of countries where, though the law is still on the books, it is never invoked.

Capital punishment has been abolished because it did not do what it was supposed to do. The reason which its spokesmen gave was that it would deter the evilly disposed, keep wicked men from committing capital crimes. In an era when a 13-year-old boy was hanged for stealing a spoon and a boy of nine was hanged for stealing a few pennies' worth of merchandise from a shop window, Lord Ellenborough, Chief Justice of England, stated the argument against repeal: "I am certain that depredations to an unlimited extent would be committed...No man could trust himself an hour out of doors without the most alarming apprehensions that on his return every vestige of his property will be swept away by the hardened robber."

Judge Ellenborough, of course, was proven wrong. But not too long ago a North Carolina judge was making the same kind of predictions before a committee of his state's legislature.

One historical fact ought to dispose of the contention as to deterrent effect. In England, among the host of crimes punishable by death, was, of course, the picking of pockets. Yet, the preamble of a law passed in the reign of Queen Elizabeth reads: ,"Whereas, persons in contempt of God's commands and in defiance of the laws are found to cut pockets and pick purses even at places of public executions while executions are being done on criminals, be it therefore enacted that all such persons shall suffer death without benefit of clergy." A sufficient commentary upon the deterrent effect of the death penalty.

Fortuanately, because certain states have been willing to experiment, we now have the light of experience. Of the seven northwest central states (Minnesota, Iowa, Missouri, North Dakota, South Dakota, Nebraska and Kansas), Minnesota and North Dakota do not have the death penalty. In 1961, the entire area's rate for homicide was 1.5 per 100,000 population. Minnesota's rate was 1 and North Dakota's was 0.9. The entire area's rate for rape was 6.4. Minnesota's rate was 2.7 and North Dakota's was 5.2. The two states having abolished a capital punishment were well below the average for the region.

The same story is true in Europe. The Scandinavian countries have lower rates of capital crimes than do Great Britain, Spain, France and Ireland, the only nations of Western Europe which retain the death penalty.

If punishment has any effect, it is due to its certainty, rather than its severity. The plain truth of the matter is that as safe a gamble as one may make, if he should commit a capital crime, he will not be executed. Juries, with a naturally tender regard for human life, refuse to convict. If convicted, the appellate courts resolve all doubts in the convicted man's favor, and, finally, parole boards and governors are humanly and properly disposed to commute sentences. Only 42 executions took place in the United States in 1963. My belief is that not more than one per cent of those brought to trial on capital charges in North Carolina ever walk that last mile to the gas chamber. And my belief is that the convictions for crimes not punishable by death is much higher than for those carrying the death penalty.

Warden Clinton Duffy of San Quentin, in his book *88 Men and Two Women*, states that he has interviewed thousands of convicted murderers and not a single one said he even remotely considered punishment at the time of the crime. Generally speaking, murder is a crime of passion where the perpetrator is not thinking of the punishment consequences.

So the argument that capital punishment acts as a deterrent will not hold water. All experience is against it. And the whole case for capital punishment rests on that argument.

What are the arguments against it?

The first appeals to our sense of fair play. It is that capital punishment is inflicted mainly on the poor—those unable to hire skilled counsel to represent them. Warden Lewis E. Lawes in his book, *Twenty Thousand Years in Sing Sing* stated: "In the 12 years of my wardenship I have escorted 150 men and one woman to the death chamber and the electric chair. In ages they ranged from 17 to 63. They came from all kinds of homes and environments. In only one respect were they all alike. All of them were poor and most of them were friendless...Thus, it is seldom that it happens that a person who is able to have an eminent defense attorney is convicted of murder in the first degree. A large number of those who are executed were too poor to hire a lawyer, counsel being appointed by the state."

The death penalty also discriminates against non-whites. This is not to say that judges and juries harbor outright prejudice against Negroes and other non-whites—although it is not farfetched to suppose that some prejudice does exist. It is rather to suggest that whatever group is at the bottom of the economic ladder will have a disproportionably higher representation in the Death House. Non-whites, being at the bottom of the ladder, pay the penalty. Thus, more than half of those executed in the United States since 1930 have been Negroes. In New York during the last five years 80% of the persons sentenced to death were Negroes or Puerto Ricans, and all but two of the 13 men actually executed were either a Negro or Puerto Rican. The same pattern exists in other states.

There is a further argument for its abolition. Nations undergo periods of upheaval, of storm and stress. This may take the form of revolution and overthrow of government, as in Russia, in Cuba and in many South American countries; or it may take the form of mass hysteria, as in Salem, Massachusetts in the early 1690's when witchcraft was the great fear, or fear of the labor movement about the beginning of this century, or fear of Communist subversion which Senator McCarthy whipped up a few years ago.

Where laws permitting infliction of the death penalty are on the books, such laws are ready and convenient tools for tyrannical or merely frightened men who suddenly come to power. So Hitler, *acting under existing law,* exterminated millions of Jews—again the despised minority. So Stalin liquidated the Kulaks, or wealthy landowners of Russia, *under the existing law.* So, *under existing law,* Castro's firing squads mowed down those who opposed his regime.

Let us here in America indulge in no vainglory. In the year 1692 ten young girls of Salem, Massachusetts accused Titubia, a West Indian slave, and two old women of bewitching them. Those accusations set off a wave of hysteria. Within four months hundreds were arrested and tried for witchcraft; 19 were hanged and one pressed to death for refusing to plead. The reaction came quickly, and, in May 1693—one year from the first accusation—Governor Phelps ordered release for all persons held on the charge of witchcraft. But he could not bring back to life 20 innocent women. They were victims of mass hysteria and a statute which prescribed capital punishment for witchcraft, a crime which existed only in the minds of the illiterate and superstitious.

All competent observers now agree that the State of Massachusetts took the lives of two innocent men when, on August

23, 1927, it executed Nicola Sacco and Bartolomeo Vanzetti for murder. They had three strikes against them when they entered the dock: they were Italian immigrants; they spoke broken English; they were active in labor and Socialist circles at a time when anti-labor and anti-Socialist sentiment was rife in Massachusetts. They were executed in spite of the confession of one Celestino Madeiros that he had participated in the crime and that neither Sacco nor Vanzetti was present. True, they were victims of mass hysteria, but that hysteria used the tool of capital punishment which lay ready to hand.

So with the Rosenbergs, husband and wife, executed for espionage, an unprecedented penalty in peacetime. It was their misfortune that they were tried at the heights of the subversion fear which Senator McCarthy had whipped up. The Rosenbergs were victims of hysteria, too, but in calmer times society had devised the tool.

The point of all this is that capital punishment would have no justification even if it were inflicted only by calm, sober, intelligent and unbiased minds operating in an atmosphere of complete tranquility. The part of wisdom is to forsee that inevitably there will be periods of turmoil, stress, upheaval, when power may be exercised by the unscrupulous or by those whose reason is dethroned by popular passion. Then the margin for error, or the opportunity for abuse, is greatly enlarged. Witness the busy guillotine of the French Revolution or Castro's firing squads. In a time of domestic tranquility, we should de-fuse the dangerous weapon of capital punishment in order that it may not, in later fevered occasions, be wrongfully employed against the innocent.

But, without regard to the temper of the times in which it is inflicted, this ancient institution has robbed humanity of its noblest spirits. Socrates, with his cup of hemlock; Jesus on the cross; Joan of Arc, Bruno, John Huss, St. Stephen. The list spans the centuries and continents. Humanity has been forever impoverished by the *lawful* execution of men and women of genius and nobility guilty of no crime.

But, at the time, their executioners, judges, jurors, hangmen, butchers all—in short, society—*thought* they were guilty, thought that the world would be better off without them. And so fallible men sustained by a belief in their infallibility think today.

Capital punishment is based upon this belief in infallibility. In the case of any lesser punishment than death, errors may be corrected. There is always the parole board or the governor who may act upon a showing that justice has miscarried, that is, when the prisoner is still alive. When death in the chair or gas chamber has closed the books, all errors are beyond correction. Scattered over this land are graves of many men, innocent of crime, whom society has crushed under its heel.

The blow falls not merely upon the condemned man. For him the agony is quickly over. But there are relatives, friends, wife, children, mother, father, perhaps, who will to the end of their days wear the mantle of shame. For the murder of one man, society murders another and condemns his survivors to endless sorrow and humiliation.

Surely a civilized state in the year 1964 has wisdom enough to meet the challenge of crime without using the tools and method of the barbarian. Surely one created in the image of God—a little lower than the angels—should not be crushed, worm-like, beneath the heel of the state.

In 1965 the North Carolina General Assembly had under consideration a bill to abolish the death penalty. Paul Green, a Chapel Hill playwright, and Wright teamed up in an effort to secure the bill's passage. In addition to personal lobbying both wrote extensively. One of the written arguments prepared by Wright was printed and placed on the desks of all Senate and House members. The bill, of course, was defeated. Excerpts follow..

SHALL NORTH CAROLINA ABOLISH
THE DEATH PENALTY?

....The real question, of course, is not whether the death penalty is a *perfect* deterrent, but whether the death penalty is a *better* deterrent than imprisonment. There are a number of different ways in which this question has been studied; what follows here is a summary of the careful discussion of the subject recently published in *The Death Penalty in America* (Doubleday, 1964, pp. 258-343), edited by Hugo Adam Bedau.)

(1) The states which have the highest rate of execution have, generally, the highest rate of murder; the states which have abolished the death penalty have among the lowest rate of murder.

(2) Abolition of the death penalty has never been followed by an increase in the rate of murder.

(3) Reintroduction of the death penalty after it has been abolished has never lowered the murder rate.

(4) When neighboring states are compared, those without the death penalty do not have a higher homicide rate than those with the death penalty.

(5) Executions in a given state do not have any apparent deterrent effect on the total number of homicides in that state: there are just as many (sometimes more!) homicides after the supposedly sobering effect of a murder trial or execution as there were before.

Individual Instances

But figures, however convincing, do not produce the impact of the human experience. The National Society of Penal Information records the following:

The hanging of the notorious Kemmler at Auburn prison, New York, a few years ago, was celebrated by 24 murders in New York, 10 in New Jersey and 10 in Pittsburgh, all within the space of thirty days.

On June 21, 1877, 10 men were hanged in Pennsylvania for murderous conspiracy. The New York Herald *predicted the wholesome effect of the terrible lesson. 'We may be certain that the pitiless severity of the law will deter the most wicked from anything like imitation of these crimes.' Yet the night after the execution of these ten men, two of the witnesses at the trial had been murdered and within two weeks five of the prosecutors had met the same fate.*

In the latter part of the year 1915, Police Lieutenant Becker and four gunmen were electrocuted at Sing Sing for the murder of Rosenthal, a New York gambler. Yet, in the early months of 1916 there were five men in the death house at Sing Sing awaiting execution for murders committed under precisely similar circumstances only a few weeks after the electrocution of these five men.

In Oregon one W.R. Lloyd obtained the idea of stealing an automobile while in the Oregon State Penitentiary for forgery; the idea resulted from conversations with the Abe Evans about the crime that had put Evans in a death cell. Lloyd killed a man while stealing the automobile and followed Evans to the death cell.

North Carolina Tragedy

In a public letter Mrs. Elizabeth Bowne Wall of High Point, North Carolina wrote:

> *In 1964 Joe Graham Hughes, a Negro, declined to gamble with the gas chamber. He pleaded guilty to the rape of an elderly white woman. Automatically he drew life imprisonment. In his jail cell after the trial the sobbing prisoner disclosed that his father 33 years ago was executed in the electric chair by the State of North Carolina for the crime of rape. This now burly Negro man was a small six-year-old child at the time.*
> *What price this boy's father's life? What deterrent?*

The Death Penalty Is Unfair In Its Application

Thomas F. Eagleton, when Attorney General of Missouri, investigated the circumstances surrounding the infliction of the death penalty, more particularly the •financial, racial and social state of the condemned. His conclusions will be of interest to North Carolinians:

It has been frequently stated that capital punishment is inflicted mainly on the poor—those unable to hire skilled counsel to represent them. Warden Lewis E. Lawes in his book Twenty Thousand Years in Sing Sing *stated: 'In the 12 years of my wardenship I have escorted 150 men and one woman to the death chamber and the electric chair. In ages they ranged from 17 to 63. They came from all kinds of homes and environments. In only one respect were they all alike. All of them were poor and most of them were friendless.... Thus, it is seldom that it happens that a person who is able to have eminent defense attorneys is convicted of murder in the first degree. It is very rare indeed that such a person is executed. A large number of those who are executed were too poor to hire a lawyer, counsel being appointed by the state...*

There can be no question of the inequality of capital punishment. Such things as race, locality, and the mood of the community are ever-present determining factors.

The Southern states have accounted for over two-thirds of all the executions in this country since 1930. During this period Florida executed 35 Negroes for rape and only one white man. Georgia executed 58 Negroes and only three white men. Of 442 executed in the country for rape, 397 were Negroes. The State of Georgia has inflicted the death penalty on more people than any other state in the union.

The National Prisoner Statistics bulletin on executions cannot be read without a realization that the exaction of this, the ultimate penalty, is a glaring example of unequal justice.

An article in the October, 1964, issue of *New South* emphasizes the same point:

The death penalty also discriminates against non-whites. This is not to say that judges and juries harbor outright prejudice against Negroes and other non-whites—although it is not farfetched to suppose that some prejudice does exist. It is rather to suggest that whatever group is at the bottom of the economic ladder will have a disproportionately higher representation in the Death House. Non-whites, being at the bottom of the ladder, pay the penalty. Thus, more than half of those executed in the United States since 1930 have been Negroes. In New York during the last five years 80% of the persons sentenced to death were Negroes or Puerto Ricans, and all but two of the 13 men actually executed were either Negro or Puerto Rican. The same pattern exists in other states.

Where the Punishment Is Death Errors Committed by Fallible Courts Are Beyond Correction

"I shall ask for the abolition of the punishment of death until I have the infallibility of human judgment demonstrated to me." This was the judgment of Thomas Jefferson nearly two hundred years ago, and it remains appropriate today.

No human instrumentality is qualified to pronounce and execute an irrevocable judgment.

Sir Jas. McIntosh declared that at least one innocent man was hanged by the high court in England every three years.

Charlie Stielow was four times brought to the threshold of death by successive reprieves and finally pardoned through the discovery of his complete innocence of any connection with the murder of which he was accused.

Lord Shaw of Dunforleime, a Scottish lawyer who addressed the American Bar Association, states that he became an enemy of capital punishment through the accidental discovery of the innocence of a client, who had been convicted of murder and whom he himself had believed to be guilty.

In Oregon, John Pender was saved from execution when his sentence was commuted in 1914 because capital punishment had been abolished by a vote of the people of Oregon; another man later admitted having committed the murder for which Pender was convicted, and Pender was given a full pardon....

As reported in *Time* for February 5, 1965, one George Whitmore of New York was arrested for rape and according to police, confessed. Whitmore, a 19 year-old Negro with an IQ of 60 was slated for trial with certain conviction in prospect when investigation revealed that his confession had been secured by duress. Another diligent policeman kept up the search for the real criminal with the result that one Richard Robles was arrested and now awaits trial. Whitmore was released. *Time* reports:

> *One of Hogan's assisants declared: 'I am positive that the police prepared the confession for Whitmore just as his lawyers charged.' And he added: 'If this had not been a celebrated case, if this case hadn't got the tremendous publicity, if this was what we so-called professionals call a run-of-the-mill murder, Whitmore might well have been slipped into the electric chair and been killed for something he didn't do.'*

The New York *Times* editorialized as follows:

> *Two years ago New York became the last of the fifty states to abolish mandatory capital punishment for premeditated murder. Now, with the public appalled by 'confessions' that turn out to be fiction, removal from the lawbooks of even the option of execution is being asked.*

> *One of the first speeches from the floor, as the Legislature finally began to get around to issues, was the appeal of Assemblyman Podell of Brooklyn for abolition of capital punishment. 'We have acknowledged redress of grievances to be a natural right,' he said. 'But the dead have no redress.'*
>
> *This is recognition of the fact that innocent men have been executed in the past, and inevitably will be in the future if the penalty remains....*

The Weight Of Informed and Competent Opinion Favors Repeal

The most authoritative study of capital punishment has been made by United Nations. In its 68-page report, issued in 1962, under the heading "Position Taken by Learned Authors," the report states:

> *It will be noted that, among the leading authorities in penal science, the supporters of abolition appreciably outnumber those who favor the retention of capital punishment. The specialists of the social sciences, criminologists, sociologists, penologists, psychologists, doctors and writers on social science and criminology are, in their great majority, abolitionists. The supporters of capital punishment, apart from a number of political figures and persons holding high public office, are generally jurists with a traditional training, and judges.*

To the above generalization there are many exceptions among politicians and jurists. In the recent successful Oregon campaign for abolition the following statements were made by public figures of national importance:

I am opposed to capital punishment for three principal reasons. The largest number of those who receive the death sentence are from the lower income brackets. This would seem to indicate that this group cannot afford the necessary legal counsel which would enable them to present an effective case in their behalf.

There is a great deal of inequity in the application of capital punishment. In other words, local customs and mores appear to influence whether one who commits a capital crime will be sentenced to death. Capital punishment is final. It does not take into account the possibility of human error, and there is no room for flexibility.

Governor Mark O. Hatfield, quoted in *Pageant*, September 1961.

I believe there is no justification, as a matter of morality, in the proposition of the death penalty for a transgression against temporal law. In my judgment, the taking of human life is the prerogative of God, and not of men.

U. S. Senator Wayne Morse, letter of March 29, 1962.

Capital punishment is a carryover from the days of torture chambers and dungeons and is incompatible with modern criminology and penology. It is merely vengeful and vindictive. It is unacceptable in a state like Oregon. I will vote 'Yes' on ballot measure one to remove this scourge from our penal code.

U. S. Senator Maurine Neuberger, letter of June 4, 1964.

CONCLUSION

The foregoing by no means exhausts the arguments against the death penalty. Perhaps of equal, or even greater, significance is the argument resting upon religious or moral grounds. There is the abuse inevitable in times of public stress or turmoil. There is the cutting off of a life without possibility of reformation or rehabilitation. There is the criminal of predisposing mental state which does not quite match the antiquated definition of insanity as a defense. The list could be indefinitely extended.

It is hoped, however, that enough has been said to aid in persuading North Carolina to join the list of enlightened states which have rejected the barbaric practice.

In an address entitled "The Crime of Punishment" at Lenoir, North Carolina, on February 8, 1972, Wright made a plea for a more humane treatment of those behind bars. The prison as now conducted, he contended, merely insured a high degree of recidivism with all pretense of rehabilitation completely abandoned. Excerpts follow.

THE CRIME OF PUNISHMENT

What do we expect our prisons to do to the inmates?

When the state prison of the state of Maine was opened the first warden proclaimed:

Prisons should be so constructed that even their aspect might be terrific ana appear like what they should be—dark and comfortless abodes of guilt and wretchedness. No more degree of punishment...is in its nature so well adapted to purposes of preventing crime or reforming a criminal as close confinement in a solitary cell, in which, cut off from all hope of relief, the convict shall be furnished a hammock on which he may sleep, a block of wood on which he may sit, and with such coarse and wholesome food as may best be suited to a person in a situation designed for grief and pentitence, and shall be favored with so much light from the firmament as may enable him to read the New Testament which will be given him as his sole companion and guide to a better life. There his vices and crimes shall become personified, and appear to his frightened imagination as co-tenants of his dark and dismal cell. They will surround him as so many hideous spectres and overwhelm him with horror and remorse.

Unfortunately, I don't have the date of this somber utterance. Probably a hundred years ago. Probably, also, and this is the real tragedy, it represented the best thought of that day.

Perhaps you may say: "Oh, yes, but times have changed." Let's test that for a moment. Let's move the hands of the clock forward to the year 1923. At that time the person most familiar with United States prisons was Joseph Fishman, for many years federal inspector of such institutions. In 1923 he wrote that when the judge sentenced a man to thirty days in jail the sentence should actually read:

> I not only sentence you to confinement for thirty days in a bare, narrow cell in a gloomy building, during which time you will be deprived of your family, friends, occupation, earning power, and all other human liberties and privileges; but in addition I sentence you to wallow in a putrid mire demoralizing to body, mind and soul, where every rule of civilization is violated, where you are given every opportunity to deteriorate, but none to improve, and where your tendency to wrong-doing cannot be corrected, but only aggravated.

Again you may say: "But that was almost 50 years ago. Times have changed." So, let us come down to the good year 1972.

President Nixon says: "No institution within our society has a record which presents such a conclusive case of failure as does our system."

Attorney General John Mitchell says: "The state of America's prison comes close to a national shame. No civilized society should allow it to continue."

Norman Carlson, director of the U.S. Bureau of Prisons says: "Anyone not a criminal will be when he gets out of jail."

Milton Luger, director of the N.Y. State Division of Youth,

says: "It would be better if young people who commit crimes got away with them because we just make them worse."

"But," you may say, "that's in benighted and uncivilized New York. In North Carolina we don't treat our young people like that."

Perhaps we approach an answer to that position in a report on the *juvenile* correction institutions of this state. From that report we quote:

> *The maximum punishment is solitary confinement in what is referred to by the administration as "the quiet room" or "the meditation room," and by children as "the tub" or "the jail." The cells for solitary confinement (or "segregation" as officials term it) are really concrete dungeons with metal doors and little observation windows. In one school a foul mattress is on the floor, and an old army blanket serves as cover. In another school there is a slab of rock for a bed. An offender must strip to his underwear; he is permitted to read only the Bible and is fed only two meals a day. A mattress is placed in the room in late afternoon and removed in the morning, leaving only the bare rock to sit on. Though the minimum permissible "segregation" period is seven days, many boys say they have spent 10 days there for a single offense, and some say they've been in as long as three weeks. This is the standard punishment for children who run away. One said he stayed in segregation for 30 days.*

How far have we come since the man from Maine—not Senator Muskie—gave his darkly pious views about prisons?

Let us indulge in no vainglory, no self-congratulation. Few would now be bold enough to express such sentiments. But the sentiments which count, which actually sway men and women, are those unuttered convictions which lie in the human heart. Our sentiments, yours and mine, are expressed by what we tolerate. How far have we come in hundred years? What do we now tolerate?

Let us search our hearts. Let us ponder as soberly as we can the answer to this question: If my boy or girl underwent such indignities would I be tolerant? If my brother or sister were in state prison, would I be indifferent?....

What about the penal system of this state?

We can't answer authoritatively since, so far as I am informed, no recent comprehensive study of the *entire* penal system has been made, though one is in prospect. We can however draw lessons from our sister states.

Judge Kenneth Love, a magistrate in Columbia, South Carolina, had sentenced 200 men to State Prison when he decided to visit that institution. He was asked: Did your visit change your feelings about your sentences? Hear his reply:

> *I think the state should take a bulldozer and push that penitentiary into the sewer. It isn't helping the prisoners one bit. That place has over 1,000 men in it and it's nothing but a powderkeg. I will not send one more prisoner to that place...I'll do anything, but I've sent my last man to that prison.*
>
> *If one of our boys over in Vietnam fell into the hands of the Vietcong and the Vietcong did to them what happens to our own people who have to go to that penitentiary, our newspapers would be all over the Vietcong for cruel and inhuman treatment.*
>
> *There are cells in there 3½ feet wide and 8 feet long, and dark, as bad as the bamboo cells in Vietnam.*
>
> *I think if the average citizen of my country went through that penitentiary, they'd have the same reaction I have.*

In Virginia, as elsewhere and in North Carolina, prison sentences usually carry reduction of time for good behavior. "Good time," as it is called, is the period during which no rules or regulations have been broken. This is, of course, a strong incentive to proper behavior. In Virginia, at least, the good time is wiped out upon decision that a rule has been broken. This occurs when a guard or other individual reports an infraction and a committee of administrative personnel finds the charge is valid.

Diabolic features of the process are that no written statement of the charge is given the prisoner; he has no right to summon witnesses or be represented by counsel; frequently the complainant is a member of the panel; rules do not seek to define offenses which may result in loss of good time further than in such general terms as "improper attitude" or "abusive language." Sometimes even the words alleged to be abusive were not stated in the guard's report.

By such crude, primitive and manifestly unjust methods, many prisoners were kept confined far beyond the time when they were eligible for parole. The ill-will or whim of a guard determined the crucial issue of liberty or protracted isolation from normal society.

It was found to be common practice in Virginia to punish inmates by use of chains, hand cuffs and tear gas; by taking away the prisoner's clothes and mattress and by requiring him to try to sleep nude on a cement floor.

Such, then, is a mere glimpse of conditions found by competent authority to exist in prisons elsewhere. I regret that no one can speak with equal authority as to our own state.

As a certain President would remark, I want to make one thing perfectly clear: I believe we have in North Carolina as enlightened a prison administration as may be found in the country. It can only do what the legislature permits it to do. And the legislature will move only in response to what the public, you and I, demand. The prison administration needs our help.

Surely we would be naive if we assumed that we here are immune to the virus which infects prisons elsewhere. And how far are we advanced anyhow from the view of the warden in Maine that no form of treatment is "so well adapted to purposes of preventing crime or reforming a criminal as close confinement in a solitary call?" What an ironic note that one holding such views should stipulate that the prisoner's only reading matter should be the New Testament. Where was it written "sick and in prison and ye visited me not?" You probably recently read that some sect was attempting to have Biblical texts engraved on prison walls. We may treat men as brutes, they say, but we shall do so with complete piety.

If we maintain in our state a prison system which dehumanizes its victims, which admittedly such systems do everywhere else, let us not blame the administration. Let us seek no scapegoats. "The fault, dear Brutus, is not in our stars; it is in ourselves."

We think and speak and write constantly of the punishment of crime. We should be thinking and speaking and writing of the crime of punishment. What one does violently to another in a moment's passion—even murder—can never equal in enormity and iniquity what society does to the offender. The criminal may act upon blind impulse but society, with a massive marshalling of all its forces, legislative, judicial and executive, with calculation and premeditation, perpetrates its own infamies.

Just how active have our churches been to halt the mass erosion of character and personality which occurs behind prison walls? One is reminded of what Voltaire said in another connection: "Ye bungling soul physicians! To bellow for an hour or more about a few flea bites and say not one word about this distemper which devours us!"

Well, what should we say?

First of all, let us admit to gross hypocrisy in pretending that prisons are instruments of rehabilitation. They are instead society's instruments of revenge, or retaliation. You do not reform a man by removing him from every humane and civilizing influence, exiling him in effect to an isolated enclave where he is thrown only with those who can only teach him more vice and crime, fill him with more bitterness toward the state, subjecting him to rigid discipline which directs his every activity.

We should make a 180 degree turn from the bitter piety of the Maine warden so that, while prisons exist, they may provide decent living conditions in an environment in which the flame of hope may be kept aglow. No longer should some present day Maxim Gorki be able to describe prison inmates as "creatures who once were men."

We should provide prison personnel of training, attitudes and motivation commensurate with their important and delicate responsibilities. They deal in the main with the illiterate, the unskilled, from predominantly minority ethnic groups. The prison population should be reflected in the composition of the guards and all others in authority.

You don't get a good guard by just picking anybody off the streets, perhaps, to pay a political debt, anymore that you get a good teacher by the same process. We need guards who *are* teachers, who have some knowledge of psychology, but who, most important of all, believe with Winston Churchill, that "if only we can find it, there is good in every human heart," and who are committed to that quest. Salaries should compare with those of the best teachers.

A recent study of federal prisons showed that guards were paid less than keepers at the Washington Zoo, leading to the conclusion that we rate prisoners lower than jackals and hyenas.

If there is one right which the American citizen prizes above all others, it is the right of privacy—the right to be free from governmental prying and snooping. Sen. Sam Ervin has performed valiantly and achieved national recognition for his services in protecting that right. An essential feature of the right of privacy is freedom from censorship of mail. We are

determined to preserve it all at all costs—*for those not in prison.*
For the man behind bars it is a different story.

Without knowledge of the North Carolina practice, it may be
stated that, certainly in Virginia, and, I believe, generally,
censorship of mail from and to prisoners is standard procedure.

What can more inhibit preservation of normal and happy
relationship with family and friends than knowledge that every
line written, every endearing expression, is reviewed by a cold,
impersonal, and, perhaps, hostile, prison guard? The free flow of
correspondence should not be chilled by knowledge that, as one
writes, a guard looks over the shoulder and that what one reads
has been tailored to pass muster before censorious eyes.

A man is sentenced to prison for a period of years. It is a
part of the crime of punishment that, for that period, we
apparently strive to strip him of every right enjoyed by the
American citizen. Then, after a period of non-existence of such
rights, we demand that he shall use them wisely upon discharge.
Prison conditions should simulate, so far as possible, conditions
of normal living in a free society.

What we have is the prison administration alone deciding
what is good for prisoners. Decision making is a necessary part
of character building. No one becomes strong or grows in grace
by having another constantly tell him what he shall or shall not
do, what is good or bad for him. That is paternalism in its worst
form. Against it men of spirit ultimately rebel. They will assert
with Woodrow Wilson "I care not how wise or good a master
may be, I will not have a master."

The answer seems to be in encouraging the formation among
inmates, in an atmosphere of calm, of an organization for their
own self-expression. Prisoners would meet in regular sessions or
assemblies at which there would be discussions of any matters of
interest and, particularly, those which affect them as prisoners.

The history of prison riots is that, as an incident of a bloody
rebellion, a list of grievance is submitted. Invariably these
grievances, or some of them, have been found to be meritorious.

Reform has been accomplished at a tragic cost in sacked buildings and snuffed out lives. How far wiser it would be to set up, in advance of the disaster, a method and procedure for dignified and orderly consideration of legitimate aspirations.

Chief Justice Warren Burger, in a recent address, made this striking suggestion:

> *The figures on literacy alone are enough to make one wish that every sentence imposed could include a provision that would grant release when the prisoner had learned to read and write, to do simple arithmetic, and then to develop some basic skill that is salable in the market place of the outside world to which he must someday return and in which he must compete. Since the best of human beings need motivation and hope, why have we thought prisoners can do without both? We should develop sentencing techniques to impose a sentence so that an inmate can literally "learn his way" out of prison as we not try to let him earn his way out with "good behavior."*

Surely this is one judicial opinion from which none can dissent.

Such are among the innovations which, we hope, may make life within prison walls more tolerable and more productive in terms of lives of those ultimately returned to normal living. In punishing crime, we are now engaged in the crime of punishment—vast, wholesome, sordid crime. "He who observes injustice and doth not protest is party to the act."

But adopt all the innovations you please, erect the most modern plants, install the most enlightened administration—the prison is still a thing of evil. Why?

Because it denies to inmates enjoyment of two fundamental human rights—liberty of movement and action and the right of decision making. Both are essential to personality and to moral growth. The prisoner conforms and becomes a mere disciplined brute or he reacts by hatred of the society which thus regulates his conduct and ultimately by riot and rebellion. The Yugo-Slav writer, Djilas, warned "Beware of the cry of the wounded soul for the hidden sore will at length erupt." Perhaps, because of their indestructible quality, it is these rebels we should hail. Who are the heroic figures, the slaves who meekly wore the yoke or John Brown and Nat Turner who led them in revolt?

We judge a person to be normal when he engages in normal activity. We should judge him to be abnormal when he engages in abnormal activity. Crime is abnormal activity. Havelock Ellis wrote "Every truly criminal act proceeds from a person who is, temporarily or permanently, in a more or less abnormal condition."

But when a person has committed an abnormal act, criminal in nature, society regards him as a normal person who has deliberately offended. He is confined with a thousand other abnormal persons—each being distinctively individual—and all are subjected to precisely the same stifling regimentation. We say "The punishment should fit the crime." It should fit the *Man* In all the universe there is none other exactly like him.

A very wise man—I think Herbert Spencer—wrote "No great thing may be done by a state which dwarfs its citizens.' Particularly in a democratic society, the aim is to magnify the citizen, to encourage his growth, to induce him to express his individuality, his peculiar and personal genius. Diversity, not conformity, is the keynote. The ideal toward which we constantly strive is a state in which there is variety of opinion, variety in religious views, political views, differences in taste and manners. We shun the conformity which means that all think or speak or act alike. We say with Thoreau that every one should march to his own drummer.

All of this for men and women who are *outside* of prison walls. But for the *confined* what say we: Lock step, wear the same garb; do as you are told, ask no questions; you will get along here only if you stifle every last spark of your initiative and individuality. You are members of a herd. Be sheep-like and you may survive. Thus does the state dwarf its citizens—when they are behind bars.

Above all else, you and I and every citizen of North Carolina should recognize the prison as an outmoded institution. Stone walls and iron bars for wild animals, perhaps, but not for men. Surely we are now sufficiently advanced in our thinking and in our knowledge of human psychology to realize that the prison is, what Hawthorne called it, "the black flower of civilization." Only in the rare case of those whose liberty would present a real and imminent danger to mankind, is confinement justified.

Surely we have intelligence enough to create substitute institutions and procedures by which men and women may be trained, encouraged and aided by society to walk erect and unafraid among their fellows.

I propose not a march on the Bastille but the development of a new attitude toward *les miserables* which tempers stern justice with compassion. When we fully comprehend the mass wreckage which prisons make of the lives of the condemned, when we fully utilize our knowledge of human behavior, and release the better and more generous impulses which lie in our hearts, then our grim dungeons, unused and vacant, shall serve only to remind us of how slow and tortuous has been mankind's long struggle upward toward the stars.

In February, 1973, the North Carolina legislature again had before it a bill to abolish the death penalty. Wright returned to the attack with a pamphlet issued jointly by North Carolinians Against the Death Penalty and the North Carolina Coalition. He used the case of a 17-year-old black girl, then awaiting execution, to point up the rank discrimination involved in legal executions. Statistically the record showed that the penalty was almost exclusively employed against blacks, the illiterate, the feeble-minded and the poor. The speech follows:

SHALL WE REACTIVATE THE GAS CHAMBER?

Those who have memories which go back to the First World War will recall articles written for the *Saturday Evening Post* by a celebrated war correspondent whose name was Samuel G. Blythe. From the scene of one of the great battles of that war Mr. Blythe wrote that one could view hundreds of dead and dying soldiers scattered over several square miles of territory without being profoundly shaken by the experience, but that a close-up view of one dead, or dying soldier produced a sense of shock and would be forever etched in memory.

Tragedy on a vast scale may be beyond human powers of assimilation. We may read of 100,000 Biafrans starving to death without being so deeply stirred. But a full page picture in *Life* magazine of one black infant with distended abdomen, arms and legs which are little more than skin surrounding bones, and eyes unnaturally glazed—such a picture produces the shock which moves one to action.

So, when we consider the death penalty we are able to endure without too great twinges of sympathy, the fact that on the Death Rows of this country 500, more or less, men and women, until the recent United States Supreme Court decision, endured the wretched deterioration of their existences, often in solitary confinement for years at a time, and deliberately isolated from every humane and civilizing influence that could bring cheer or hope. Perhaps a more intimate acquaintance with one of the victims of society's moral insensibility may bring the whole issue of capital punishment within our comprehension. Not comprehension alone, because comprehension is merely a mental concept. I would hope that the experience would stir the humane and generous impulses which, we must believe, lie within every heart.

When the Supreme Court acted there was the general feeling that, at long last, the gas chair could be dismantled. But, here and there throughout the state voices are raised—even in the General Assembly—seeking to preserve and re-activate that symbol of a discredited institution. The struggle to introduce sanity and humanity into treatment of those who break the law must be continued.

Let us then, in obviously the most superficial way, turn out attention to one occupant of what was, and may again become, North Carolina's Death Row. Incidentally, that name for the group of cells in North Carolina's State Prison was chosen with intuitive wisdom. Occupancy there was a kind of living death. Mentally, morally, spiritually, the occupants were already entombed.

Marie Hill, at age 17, presumed by the state to lack the intelligence to vote, or to drive an automobile, or to marry, without her parents' consent, was condemned to death by the very society which indulges these presumptions. The state presumes, also, that she was sufficiently stable and adjusted to control her emotions, to subdue the wild passions of her adolescent years, and to reflect, in her moment of temptation, upon the ghastly consequences of her action.

Marie was born June 16, 1951, in a Rocky Mount Negro slum. Her unwed mother, Mary L. Hill, gave her to Maggie Joyner, when Marie was still an infant. Then the mother disappeared.

When Marie was six months old, John Lesesne, her father, married Mrs. Joyner's daughter, Arilla. He moved into the Joyner house where Marie grew up. There were two bedrooms, one of which also served as a kitchen. The bathroom is on the back porch. Her natural father worked as a truck driver for a bottling company and his wife worked as a sweeper during the tobacco harvesting season. These were the custodians of the little girl. Apparently they were kind to her but unable to give her the care and attention that she should have had.

Society was early put upon notice of the tragic career that lay ahead. When Marie was 13 she was arrested and convicted for stealing $220.00 from the cash register of a local store. Nine months later she was arrested and convicted of auto theft and forging checks for $35 and $45. Three months later she was accused of knifing a boy at a dance. Authorities dropped the charges, however, and she was tried only for auto theft. This time she was sent to the State Training School in Kinston.

She was released the next spring and returned home, a drop-out from school and without a job. Then, on October 7, 1968, apparently in company with two other girls, she robbed and killed the white owner of a grocery store a few blocks from her home. Such are the dreary annals of her life.

It is easy, as some of her neighbors did, to accept the hypothesis that Marie was a "bad girl" or "mean" as one of her teachers described her. This, of course, is society's lazy answer to crime. It saves us from the hard necessity of thinking—what caused her to develop as she did, what curative processes should the state have employed, to what extent is the state remiss in not heeding the danger signals which flashed early in the girl's life?

Marie Hill is important, not only in her own right as a human being, but because she is typical of the hundreds who have marched the last mile. How is she typical?

First of all she is *black*. The Attorney General's report shows that in North Carolina for the years 1962 through 1967 inclusive, more whites (8786) than blacks (7190) were charged with the capital offenses, in the superior and inferior courts of North Carolina; and more whites (7427) than blacks (5077) were convicted of these crimes.

But, while whites lead in the number of *arrests* and *convictions*, the story is entirely different when *executions* are considered. Since 1953, when the General Assembly authorized the solicitor to accept a guilty plea in a capital case, eight persons have been executed in North Carolina—all blacks.

Since 1910, only two white men were ever sentenced to death for burglary, and both of them won new trials and life sentences. On the other hand, 36 blacks have been sentenced to death for burglary and 10 have been executed.

The same is true of rape. More whites than blacks in North Carolina are convicted of rape but the death penalty is reserved in large part for the blacks. Nineteen whites have received the death penalty of whom eight were executed. In contrast 117 blacks have received the death sentence of whom 68 were executed.

Marie is not only black, she is a *minor* and here the same statistics tell the same racial story. Thirty-two minors have been sentenced to death in North Carolina, 9 white and 23 black. Four of the whites went to their death—the most recent in 1936. In contrast 20 of the 23 blacks went to their death.

More than incidentally, Marie was joined on Death Row by another minor, a 16-year-old Negro boy named Robert Louis Roseboro of Cleveland County. Possibly our Chambers of Commerce could have claimed a new first for North Carolina—the two youngest persons in the nation on Death Row. Since minors are not old enough to vote, but may be drafted into the Army, or sent to the gas chamber, they are deemed old enough to kill or be killed by the state. I hope there is no truth to the rumor that the state is planning, if the death penalty is revived, to establish a Death Row kindergarten.

Marie Hill is a *female*, and again the racial story is repeated.

North Carolina has sentenced six women to the death chamber: one white and five black. The white women was commuted by the governor; in contrast two of the blacks were executed and three had sentences commuted by the governor.

Marie Hill lived in Rocky Mount, located in the counties of Nash and Edgecomb. Fourteen persons have received the death sentence in these two counties—six whites and eight blacks.

One of the six whites was executed but five of the eight blacks were executed.

Marie Hill was convicted of *murder*. Since 1910, North Carolina has imposed the death penalty for murder on 494 persons: 159 whites and 335 blacks. Of the 159 whites sentenced to death, 68 have been executed. Of the 335 blacks sentenced to death, 206 have been executed. In short, of the whites sentenced to death, the odds are 50-50 as to the gas chamber; of the blacks sentenced to death, the odds are two to one· in favor of the gas chamber.

Marie Hill was *uneducated* except in the most limited way. She was a dropout from the eighth grade, from which she missed 87 out of 180 days. She had a D or D- average. Again she is typical. Records over a 15 year period showed admissions to State Prison had an average of 7.47 years of schooling; death row admissions, 4.65 years; those executed, 4.54 years.

North Carolina has thus sent to its gas chamber the products of its own failure to educate.

(I want to acknowledge with gratitude that these statistics have been supplied me by Professor Dan H. Pollitt of the Law School of the University of North Carolina.)

If Marie Hill should have been executed she would be:

(1) The first minor executed since 1944 (the last white minor was executed in 1936);

(2) The first woman executed since 1944 (no white woman has ever been executed in North Carolina);

(3) The first female minor ever executed in North Carolina.

We ought not to end this discussion of the Marie Hill case without mention of another factor in which she is typical. Happily, this has nothing to do with race. It applies to all of that company of the condemned, whether white or black, minor or adult. She is *poor* and she lacks friends in high places. She had no funds with which to employ the best available counsel, psychologists or psychiatrists and expert testimony to be furnished by others. She had no well placed friend who might "intercede" for her, or "pull wires", or "to say a good word" to the prosecuting attorney or judge. She faced her ordeal tragically alone, unsupported except for the feeble voices of little men and women of little consequence in influencing the judicial process or combating the awesome power of the state. In all respects, again her case is typical.

Michael DiSalle, former governor of Ohio, has written that "During the four years as governor, I was never asked to pass on a clemency request of a gangster, syndicated racketeer or hired killer; none of them got the death penalty."

Who, then, does get the death penalty?

Playwright Paul Green says that the death penalty is "wrought against the poor, the murky minded, the unfortunate."

Warden Lewis E. Laws of Sing Sing has said, "In the twelve years of my wardenship I have escorted 150 men and one woman to the death chamber and the electric chair. In ages they ranged from 17 to 63. In only one respect were they all alike. All of them were poor and most of them were friendless."

I shall not labor the point. I dare say that not a person in this state can recall the case of a wealthy man or woman in North Carolina ever having walked the last mile to the gas chamber.

North Carolina is, we proudly assert, a civilized state. We maintain all of the trappings and institutions of a civilized society—schools, synagogues, churches, hospitals, libraries and the like.

We have been reared under the influence of Judeo-Christian ethics. Undoubtedly we respond to humane impulses. We have societies for the Prevention of Cruelty to Animals. Long ago we outlawed bear-baiting because of cruelty inflicted upon the bear. We outlawed cock-fighting because it resulted in the death of a few roosters.

Let us hope this is not the only motive for suppressing such primitive sports. Surely, in enacting such legislation, we were moved also by the conviction that to witness such exhibitions had a debasing and demoralizing influence upon the spectators. How many more decades must pass and how many more lives must be snuffed out by state-designed executions of human beings before we realize that such legalized taking of human life has its own debasing and demoralizing effect upon the society which orders them and upon all of us for whom the executioner acts as our agent?

And how much longer must we wait before we realize that out own inaction as citizens in the presence of this infamy has a corrosive effect upon our own characters?

It is written in the Talmud: "He who witnesses injustice and does not protest is a party to the act."

Solon was asked "When will there be perfect justice in Athens?" He replied: "When those who have not suffered injustice are as indignant as those who have."

For those who may be disposed to yield to humane impulses perhaps a word of caution is advisable. There is a cynical school of thought which holds that people having such concern and, particularly, those who are opposed to the death penalty, are mere sentimentalists, emotional, soft-brained, soft-hearted do-gooders—I believe the phrase is "bleeding hearts"—while those in favor of retaining the death penalty are unemotional and entirely rational.

Just the reverse seems to be true. The individual who can

think of nothing better to do with a man than to kill him, who goes about shouting "Kill him, kill him." is the highly irrational and emotional individual. He is giving expression to the oldest of the human emotions—revenge, retaliation. We who say: "Study this man, study his background, his environment, his ancestry, his education, all of the forces which made him what he is, and you may, in time, come up with the cause of the atrocities which shock us." Knowing the cause, society may take steps to prevent such crimes. That seems to be the rational, the scientific, the unemotional approach to crime. It is the approach of medicine and all the other sciences....

It seems appropriate that not merely the rationality, but also the morality of state action should be considered. Here is the state giving to all its citizens the age-old injunction, "Thou shalt not kill," saying, in effect, that the most horrible of all crimes is the premeditated taking of human life. Yet the state itself, above all others offers the classic example of premeditation. A man is arrested on a charge of murder. Months, or even years, may elapse between his arrest and the trial. There is your period of meditation. And then he is convicted and other months or years elapse before the execution date rolls around. There the state has had years of premeditation over the problem of taking human life. You cannot imagine any individual, however depraved and sadistic, keeping his victim confined and biding his time over a period of years, before striking the fatal blow.

Everyone of us must ask himself the question: "Is it fair that the state should adopt a code of conduct for itself that it denies to the citizen? If individual citizens have no right in themselves to take human life, except in self-defense, can they, by merely joining themselves together in an organization called the state, create that right in the organization? If the individuals do not have that right in themselves, what title deeds can the state show to its right to take human life?

Surely, if anything, the state should be held to an even higher standard of conduct than it requires of the citizen. The state is the great teacher. The citizen is the pupil. Example is more powerful than precept. So, when the state sets the example, why should it express surprise that the citizen has adopted for himself a code of conduct approved by the state? The somber truth is that executions breed murder and it is illuminating that no nation which has abolished the death penalty has ever, thereafter, begun a war.

Is it moral for a state to require of its citizens a standard of conduct to which it itself does not adhere?

Advocates of the death penalty would revise the ancient law to read: ,"Thou shalt not kill, unless thou art a state"; "Revenge is mine, saith the state, I will repay"; "The Lord giveth and the state taketh away. Blessed be the name of the state"....

Our obligation is to identify ourselves with the state which condemns. The executioner is our agent. In a larger sense you and I, as citizens, if we remain quiescent, throw the switch, or drop the pellet in the pan of liquid. We are the executioners.

And in a larger sense, we must identify ourselves with the man strapped in the oaken chair, if there is any validity to our religious convictions, that man is our brother. John Donne was right. He is part of the main. When we have reached the last ultimate peak of moral grandeur we will be at one with this man and feel that it is we whom society is putting to death. When he dies, the bell tolls for us too.

Because, as a young reporter, Wright frequently visited State Prison in Columbia, South Carolina, he became somewhat familiar with prison conditions, at least in that institution. While he never practiced criminal law, as a lawyer he observed the crude procedure by which sentences were imposed. Some knowledge of the thoroughly unscientific method of imposition which sent men to prison for a term of years, as well as the nature of prisons and their effect on inmates, prompted him in 1971 to advance a completely new concept of the sentencing procedure. His ideas are set forth in the following essay.

CRIME AND PUNISHMENT

Ten years at hard labor in State Prison.

Every day except Sunday throughout the United States these or similar words are being spoken by black robed figures from a bench elevated some feet above the person to whom they are addressed. The words profoundly affect that man and members of his family. Presumably, also, they have some theoretical effect upon society.

The drama is probably as old as criminal law itself, certainly as old as prisons. For centuries the characters, judge and felon, have played their roles. Different judges and different felons, to be sure, but the stage and script are unvarying.

Since the first such sentence was spoken revolutions have shaken the world. Empires have risen and fallen. Science has supplanted faith and superstition. Human slavery has perished. In many areas and facets, with advance in civilization, have come new methods and techniques designed to mitigate savage and barbaric practices. But the old formula for treatment of the prisoner persists.

Society insists that the way to prevent crime is to punish the law breaker. How does it go about the task of assessing punishment?

The process begins with the legislature. A hundred or two-hundred men, representatives and senators, assemble in the state capitol. Probably not a one has ever served a prison sentence. Hence he legislates about a matter of which he has not actual, personal knowledge or experience.

Few, if any, of the members are psychologists, sociologists, penologists, former prison officials. Hence they legislate without even theoretical, to say nothing of practical, acquaintance with the mental or emotional states which induce commission of crime or of the effects of prison sentences upon those confined.

On a certain legislative date they decree, as to a child still in his mother's womb, that, when he is of age, if he should commit murder, he shall be electrocuted or sent to prison for life.

No two individuals, except in the rare case of identical twins, have precisely the same heredity. Without exception, no two individuals have precisely the same environment in the sense of the myriad forces which beat upon and mold human beings. No two individuals have the same subliminal urges, the same weaknesses, the same strengths, the same capacity to control their conduct. The law agrees that no two thumb prints are exactly alike but assumes that, insofar as criminals are concerned, in every respect except their thumbs, they are exactly alike. Such is the basic postulate upon which the legislature acts.

Legislatures, which thus deny the diversity of individuals, are themselves classic examples of diversity. One must pore endlessly over the statutes of the fifty states to come up with instances in which the same criminal acts receive the same punishment.

There is complete lack of uniformity, for example, in what crimes are regarded as capital offenses in those states which retain the death penalty. Murder is the only constant. Kidnapping is a close second. But rape is a capital crime in only 17 states, largely in the South. Other crimes which are regarded as capital in few states include duelling, robbery, attempted murder of the President, lynching, burglary, arson, trainwrecking, perjury, treason, bombing and attempted rape.

Legislation in regard to drugs and pornography provides punishment ranging from a fine of $50 in some states to ten years in prison in others.

The services of a computer would be required to find—if it be possible—two states having identical punishments for the same offenses. But the legislative responsibility is to determine what constitutes a crime and what, within limits, shall be done with the felon. Rarely, if ever, do two states provide the same answers.

The legislature, having performed its function, the next key factor in imposition of sentence is the trial judge. In some cases, where sentences are mandatory, he has no option. In nearly all others, he acts within limits set by the legislature—say five to ten years in the discretion of the court. In this area of discretion, the qualifications of the judge—his learning, temperament, experience and character—these powerfully act upon the fateful words he shall utter.

The judge labors under the same limitations which afflict the legislator. He has never been confined in a jail, so he has the most superficial and second-hand information about what Hawthorne described as "the black flower of civilized society, a prison." The effects of confinement for varying periods—five, six, or seven years up to ten—are completely beyond the judge's ken.

That is true of the effects generally upon the mythical average man. But the judge deals with a lone and distinctive individual, the like of which doesn't exist anywhere else on the globe. As Rene Dubos wrote in *So Human An Animal*:

Each human being is unique, unprecedented, unrepeatable. The species Homo Sapien *can be*

> *described in the lifeless words of physics and chemistry, but not the man of flesh and bone. We recognize him as a unique person by his voice, his facial expressions, and the way he walks—and even more by his creative response to surroundings and events.*

The judge subscribes to the official credo that confinement for a fixed period in "the house of the dead," as Dostoyevsky described the prison, results in reformation. Our present treatment of prisoners rests upon a curious assumption; that is, that if one who has committed a crime is shut up with others of his kind or worse, deprived of contact with family and friends, assigned a number, subjected to discipline which directs every detail of his conduct, allowed to perform none of the functions of citizenship—such a one, after an arbitrary period, will return to society as a useful citizen.

First as lawyer and later as judge, the man on the bench has been conditioned to this view of how the transgressor should be treated. The humanities are no part of the law school curriculum. The realities of legal practice and judicial experience do not tend to soften temperament. Worship of precedent, whatever its values, does not operate to development of innovative and imaginative temperaments. So many years in prison as treatment of the criminal is among the most ancient and esteemed of precedents.

De Tocqueville commented upon the blighting effect of *stare decisis* upon the personality of the practioner. He wrote:

> *This predisposition (to adhere to precedent) has an effect upon the character of the legal profession... The English and American lawyers investigate what has been done; the French advocate inquires what should have been done; the former produce precedents, the latter reasons. A French observer is surprised to hear*

how often an English or an American lawyer quotes the opinions of others and how little he alludes to his own...This abnegation of his own opinion and this implicit deference to the opinion of his fore-fathers...this servitude of thought which he is obliged to profess, necessarily gives him more timid habits and more conservative inclinations in England and America than in France.

The judge brings to his high office the bent of mind, the habits, the predilections, the mental impedimenta accumulated in large part in law school and legal practice. Rarely is he a psychologist or sociologist in even an amateurish sense. It may be fairly said, therefore, that he has only the most rudimentary knowledge of the effect of his decision upon the prisoner or upon society.

But, as he approaches the awesome decision about what shall be done with the prisoner, the gravest difficulty under which he labors is his ignorance of the man in the dock. Upon him the blow will fall. What manner of man is he anyhow?

The judge has observed the man for the few hours or few days the trial has lasted. Under strict rules of evidence, the information spread before the judge relates only to the circumstances surrounding commission of a crime. The camera has been focused only upon one act of an entire life, an obviously reprehensible and sordid act. Of that act the jury has said the defendant is guilty.

The only aid to the judicial discretion, found in some jurisdictions, is the report of an investigative officer, covering such elementary matters as prior record, schooling, marital status and the like. These are the bare facts about the man, facts as distinguished from truth. From his own observations and this superficial report the judge decides on a figure somewhere between five and ten years. A kind of judicial roulette.

It is no disservice to the judiciary to state that the

temperament of the judge, the state of his health, the social circles in which he and the prisoner move, the class consciousness, his like and dislikes, his subconscious prejudices, "the complex of instincts and emotions and habits and convictions, which make the man, whether he be litigant or judge"—all these and more enter into the sentence he will pronounce.

In the cases of two men convicted separately of precisely the same crime but being sentenced by different judges, it would be assumed that the sentences would be the same. That result by no means follows. One judge may give five years and another ten for the same offense committed under similar circumstances. The judge is the resultant of forces which have developed propensities and attitudes which find expression in the sentences he pronounces. However honorable his intentions and however zealous to do only what is right, no judge can totally divorce himself from subconscious motivations.

Every criminal lawyer is aware of judicial limitations. The defense attorney maneuvers to get his case before a sympathetic judge; the prosecutor seeks out the "hanging judge." The shrewd felon hires a lawyer who is the golf companion of the man who will pronounce the sentence. After all, judges are human beings. The tides which engulf ordinary mortals must at least lap at the feet of the judge.

Such, then, are the human factors which enter into imposition of sentence. The duration within limits fixed by legislators; the exact period fixed by judges. Both act from lack of knowledge of the institution to which the prisoner is consigned. Both act from profound ignorance of the man consigned. The alarming percentage of those returning to prison for subsequent crimes proves the ineffectiveness of the system.

So long as punishment is the dominant motivation for imprisonment and so long as imprisonment is the only mode of punishment, just so long will prisons be crucibles of crime, just so long will society engage in the mass erosion of character and personality which daily occurs within prison walls.

Both basic postulates must be abandoned. Treatment, rather than punishment, should be the motive. Alternatives to prisons must be provided. Knowledge of prison and prisoner must supplant ignorance.

On December 7, 1927, Governor Al Smith of New York proposed a bold and revolutionary approach to the whole area to treatment of those convicted of crime. Governor Smith was not a jurist but his intuitions and perceptions were deep and brilliant. In an address before the New York State Crime Commission he said:

> *I have for some time, because of my direct experience with the results of the administration of criminal justice, become deeply impressed that we could make a great stride in the direction of real justice if we changed somewhat our methods of administering it. We are dealing with human beings, no two of whom are ever under normal circumstances exactly alike. How much more are they likely to differ under abnormal situations. We have progressed in our knowledge of the processes of the human mind and the influence on it of physical conditions. I would like to see that knowledge applied to the determination of the kind and duration of punishment best adapted to bring about the restoration of delinquents to normal social life.*
>
> *Because of my belief that justice sometimes miscarries because those charged with determining guilt are often affected by the thought of the sentence to be imposed for a given crime, I would suggest that the Crime Commission give careful study and consideration to a fundamental change in the method of sentencing criminals. After guilt has been determined by legal process instead of sentence being fixed by judges according to statute, I should like to see*

offenders who have been adjudged guilty detained by the state. They should then be carefully studied by a board of expert mental and physical specialists who after careful study of all the elements entering each case would decide and fix the penalty for the crime. I realize the complexity of such a fundamental change. It probably requires even constitutional amendment. Therefore I recommend that your Honorable Bodies request the Crime Commission to report to you after due and careful study of the proposal, whether such a change is advisable and how it can be brought about. It appeals to me as a modern, humane, scientific way to deal with the criminal offender.

Governor Smith's proposal hardly requires elaboration but perhaps comment upon its advantages over the present system may be permissible.

At present the juror, meditating guilt or innocence, must have in consciousness the inevitable consequence of his verdict. Free-.dom if not guilty; the prison for a fixed period if guilty. He may be inspired or deterred by contemplation of the result of his action. His verdict in many instances must be affected by such contemplation.

Governor Smith's plan presents no such predetermined consequence of a guilty verdict. The juror acts in the knowledge that the result to the prisoner will be determined impartially by those not party to the trial and, hence, unmoved by the emotions the trial engenders. Possibly the guilty person may go to prison for an indeterminate period; possibly he may go to a mental or other institution; possibly still other dispositions of his case may be made. There would be removed from the jury every consideration of what punishment may be meted out; their concern would be limited entirely to determination of guilt or innocence.

Who would decide what should be done with the guilty and

what should be the objective?

Governor Smith's "suggestion embraced the constitution of a board of the highest salaried men...properly composed of or constituted of psychiatrists, alienists, lawyers and students, and that the final disposition of the man's punishment should be in the best interests of the state and of the man himself."

Forty-four years have elapsed since the Governor made his proposal. Penology as a recognized area of science has in the meantime become firmly established. No doubt, if he were now advancing his suggestion, one or more penologists would be included in the make-up of the board. Statistical and other information throwing light on the results of varying methods of handling men are now available. New tests disclosing personality traits, hidden talents, unsuspected skills, are the familiar tools of personnel executives and employers. During the detention period following conviction the accumulated knowledge and newly devised techniques could be employed to come up with the best answer to the question of what should be done with this man.

What is now done? As a broad generalization, on arrival at state prison he is given prison clothes, a number, a physical examination, and assigned to such work as is available. There is little thought of what he can do best—little thought, in fact, of what he can do at all. The varieties of prison employment are obviously and necessarily limited. A man of special gifts in a specialized area is consigned to idleness or work at unfamiliar and uncongenial tasks. This doesn't make for a happy prisoner or easy discipline.

If such an imaginative plan as Governor Smith proposed should be adopted, the state should be braced for novel experiments. Since it is already established that much crime is the result of mental disease or mental states not quite meeting strict legal tests of the defense of insanity, many condemned men would be sent, not to prison, but to mental or psychiatric institutions. Others might go to specially operated work camps where they could be employed at tasks with which they are familiar or given training at tasks for which they are suited—all with a view to fitting them to function in a normal society upon their discharge.

After its observation of the prisoner during the detention period following conviction, after its examination of his background, his limitations and qualifications, after its original determination of his treatment, the board would not wash its hands of the prisoner. It would continue to have him in theoretical custody. Its original estimate may have been mistaken. It has reserve authority to amend, alter or reverse as circumstances dictate. Always the prisoner would have the hope-inspiring knowledge that those most familiar with his special conditions or problems have him in consciousness. He is not society's forgotten man.

When and only when the time arrives that the board feels the prisoner may be safely discharged, it would make that determination. The decision would not have been made by a legislative act passed perhaps before the man was born, or by a judge who observed him only during the course of a trial.

Those were decisions as to an impersonal, statistical man, not a unique, individualized human being of blood and bone as distinct in his personality from every other human being as in his thumb prints.

The investigation by the board, essential to an understanding of the man, would have included meticulous examination of heredity and environment in the broadest sense, including all factors which might have accounted for criminal behavior. Its observations of the man during his period as a technical prisoner would throw further light upon the motivations of his anti-social conduct. A vastly significant by-product of this study of the criminal would be the study of crime. Begin by asking: Why did this man kill? The answer as to one man may mean little. The answers as to a thousand men who killed may give the key to the various causes of homicide. As in the case of any disease, when the cause is known the cure follows.

Revolutionary? Governor Smith's proposal doubtless is. It is the scientific approach to crime. Science is always revolutionary in that it disturbs accepted dogma. Mounting crime rates refute the validity of our ancient conceptions of crime and punishment. It is time for drastic change.

WHAT IF WE SUDDENLY WENT DECENT?

Robert Yoakum, in one of his columns entitled "What If We Suddenly Went Sane?" in the Washington *Post* some years ago, reviewed E.M. Forster's *Two Cheers For Democracy*. Forster, a profound and brilliant Englishman, was mildly pessimistic about the future of democratic government. He wrote: "The climate is political, and the conclusion is that, though we cannot expect to love one another, we must learn to put up with one another. Otherwise we shall all of us perish."

Again, in 1939 Forster wrote: "No millennium seems likely to descend on humanity. No better and stronger League of Nations will be instituted; no form of Christianity and no alternative will bring peace to the world or integrity to the individual; no change of heart will occur."

At that point Yoakum, the reviewer, takes over:

"But what if....;? What if suddenly, inexplicably, joyously, a change of heart should occur? From Forster's 1939 essay What I Believe, *let's put his words into the mouths of today's thinkers and doers. Hang on, please."*

Yoakum has then Vice-President Spiro Agnew using Forster's words to tell applauding newspaper editors: "Democracy has another merit. It allows criticism, and, if there is not public criticism, there are bound to be hushed up scandals. That is why I believe in the press, despite all its lies and vulgarity."

Then Senator Strom Thurmond uses as his sentiments for insertion in the *Congressional Record* Forster's words: "Tolerance, good temper and sympathy—they are what matter really, and, if the human race is not to collapse, they must come to the front before long."

The Yoakum article contains other examples of utterances by

public figures who suddenly went sane. All of this suggests a parallel. A brief digression is in order.

The granting of amnesty has many precedents in American history. It is part of President Carter's program and, the Barry Goldwater's notwithstanding, will no doubt occur in one or another form.

Those who evaded the draft and those who deserted were breakers of the law. Yet the sense of "charity for all," in Lincoln's words, will prevail.

Now, let us suppose that governors of certain Southern states suddenly went decent, suddenly had an accession of good manners. felt obliged to act officially as a gentleman who had wronged another would act.

Here, without charge, is a proclamation he might issue:

> *WHEREAS the State of   by its laws supported and enforced the institution of slavery until the year 1865 when war and a presidential proclamation accomplished its end, and*
>
> *WHEREAS the State of   by its laws supported and enforced separation of the races, termed segregation, until Supreme Court decisions accomplished its end, and*
>
> *WHEREAS many black citizens used constitutionally declared civil liberties of assembly, protest, organization and demonstration to secure legal enforcement of their rights to share and enjoy full participation in government and all those privileges and immunities which citizenship confers, and*
>
> *WHEREAS their constitutionally approved efforts and activities, in a shameful number of instances, were met with legal resistance and prosecution by this state, resulting in fines or imprisonment, and by countless individual acts of violence, intimidation, foreclosure, terminated tenancies and employment, penalties for*

membership in organizations of their choosing, and in unpunished murders, and

WHEREAS many black men and women of spirit, unable or unwilling to endure such indignities, left their native state in search of environments more conducive to normal growth for themselves and their children,

NOW, THEREFORE, I   , as Governor of the State of   , in an effort, insofar as words may do so, to rectify the wrongs governmentally inflicted or condoned, as well as those committed by misguided individuals, do hereby issue this admission of, and apology for, all such evil and irrational public and private acts.

If it is found legally permissible, I advise and recommend that all police or court records of those arrested or brought to trial for offences arising out of peaceful acts of protest, assembly, petition or demonstration by those seeking to assert their legal rights be forthwith expunged.

IN WITNESS WHEREOF I have hereunto set my hand and caused the great Seal of the State to be affixed this   day of   , 19 .

It is to be noted that amnesty as conferred by Lincoln and other presidents was an act of grace in favor of those who had broken the law. The proclamation herein proposed is in favor of those who suffered because the state and society had broken the law. They are not the offenders; they are the offended.

There is an Italian proverb which declares: "He never pardons those he injures." George Herbert in 1640 wrote in *Jacula Prudentia*, "The offender never pardons." Dryden in 1640, in "The Conquest of Granada," put the idea in verse:

> *Forgiveness to the injured does belong*
> *But they never pardon who have done wrong.*

Never is a long time. Events move swiftly. Men of enlightenment and vision now occupy governors' chairs in some Southern
states. They must have a sense of shame for what occurred in
their states.

Don't sell the proclamation short.

Marion A. Wright

Linville Falls, N.C.
July 17, 1977